THE DOWN GOES BROWN HISTORY OF THE NHL

THE
DOWN GOES BROWN
HISTORY OF THE NHL

THE WORLD'S MOST BEAUTIFUL SPORT, THE WORLD'S MOST RIDICULOUS LEAGUE

SEAN McINDOE

RANDOM HOUSE CANADA

PUBLISHED BY RANDOM HOUSE CANADA

www.penguinrandomhouse.ca

Library and Archives Canada Cataloguing in Publication

McIndoe, Sean, author
    The Down goes Brown history of the NHL : the world's most
beautiful sport, the world's most ridiculous league / Sean McIndoe.

Issued in print and electronic formats.
ISBN 978-0-7352-7389-4
eBook ISBN 978-0-7352-7391-7

    1. National Hockey League—History. I. Title.

GV847.8.N3M423 2018   796.962'64   C2018-902690-1
                                                 C2018-902691-X

Book design by Rachel Cooper
Cover photo: © Frank Prazak / Hockey Hall of Fame

Printed and bound in Canada

10 9 8 7 6 5 4 3 2 1

Penguin
Random House
RANDOM HOUSE CANADA

To my parents,
Bob and Judi McIndoe

CONTENTS

INTRODUCTION

It's not just you. This league has always been a little bit off.

THE NHL IS A WEIRD LEAGUE.

Every hockey fan has had this thought. One moment, you're in awe of the speed, skill and intensity that define the sport, shaking your head as a player makes an impossible play, shatters a record or sobs into his first Stanley Cup. The next, everyone's wearing earmuffs, Mr. Rogers has shown up and guys in yellow raincoats are officiating playoff games.

That's just life in the NHL, a league that can't seem to get out of its own way.

No matter how long you've been a hockey fan, you've known the sinking feeling that maybe, just maybe, some of the people in charge here don't always know what they're doing. And at some point, you've probably wondered: Was it always like this?

The short answer is yes.

As for the longer answer, that's this book.

I was born in Australia and lived in California until I was almost five, so when it came to being a hockey fan, I had some catching up to do. Once I arrived in Canada it didn't take me long to fall in love with the game, and by the time the Islanders dynasty was giving way to Wayne Gretzky and the Oilers, I was hooked. I dove into the game's history, reading anything I could get my hands on and listening to older fans tell the stories of the legends who had come before my time.

But there was another half of the fan experience, and it was one I didn't often see reflected in the reference books I signed out of the school library. This part came in bits and pieces, from throwaway lines in Sunday columns and rambling stories from late-night sports radio callers and offhand anecdotes by colour commentators late in blowouts. And it seemed to send a clear message: The game's history was filled with epic stories of dramatic moments and heroic performances, to be sure. But there was also plenty of weird stuff that happened in between.

Once I hit my forties and was able to make a career out of writing about hockey, that's the kind of stuff I made sure to mention. To this day, I'll drop in a passing reference to some strange moment or circumstance and find that readers often have no idea what I'm talking about. Some assume I'm joking; others accuse me of making stuff up. I'm not. The NHL has featured so many weird side notes over the years that the story doesn't feel complete without them.

That's where this book comes in. The idea here is to trace the history of the NHL from its earliest days as a four-team organization (that almost immediately shrank to three when an arena fire left one team homeless) to its current iteration as a multibillion-dollar monstrosity. We'll look at the story from a fan's perspective—from yours and mine—and cover the best, the worst and (especially) the downright odd. This book is about the moments that brought you out of your seat, but also the ones that left you just shaking your head. Because Lord knows, the NHL has given us plenty of both.

To tell that tale, we'll have to go back to the start, more than a century ago.

IN THE BEGINNING

Let's all start a hockey league—but not with that guy

OUR STORY BEGINS THE WAY ALL THE TRULY GREAT ONES do: with a bunch of guys sitting around trying to figure out how to ditch the loser in the group that nobody likes.

By 1917, the year the NHL was born, there had already been several attempts to form professional ice hockey leagues in North America, with varying degrees of success. The Western Pennsylvania Hockey League had become the first to pay some of its players, in 1902, and soon it morphed into the International Professional Hockey League, the sport's first fully professional circuit. The IPHL didn't last long, running from 1904 to 1907, but it spawned plenty of imitators.

In those early years, the Eastern Canada Amateur Hockey Association had emerged as the sport's most successful league. "Success" in those days was relative, and like most of the era's leagues, the ECAHA struggled through financial challenges and team instability. The league lasted four seasons, until 1909, when a dispute broke out involving its most successful franchise.

The Montreal Wanderers had won three ECAHA titles, but new owner P.J. Doran announced his intention to move them to the Jubilee, a smaller rink that he also happened to own. The other owners objected, and the infighting led to them forming a new league, called the Canadian Hockey Association, without Doran or his team.

Needless to say, this didn't sit especially well with the Wanderers. In response, they formed their own league to compete with the CHA. Jimmy Gardner, the Wanderers' former star player and soon-to-be coach, approached an industrialist named Ambrose O'Brien, whose application to join the CHA with a team in Renfrew, Ontario, had been rejected. The two quickly put together a rival league, named it the National Hockey Association, and granted four franchises at their initial meeting on December 2, 1909.

Days later, the fledgling NHA and CHA both held organizing meetings at the Windsor Hotel in Montreal. Merger overtures were made, but the CHA rejected any such talk. That turned out to be a mistake. Within weeks, the CHA folded and two of its franchises were absorbed by the NHA. The new league, now featuring seven teams, began play in January. Over the next five years, despite the challenge of a world war and competition from the rival Pacific Coast Hockey Association, the NHA was able to establish itself as hockey's premier league, featuring franchises that would later become the Ottawa Senators and Montreal Canadiens. But by 1915, the fledgling league had a problem, and its name was Eddie Livingstone.

Livingstone came to own both of the league's Toronto teams, the Blueshirts and the Ontarios, the latter of which would later be renamed the Shamrocks. The rest of the NHA's owners didn't like the idea of both Toronto franchises being owned by the same man, let alone one as prickly as Livingstone. As D'Arcy Jenish describes him in his excellent 2013 book *The NHL: A Centennial History*, Livingstone "had the gentle demeanour of a pastor but the fastidious personality of a tax collector or customs agent."

Livingstone continuously struggled to find enough players to fill both rosters, which led to the demise of the Shamrocks in 1915. But even with their chief issue seemingly resolved, the league's troubles with the Toronto owner were hardly over. There were arguments over player rights, including an aborted trade of star Cy Denneny, and accusations that his teams played too rough a style. Tensions were high enough that Canadiens owner George Kennedy occasionally tried to fight Livingstone. The two never did come to blows, as far as we know, which was probably good news for Livingstone, given Kennedy's background as a professional wrestling promoter.

By November 1917, the rest of the NHA had finally had enough and voted to suspend the Blueshirts franchise. When Livingstone responded by suing the NHA, the rest of its owners came up with a novel solution: They shut down the entire league. And then, days later, they started a new one. In a meeting—once again at the Windsor—on November 26, 1917, the National Hockey League was formed. At the time, legendary hockey writer Elmer Ferguson asked Kennedy if Livingstone had been invited to join the new league. "I guess we forgot," the Canadiens owner deadpanned.

The new NHL was, in the eyes of the men who created it, just a stopgap until Livingstone dropped his lawsuit and they could reform the NHA. They gave it a year or two at most. It featured five teams—the Canadiens, Senators, Wanderers, Quebec Bulldogs and a new team in Toronto that didn't yet have a name but did fulfill the league's key requirement for acceptance: not being owned by Eddie Livingstone. The Bulldogs, in true early-twentieth-century hockey fashion, didn't make it to opening night, leaving the league to take the ice with four teams.

The very first games in NHL history were played on December 19, 1917, as the league debuted with a pair of contests. In Montreal, the Wanderers held on to beat Toronto by a final score of 10–9, with defenceman Dave Ritchie scoring the first goal in league history just a minute into the action. In addition to its historical importance, the game stands to this day as the greatest win in the Wanderers' entire NHL history . . . unfortunately, as we'll see in a moment. Meanwhile, the league's other Montreal franchise was earning a win of its own in Ottawa. The Canadiens topped the Senators 7–4 in front of a packed house of six thousand fans. That win featured five goals from "Phantom" Joe Malone, who would soon emerge as the league's first superstar by scoring forty-four goals in just twenty games.

For years, it was an open question as to which of these two games was actually the league's first, since official start times weren't well documented back then. But according to recent research by hockey historian Randy Boswell, the contest in Montreal earned "first-game" honours by about half an hour, owing partly to a last-minute contract dispute between Senators players and management that saw two Ottawa stars, Hamby

Shore and Jack Darragh, fail to agree to terms and join the game until after the first period was over. Yes, the NHL didn't even make it to its first opening faceoff without a labour dispute.

As those two final tallies attest, those early games tended to be high-scoring. The league averaged just under ten goals per game in its first season. Part of that was due to the era's goalies, who wore tiny pads and weren't anywhere near as big or athletic as their modern counterparts. They also weren't very skilled. Early scoring star Babe Dye's signature move was simply to get a hard shot away quickly; that was enough to allow him to rack up repeated thirty-goal seasons and to regularly score from his own side of the red line against flustered goalies who hadn't seen the puck coming.

Other early stars included Montreal's Newsy Lalonde, a two-time scoring champ, and Ottawa's feared combo of Cy Denneny and Frank Nighbor, the latter of whom earned the first Hart Trophy as league MVP in 1924. Nels Stewart won the Hart twice, including in his first season in 1925–26, and King Clancy and Sprague Cleghorn became the NHL's first blueline stars. In goal, Montreal's Georges Vézina and Ottawa's Clint Benedict shone early, while Canadiens star George Hainsworth emerged as the league's top netminder later in the 1920s. Hainsworth's best season came in 1928–29, when he posted a ridiculous goals-against average of 0.92. That number didn't make him all that much of an outlier by the end of the '20s , though, as the first decade of action in the new league had seen scoring plummet to under three goals per game thanks to improving goaltenders and rapid advances in defensive strategy. The offensive stagnation was enough of an issue for the NHL to adopt a rad-ical rule change: allowing the forward pass. The change was a big hit, with the *Ottawa Citizen* crowing that "the days of strictly defensive hockey have passed and the grand old winter pastime will come back to its former popularity."

The forward pass opened up the game for a new generation of scoring stars in the 1930s, such as Boston's Dit Clapper and Cooney Weiland, Montreal's Toe Blake and the Toronto Maple Leafs' "Kid Line" of Charlie Conacher, Busher Jackson and Joe Primeau. Eddie Shore became the first defenceman to win multiple Hart Trophies, capturing the honour four times—a mark that has been surpassed by only Wayne Gretzky and Gordie Howe.

The likes of Vézina, Blake and Shore bore little resemblance to the stars of today's NHL. Not only was the game markedly different, but there was no marketing machine to promote the league's first franchise players, and certainly no players' union to fight for their rights. Many worked second (and even third) jobs to make ends meet. Today, some fans haven't so much as heard names like Howie Morenz; most couldn't pick Babe Dye out of a lineup.* But these were the players who built the league into what it would become, and set the stage for future generations to reap the benefits by standing on their shoulders.

Like its stars, the NHL's standings in those early years didn't look much like what today's fans are used to. In each of the first four years, the season was divided into two sections—each was called a "half," although 1919–20 was the only season in which both halves contained an equal number of games. The team with the best record in each half would face each other in a final series for the overall league championship.

The very first NHL championship was won by the still-nameless Toronto team in a two-game, total-goals series against the Canadiens in 1918. Despite that initial success, Toronto struggled financially the next season, temporarily shutting down operations and watching from the sidelines as the Canadiens took the title in 1919. The Senators followed that by becoming the first team to win both halves of the season in 1919–20 and then becoming the league's first repeat champion in 1921. The half-season format was dropped in time for the 1921–22 season and replaced with a full-season schedule that saw the best two teams face off for the championship. The 1922 title went to the Toronto squad, now known as the St. Patricks.

You'll notice a distinct lack of references to the Stanley Cup so far. That's because hockey's most famous trophy wasn't exclusively reserved for the NHL until 1927. The trophy was originally commissioned in 1892

---

* Which is a shame, because he may have had the greatest hair in NHL history; the guy looks like somebody put a more stylish Henrik Lundqvist in a time machine.

by Lord Frederick Stanley of Preston, a British politician who was then serving as Canada's governor general. Stanley and his family were avid sports fans and had become enamoured with hockey while in Ottawa. He positioned his trophy as a challenge cup,* and that's what it remained until 1913, when the NHA and PCHA agreed that their respective champions would face off for the Cup.

The NHL continued that tradition, with its champion facing the winner of the PCHA (and later the Western Canada Hockey League) at the end of every season. The exception came in 1919, when an outbreak of Spanish flu forced the cancellation of the final series. Several Canadiens players were overtaken by the illness, and defenceman Joe Hall died. It would be the only year in the NHL's history that the Stanley Cup was not awarded until the 2005 lockout.

Beginning in 1927, the NHL assumed unofficial ownership of the Cup, and it was awarded directly to the league champion in every subsequent season. For the next fifteen years the trophy made its way around the NHL, never stopping very long with any one team. The only back-to-back winners were the Canadiens in 1931 and 1932 and the Red Wings in 1936 and 1937. But while the Cup changed hands frequently, it was increasingly being contested by the same group of teams. Apart from the 1927 Senators and 1935 Maroons, all other early-era Cup champions would go on to become the "Original Six."

Of course, we're getting ahead of ourselves here, because before it could field the Original Six, the league had to get off the ground with an original *four*. When the Quebec Bulldogs failed to ice a team ahead of opening night in 1917, it left the fledgling NHL with a pair of franchises in Montreal—the Wanderers and Canadiens—and a team each in Ottawa and Toronto. The Wanderers boasted a rich pre-NHL history, having been Stanley Cup champions in 1906, 1907, 1908 and 1910. During that first season in 1917–18, they expected to battle toe to toe with the cross-town Habs for the city's affection.

---

*   Meaning any team could challenge the current champions for it.

The rivalry lasted four games.

On January 2, 1918, the arena that both Montreal teams called home burned to the ground after a fire started in the ice-making plant. The Wanderers franchise was already struggling, having won only its first game while watching star players walk away from the team. Now, it found itself with nowhere to play.

The arena fire was the NHL's first crisis, and it was literally an existential one. If the new league lost both Montreal teams, it would almost certainly have to fold, having lasted mere weeks. Fortunately, the Canadiens quickly found a temporary home at the Jubilee Arena.* Unfortunately, the Wanderers were left adrift. With no meaningful offer of help coming from the NHL's other members, the team ceased operations. The NHL was only a few games old, and it had already lost its first active franchise.

Like the Wanderers, the Ottawa Senators entered the league as a dominant squad that had won several Cup titles in the challenge era only to see its first NHL season get off to a rocky start.** The loss of the Wanderers, a longtime pre-NHL rival, also hurt, and there was some question as to whether the iconic franchise, which could trace its roots back to the 1880s, would survive. It did, and even thrived for a time, winning four more Stanley Cups in the 1920s. But the 1930s brought hard times. The Senators were forced to miss the 1931–32 season, and by the end of the 1933–34 campaign, they had finished last in consecutive years and were rumoured to be looking to merge with another franchise.

Instead, they moved to St. Louis, where they became the Eagles. That led to threats of a lawsuit by the St. Louis Flyers, an existing minor-pro team that claimed that a previous agreement with the NHL granted them exclusive rights to the territory. The Eagles were eventually allowed to play when the Flyers relented, but they survived for just one season. At the end of the 1934–35 campaign, the team was sold back to the league and

---

* The Jubilee burned down in 1919, because NHL hockey in Montreal always seems to end with something catching fire.

** Including the financial dispute with Shore and Darragh that provided some ironic foreshadowing of the Rod Bryden and Eugene Melnyk eras.

disbanded. That was the official end of the original Ottawa Senators, which technically has no direct connection to the modern iteration. But that doesn't stop today's Senators fans from celebrating that early history—and claiming those old Stanley Cups as their own.

The demise of the Wanderers and Senators left just two of the four teams from the NHL's earliest incarnation in operation. Both are still going concerns today. You've probably heard of them.

The Montreal Canadiens are the only existing NHL team that predates the league itself. They were founded along with the NHA in 1910 as a francophone rival to the Wanderers and had already won their first Stanley Cup by the time the NHL was formed. While the franchise would go on to become the most successful in league history, its first decade in the NHL was fairly unremarkable. The Canadiens won three league titles and the 1924 Stanley Cup, and were competitive throughout—with the exception of the 1925–26 season, which saw them finish dead last.

The following year would stand as a turning point. Ahead of the 1926–27 season, the team moved from the Mount Royal Arena—its home since the 1919 fire that claimed the Jubilee—to a newer, bigger building known simply as the Forum. Over the next five years, they finished first in the league four times and won the Stanley Cup in 1930 and 1931.

That would be the team's last taste of postseason success until the Original Six era; from 1932 until 1941, the Habs* lost ten straight playoff series. By the late '30s, there was even some concern about the franchise's long-term viability as a result of low attendance. But the crowds returned, and the team enjoyed slightly more success from 1942 on—something we'll get to in a few chapters.

The Toronto Maple Leafs can also trace their roots back to the NHL's first days, although they weren't yet called the Leafs in 1917. Originally, the team didn't have a name at all—even when it won the league's first

---

* The nickname "Habs" is short for "*Habitants*," and seems to have appeared in the mid-'20s. Despite what you may have heard, the *H* in the famous Canadiens logo doesn't actually stand for *Habitants*, but rather *hockey*.

title, it was officially just "Toronto."* Fans and media of the day often referred to them as the Blueshirts, even though they weren't technically linked to Livingstone's old NHA squad. Later, they would become the Arenas (which the NHL retroactively recognizes as the name of the 1917–18 team) and then the St. Patricks. The Maple Leafs name wouldn't arrive for nearly a decade, and its creation was at least partially the fault of our old friend Eddie Livingstone.

As late as 1927, Livingstone was still causing headaches for the Toronto franchise, filing various lawsuits and generally making as much of a nuisance of himself as possible. Team ownership was said to be considering a move to Philadelphia, which would leave Toronto without an NHL team. That's when businessman Conn Smythe stepped in to form a group to buy the club and keep it in Toronto. Among Smythe's first acts as team owner were the adoptions of the now-iconic blue-and-white colour scheme and the even more iconic nickname. There's some dispute over exactly where the name came from. The generally accepted story is that it honours a World War I military regiment, although the fact that the name was also being used by Toronto's successful International League baseball team (which won a pennant in 1926) probably didn't hurt.**

Under any of its four handles, the Toronto team didn't exactly enjoy sustained early success. After capturing that 1918 Cup, they won just two more before 1942, the beginning of the Original Six era—once as the St. Patricks in 1922, and again as the Maple Leafs in 1932. But despite the lack of overall success, the franchise reached an important milestone in 1931 with the construction of Maple Leaf Gardens. Built in just five months and financed in part thanks to a clever offer to the construction

---

* This wasn't all that unusual. Even the Ottawa franchise, which had been called the Senators long before arriving in the NHL, was officially the Ottawa Hockey Club and was occasionally referred to as simply "the Ottawas."

**   For the record: No, the Toronto Maple Leafs' name is not grammatically incorrect. While it's true that the plural of "leaf" is "leaves," the team isn't named after those things that grow on tree branches. The Toronto Maple Leaf Hockey Club is a proper noun and the regular rules of pluralization don't apply. Stan and Scotty Bowman are the Bowmans, not the Bowmen, and Don Cherry's family members are the Cherrys, not the Cherries. Similarly, a group of Maple Leaf players are Leafs.

workers of stock in lieu of wages, the Gardens opened that November and immediately rivalled the Forum as the league's most impressive arena. And the timing couldn't have been much better, as the 1930–31 season had brought with it Toronto's first real superstar.

Building the Gardens on such a tight schedule was a financial risk for Smythe, but landing King Clancy for the Leafs took a gamble that's almost too strange to be believed. For the first nine seasons of his career, Clancy had starred with the Senators. But with the Ottawa franchise desperate for a cash infusion to kick off the 1930s, Sens ownership agreed to sell Clancy to Smythe's Maple Leafs for thirty-five thousand dollars. Straightforward enough, right? Well, just as straightforward was the fact that Smythe didn't have the money. So, the Leafs owner did the only reasonable thing: He bought a winless racehorse named Rare Jewel for two hundred and fifty dollars, entered her in the prestigious Coronation Futurity Stakes and cheered her to victory at 106–1 odds. The winner's purse (supplemented by a well-placed bet or two) gave Smythe the cash he needed to bring Clancy to Toronto. The talented blueliner led the team to a Stanley Cup in his second season in the Big Smoke.

Between their new star and their new home, the Maple Leafs were set to survive the ups and downs of what was still a relatively new league, pressing alongside the Canadiens towards what would become the Original Six era. As we'll see in the next chapter, a few of the other teams that tried to join them didn't meet with quite as much success.

RULES ARE RULES

Today's rule book may not be perfect, but it's come a long way

IN THIS BOOK, WE'RE GOING TO TAKE A MOMENT BETWEEN each chapter to explore some of the league's historical oddities. This isn't the important stuff; you can skip it all without missing anything fundamental to your understanding of the league. But sometimes the weird stuff is the most fun, and for that reason alone, I believe it's worth taking a page or two to explore it.

For starters, let's take a moment to appreciate the noble NHL rule book.

Nobody likes the rule book. Either it's being cited to enforce unfair penalties against the well-meaning (i.e., your team), or it's being outright ignored in the service of blatant cheaters (everyone else). Modern fans think the rule book is awful. But dare to suggest an improvement and you'll quickly find out that they also don't want it to ever change.

But over the years, it *has* changed. A lot. And that's a good thing, because some of the old rules were truly bizarre.

For one, the sport used to feature an extra skater for each team called a "rover." As the name implies, this player was free to go wherever he thought he was needed. The position was never featured in the NHL, but it was widely used elsewhere into the 1920s, including at the Olympics. The Hockey Hall of Fame lists nineteen inductees as having played the position at some point in their careers, including Newsy Lalonde and Cyclone Taylor.

Penalties were another aspect of the game that was handled differently in the early days. Minors were three minutes instead of two, and if a player was kicked out of the game, his team played shorthanded the rest of the way. Goaltenders originally had to serve their own penalties, leaving the team's other players to temporarily mind the net. (Backup goalies weren't widely used in the league's early days, which led to some interesting situations when starters were hurt or otherwise unable to play. New York Rangers coach Lester Patrick famously had to strap on the pads one night in the 1928 Stanley Cup final, helping his team to an overtime win.) And penalty shots once came in the form of a blast from a specific spot exactly thirty-eight feet in front of the goal line.

Even better, many of those penalties could be called for infractions we wouldn't recognize today. A Montreal Forum programme published in 1934* included calls for such transgressions as moving before a faceoff, a positioning rule called "anti-defence" and, best of all, "loafing."

So, the next time you're at an NHL game and everyone around you is yelling at the officials over an obvious dive or yet another interminable video review, mix it up a little: Start screaming about a missed call for loafing. The refs may not know what you're talking about, but it will bring back some memories for the ninety-year-old in the next section.

---

* Recently uncovered by NHL historian Dave Stubbs.

2

THE FORGOTTEN TEAMS

We all know the Original Six.
But what about these NHL teams that came before?

IF YOU'RE A HOCKEY FAN, YOU KNOW ALL ABOUT THE Original Six, the group of teams that represented the sum total of NHL hockey between 1942 and the league's expansion in 1967.

You really have no choice. Today, the league insists that the Toronto Maple Leafs, Montreal Canadiens, New York Rangers, Detroit Red Wings, Chicago Blackhawks and Boston Bruins be treated with reverence. Their histories are recounted in hushed tones. Games between them get extra attention. They are clearly in a category of their own, separate and just slightly elevated above the rest of the league.

And rightly so, because the Original Six is just a flat-out cool concept. The fact that the NHL was such a small outfit for so long sets it apart from the other major North American sports leagues, and the stability that came with having the exact same lineup of teams in place for a quarter century allowed fans to fall in love with a familiar product. Hockey fans adore the Original Six, as well they should.

But given all that reverence, it often comes as a surprise to new fans to learn that the Original Six weren't really the NHL's original teams. Only one of them was even around (under its current name) when the league officially formed back in 1917, and over the first twenty-five years of the NHL's history, franchises appeared, folded, moved and changed identities almost constantly. That "original" lineup of six didn't actually appear until the NHL had already seen eleven other teams come and go.

After the Montreal Wanderers made their early exit, the NHL's three-team era lasted for two seasons before the league expanded for the first time by welcoming the Quebec Bulldogs back for the 1919–20 season. In what would serve as both a reminder of the Bulldogs' first kick at the NHL can and an omen for the next century or so of expansion attempts, it didn't go all that well.

The Bulldogs weren't an expansion franchise in the modern sense; rather than starting from scratch, they were an existing team based in Quebec City with a history in the NHA and other leagues. But they'd been dormant for two years before taking the ice in the NHL, and star player Joe Malone had joined the Canadiens in the meantime. Malone returned to the Bulldogs for that 1919–20 season and led the league with thirty-nine goals and forty-nine points in only twenty-four games, but his standout play wasn't exactly contagious—the team won just four games and finished dead last.

That first season would also be the Bulldogs' last, as poor attendance and shaky financials doomed the club. The league took control of the team in 1920 and moved it to Hamilton, where it became the Tigers. Hamilton brought somewhat more success than the team had enjoyed in Quebec City; the Tigers were at least a viable franchise for five years. They weren't very good, mind you, and missed the playoffs in each of their first four seasons. At one point, the league ordered its other teams to supply the Tigers with better players in the hopes of making them competitive. Even that didn't help much. By the time the 1925 Stanley Cup was awarded, the NHL's first foray into Hamilton had come to an end.

Despite the Tigers' struggles, the Canadiens, Senators and Arenas/St. Pats were competitive, and the NHL had better luck when adding two new teams in 1924, both of which stuck around for awhile. One was the league's first American franchise, the Boston Bruins, who of course earned a place among the Original Six. The other didn't last quite as long, but did manage a respectable run of fourteen years. That would be the NHL's third Montreal-based franchise, the Maroons.

With the Canadiens by now a reasonably established success among Montreal's francophone residents, the Maroons were intended to pick up where the Wanderers had left off as the team of choice for the city's English-speaking population. The plan largely worked, and the Maroons played in front of sold-out crowds while establishing themselves as one of the league's most successful teams. They won Stanley Cups in 1926 and 1935—the last non–Original Six team to win it until the 1970s—and produced future Hall of Famers like Babe Siebert and Nels Stewart, who retired in 1940 as the NHL's all-time goal-scoring king, a title he held until Maurice Richard broke his record in 1952.

While the Maroons were a successful team over their fourteen-year history, their greatest contribution to the NHL came in their very first season. Needing a new arena,* the team built the largest in the league at the corner of Sainte-Catherine Street and Atwater Avenue. The building was christened the Forum, and it would go on to become the most famous cathedral in hockey history. While it will be forever linked with the Canadiens, the Forum opened in 1924 as the exclusive home of the Maroons; the Habs wouldn't move in to join them until two years later.

Tough economic times eventually caught up with both Montreal teams, but the Maroons were hit hardest. By 1937, they were struggling badly and in danger of moving. They finished the 1937–38 season, but suspended operations afterwards. As occasionally happened in those days, the team technically remained in limbo until the league officially cancelled it in 1947, meaning that even during the early years of the Original Six era, there were actually more than six teams on the books.

With the Bruins and Maroons on board, the 1924–25 campaign was notable for being the only one in the pre–Original Six era to include exactly six teams. That off-season, the league moved the Tigers to New York, where they became the Americans, and added a new franchise in

---

*   Preferably one that wouldn't burn down.

Pittsburgh. The Americans gave the NHL its first entry into the world's biggest market, and they were the first team to play at a brand-new arena called Madison Square Garden. They also gave the league one of its early legendary characters: team owner "Big Bill" Dwyer. Officially, Dwyer was a New York entrepreneur. Unofficially, he was a mobster and bootlegger. Flush with money, Dwyer was more generous with his players than other owners. His relationship with opposing players wasn't quite as friendly. According to legend, Detroit goalie Alec Connell almost got himself killed by socking a crooked goal judge at the Garden who also happened to be a member of Dwyer's gang, leading to a failed hit attempt that night.

Joined at the Garden by the more-enduring Rangers a year later, the Americans had a reasonably good run of their own, lasting until the 1941–42 season. A combination of the league's endemic financial problems and the outbreak of World War II led to the team's demise, although like the Maroons, they lingered on as a ghost franchise for years before being officially folded. The Americans played their final game after seventeen seasons. All told, not a bad little run.

The new team in Pittsburgh wasn't quite as successful. Creatively named the Pirates after the city's established Major League Baseball team, the franchise lasted just five seasons. It was a decent team for at least a few years, riding Lionel "The Big Train" Conacher to playoff appearances in two of its first three seasons.* But in 1928–29, the Pirates managed just nine wins in forty-four games. They were even worse in their final season, going 5–36–3 while selling off players to make ends meet. They were relocated to Philadelphia to become the Quakers before the 1930–31 season. That was intended as a temporary move, but not quite as temporary as it turned out. The Quakers lasted just one season, winning four games, before folding. The NHL wouldn't return to Pennsylvania for thirty-six years.

---

*   Conacher was one of the era's first multisport stars, also excelling at football and baseball, and was voted the greatest Canadian athlete of the half century in 1950. Even back then, Canada's biggest stars had a knack for ending up in Pittsburgh.

The 1926–27 season saw the biggest expansion yet, with the league adding three teams in the Rangers, Chicago Black Hawks and Detroit Cougars. Finally, each of the Original Six teams was in place, although it would take awhile for Detroit to become the Red Wings—they would also be known as the Falcons before finally settling on their permanent moniker in 1932.

That 1926 expansion—the league's last for forty-one years—left the NHL with ten teams divided in the standings into an American Division featuring Boston, Chicago, Detroit, Pittsburgh and the New York Rangers, and a Canadian Division featuring Toronto, Ottawa, both Montreal teams and the New York Americans. Yes, the league put a New York team in the Canadian Division. Yes, the team was even called the *Americans*. When it comes to drawing up divisions, the NHL has struggled with the concept of geography. This will turn out to be a theme.

Those ten teams would be whittled down to seven by the 1941–42 season, as the Maroons, Senators/Eagles and Pirates/Quakers all made their exits. The Americans followed in 1942 (although some consideration was given to the idea of the team returning within a year or two, it never happened). The NHL was back down to six teams.

There were no grand ceremonies or declarations of a new era when the Americans vanished. It simply felt like yet another change for a league that was getting used to them. But, though nobody knew it at the time, after twenty-five years of near-constant flux, stability had finally arrived in the National Hockey League. The Original Six era had begun.

THE BEST TEAM TO EVER MISS THE PLAYOFFS

You think the modern-day NHL gives Hamilton a rough ride?

THE CITY OF HAMILTON, ONTARIO, HAS QUITE THE HISTORY when it comes to hockey. It has played host to teams in the American Hockey League and at the major junior level, as well as tournaments such as the 1986 World Junior Championship. And in 1987, the Steel City was the scene of Mario Lemieux's historic goal against the Soviets to win the Canada Cup. Many fans still view that game as one of the greatest ever played.

But when it comes to the NHL, Hamilton's luck has been significantly more hit-and-miss. It seemed like the city was on the way to getting an expansion team back in the mid-'80s, when Copps Coliseum opened and was instantly hailed as one of the better arenas in North America, but that team never arrived. And tech giant Jim Balsillie's ongoing efforts to lure an existing team to the city, which peaked in 2009 with the Make It Seven campaign, gathered plenty of fan support but ultimately died, largely due to lack of interest from the league.

So maybe it will make disappointed fans in Hamilton feel better to know that there really was a time when the city had its own NHL team. And given how well it went, it might be just as well that you probably won't be getting another.

As we saw in chapter 2, the Hamilton Tigers weren't very good over their first four years in the NHL. Debuting in 1920, they won just six times over the course of the twenty-four-game season. They increased that total to seven in 1921–22, dropped back down to six a year later, and then managed an unprecedented nine wins during the 1923–24 campaign. None of those teams made the playoffs.

But the 1924–25 Tigers finally clicked. They won nineteen of their thirty games and finished in first place in the six-team league. Finally, NHL playoff hockey would be coming to Hamilton.

Well, not so fast.

After adding two new teams the previous summer, the NHL had lengthened the regular-season schedule. The league had also made it clear that all playoff revenue would go directly into the pockets of the team owners. Those changes didn't sit well with some players, who had the crazy idea in their heads that extra work should translate into extra pay.

And so, at the end of the regular season, the Hamilton Tigers walked off the job. They demanded more money, including a share of the playoff revenue they were about to generate. Led by team captain Shorty Green, the players demanded that each receive a two-hundred-dollar raise before they'd take the ice for another game.* Pay up, the players essentially said, or you can go ahead and have your postseason without the league's best team. To which NHL president Frank Calder replied: We'll take the second option.

Calder wasn't much for compromise, at least when it came to negotiating with the league's workforce, and when it became clear that the players weren't bluffing, he dropped the hammer. Calder fined each striking player the same two hundred dollars they'd been demanding and suspended the entire team.

The 1925 playoffs went ahead as scheduled—without the Tigers. The season was supposed to introduce a three-team playoff system in which the league's second- and third-best teams would face each other in a semifinal, with the winner taking on the first-place squad. With the Tigers sidelined, the semifinal between the Canadiens and St. Pats ended up being for the league title. The Canadiens won.

As for the Tigers, the team never played another game in Hamilton. The franchise was sold to Dwyer and moved to New York, and any man involved in the strike was forced to write an apology letter to Calder before he could play again. Nearly a century later, the NHL has yet to return to Hamilton.

---

* One version of the story, as told by Ron Corbett in a 2013 *Ottawa Sun* article, has the Tigers making the decision to strike over a few drinks in the bar car on the train ride home from their last regular-season game.

Writing in the *Toronto Star* in 2009, historian Myer Siemiatycki called the Tigers "the best NHL team never to win the Stanley Cup." Would that still be the case if not for the players' strike? And if the Tigers *had* won a Cup, would the NHL have stayed in Hamilton, and maybe even lasted there to this day? We'll never know. But while fans in the city may never get the team they've been longing for, at least they can lay claim to some dubious NHL history: the only first-place team to ever miss the playoffs.

3

THE DAWN OF THE ORIGINAL SIX

Through wartime, scandal and three league presidents,
a golden era begins

WHILE TODAY'S FANS CAN LOOK BACK ON THE 1942–43 season as the dawn of a new era, it hardly felt that way at the time. The constant birth, death and relocation of teams had left the NHL's long-term survival far from certain. What's more, World War II was playing havoc with teams' rosters and bottom lines, to the point that there was serious talk about suspending operations in 1942 before the Canadian and US governments urged pro sports leagues to continue.

Many of the era's biggest names would seem unfamiliar to modern fans, given how the league tends to skip over the period when promoting its history. The league's top scorers in 1941–42 had included such players as Phil Watson, Red Hamill and Don Grosso. The postseason all-star teams featured names like Pat Egan and Bucko McDonald. The Hart Trophy went to Tommy Anderson of the Americans, a team that ceased to exist over the off-season. As it turns out, they took Anderson's NHL career with them. He ended up enlisting in the army and spent the next three seasons playing in the Calgary National Defence Hockey League; he didn't appear in the NHL again.*

The impact of the war was reflected in the standings as well. Due

---

* As of 2018, Anderson, Al Rollins and José Théodore remain the only Hockey Hall of Fame–eligible Hart Trophy winners not to have been elected.

to travel restrictions, the league did away with overtime periods as of November 1942, resulting in a spike in ties. Regular-season sudden death wouldn't return until 1983.

Still, the players who were available put on a decent show. The Detroit Red Wings took first place in 1942–43 with a 25–14–11 record, then rolled to a Stanley Cup by knocking off the Toronto Maple Leafs and sweeping the Boston Bruins.* Only the New York Rangers were truly bad, managing just eleven wins while finishing dead last, nineteen points behind the fifth-place Chicago Black Hawks. They'd be even worse the next year; having lost nearly half their roster to the war by 1943, the Rangers suffered through what might be the worst season in NHL history. They started with a fifteen-game winless streak and outdid themselves to close out the year, failing to earn a *W* over a twenty-one-game stretch. In between, they won just six times, and at one point they were beaten 15–0 by the Red Wings, the biggest blowout in league history. They wouldn't win a playoff round for the rest of the decade.

For their part, the Montreal Canadiens puttered along to .500, ending with a 19–19–12 record on their way to a quick playoff exit. It was actually the team's best finish in years—they'd ended up in either sixth or seventh place in each of the last four seasons and hadn't won a Stanley Cup since 1931—but that was about to change, largely thanks to a rookie winger who made his NHL debut in that first Original Six season.

Maurice Richard was born in 1921 and grew up in Montreal's Bordeaux neighbourhood, a rough area in the city's north end perhaps best known for its prison. He was the oldest of eight children, and his family was poor. He began to garner attention for his hockey skills while studying to become a machinist, and by 1938 was considered a future star. He signed with the Montreal Canadiens farm team in 1940, but suffered two fractures in his first two seasons, delaying his NHL debut until 1942, when he was twenty-one years old.

---

* That loss earned the Bruins the O'Brien Cup, a now-forgotten trophy awarded to the playoff runner-up from 1939 until it was retired in 1950.

That debut season was largely forgettable; Richard played just sixteen games and scored only five goals before a broken leg sidelined him. It was his third major injury in as many years, and there was speculation that he was too fragile to last in the league—concerns that turned out to be unfounded, as he stayed healthy for most of the rest of his career. Richard's follow-up was anything but forgettable; he established himself as a star by scoring thirty-two goals in 1943–44, and then achieved immortality with his fifty-in-fifty season in 1944–45.

Meanwhile, another newcomer was playing perhaps an even bigger role in Montreal's ascent. Goaltender Bill Durnan arrived as a twenty-seven-year-old rookie in 1943 and immediately established himself as the league's best at the position, earning the Vézina Trophy and first-team all-star honours in each of his first four seasons. Adding Durnan and Richard to a roster that already featured veteran stars like "Toe" Blake and Elmer Lach was enough to create the first true powerhouse of the Original Six era. The Canadiens led the league in points every year between 1944 and 1947—including topping the eighty-point mark twice (in a fifty-game schedule)—and that dominance produced Stanley Cups in 1944 and 1946.

Hot on Montreal's heels, the Maple Leafs captured the trophy in 1945, then closed out the decade with three straight wins from 1947 through 1949. Those Leaf teams featured stars like Syl Apps, Teeder Kennedy and Turk Broda, and while they only topped the standings in the regular season once in the decade, they had a knack for coming through in the playoffs. That was best exemplified by the 1948–49 team, which actually finished under .500 and barely claimed the league's fourth and final play-off spot before winning all but one of its playoff games on the way to another title.

While that championship was good news for the Maple Leafs, the 1948–49 season almost brought an even bigger prize to Toronto. Determined to improve his team by importing some star power, Conn Smythe made a push to purchase Maurice Richard's contract from the Canadiens. By this point, the Rocket was already one of the game's brightest stars, a four-time first-team all-star with a Hart Trophy to his name. It wasn't unusual for NHL owners to float the idea of purchasing star players, but this time the news leaked and Toronto's *Globe and Mail* newspaper even ran a doctored photograph of Richard in a Maple Leafs uniform. The prospective deal created quite a stir in both cities, but the Canadiens eventually turned Smythe down, leaving fans to chew on one of the great "what if?" scenarios in NHL history.

While there was finally some consistency to the lineup of teams after the departure of the Americans, the 1940s still brought their share of changes and challenges to the NHL. The league went through three presidents in the decade, as Frank Calder passed away in 1943 and his successor, Red Dutton, quit in 1946, paving the way for Clarence Campbell to begin a thirty-one-year reign. By the middle of the decade, some of the game's former stars were returning from their military duties. The league expanded its schedule to sixty games and began introducing many of what are now traditional hockey sights and symbols, including red goal lights, hand signals for penalties and captains wearing a *C* on their jerseys.* The decade also saw the debut of the all-star game as an annual tradition. The game pitted the defending Cup champions against a roster of stars from the remaining five teams, and was typically scheduled to be played before the regular season began. The first official all-star game was played on October 13, 1947, in Toronto, with the league's best taking on the Cup champion Maple Leafs. Newspapers breathlessly reported that the game would feature nearly a million dollars' worth of talent. The all-stars won 4–3 in front of a sellout crowd at Maple Leaf Gardens.

Considerably less breathless was the response to the story that closed out the decade: the Billy Taylor/Don Gallinger gambling scandal.

Taylor was a playmaking forward who'd broken into the NHL with the Maple Leafs during the 1939–40 season. He spent five seasons in Toronto, winning a Cup in 1942 and posting sixty points in 1942–43,

---

* Initially, goalies were allowed to be captains, and Durnan briefly held the honour for the Canadiens. In 1948, the league banned goaltenders from exercising the duties of captain; Roberto Luongo held the role for the Vancouver Canucks from 2008 to 2010, but couldn't wear a *C* or discuss calls with officials.

before a trade sent him to Detroit three years later. He had a career-best sixty-three points in his lone season with the Red Wings, leading the league in assists in the process. That included a seven-assist game, establishing an NHL record that was unmatched until the 1980s, when Wayne Gretzky tied it on three occasions.

Gallinger made his NHL debut with the Bruins during the 1942–43 season. At just seventeen years old, he was one of the youngest players in league history, and he remains the youngest player to ever score a playoff overtime goal thanks to his winner against the Canadiens in that year's semifinals. Despite losing time to military service, he'd established himself as a full-time NHLer by 1947, at which point he was still just twenty-two years old. It would end up being his final year in pro sports.

Shortly before the 1947–48 season began, Taylor was traded to the Bruins, where he eventually roomed with Gallinger. Both players had reputations as gamblers, and Gallinger had already been betting on the Bruins—always to win, he'd later claim. Taylor apparently convinced him they could both make more money betting against their own team. Pro athletes gambling on their own games had been considered a serious breach of ethics at least as far back as the Black Sox scandal that arose during the 1919 World Series and nearly brought down Major League Baseball. The NHL had been taking accusations seriously for years, and in 1946 the Maple Leafs' Babe Pratt had served a nine-game suspension for betting on Toronto.* NHL president Clarence Campbell had made it clear to teams and players alike: no betting on games. But that message apparently didn't deter Gallinger and Taylor, who were caught late in the season. Taylor had been traded to New York by then, but the Bruins had their suspicions about him and Gallinger, and those were confirmed by a police wiretap. When the two players continued to deny any wrongdoing, Campbell suspended them indefinitely, swearing they'd never play in the NHL again. Neither ever did. While the bans were formally lifted in 1970, they remain the longest suspensions in NHL history.

---

* Pratt was inducted into the Hockey Hall of Fame in 1966 and Gallinger's son later told *The Hockey News* that Pratt's light sentence had always bothered his father.

———

By the time the 1950s arrived, the Maple Leafs had built a dynasty, Richard was the sport's biggest star, Campbell was ruling with an iron fist, and—perhaps most important of all—the NHL was a successful and, at long last, stable operation. But there was more change to come. And a major agent of it would arrive from Detroit in the form of a twenty-one-year-old kid named Gordie Howe, who was in the middle of a breakout season for the Red Wings.

THE ORIGINAL . . . SEVEN?

The NHL's forgotten decision to add a seventh team in 1952

THE ORIGINAL SIX ERA COULDN'T LAST FOREVER. FINANCIAL realities would eventually force the league to catch up to the rest of the sports world and expand. But there was something simple and almost romantic about the same six teams taking the ice for a generation—something that still tugs at hockey lovers' heartstrings more than half a century later.

And that's probably why you rarely hear about the time in 1952 when the NHL approved a seventh team . . . in Cleveland.

It actually wasn't as crazy as it sounds. These days, Cleveland's two-year NHL foray in the late '70s is a punchline. But in the early 1950s, the city had been chasing a team for years and its efforts were taken seriously—in a 1935 article in the *New York Herald Tribune*, one of the owners of the Montreal Canadiens was quoted as suggesting the team might be better off moving to Cleveland. At the time, pro hockey was thriving in Ohio. That was largely due to the American Hockey League's Cleveland Barons, who'd won the Calder Cup in 1951 and were playing to packed houses at the old Cleveland Arena. And so, in 1952, the Barons made a push for a spot in the NHL.

The league's board of governors considered the offer and, after some debate, emerged with a decision. On May 14, 1952, the owners announced that the Barons were in. The NHL's six-team era was over.

Sort of.

To gain admission, the Barons would have to meet certain "financial conditions," announced NHL president Clarence Campbell. As long as they did that by June 1, the president assured fans, "it is almost a certainty they will be in the NHL next season." The specific targets weren't made public at the time, but years later they were reported to involve the Barons securing five hundred thousand dollars in capital. Their backers weren't able to get that cash—by some accounts, they never even came close—and the NHL eventually withdrew its approval of the franchise. Almost as quickly as it had made it in, Cleveland was back out, and the six-team era continued.

In a 1966 interview, Campbell told the Associated Press that he had been confident enough in the Cleveland offer that he had already drawn up a new league schedule that included the seventh team. While he acknowledged that other markets had approached the league at various points in the Original Six era, he claimed that the Cleveland bid was the only one the NHL actually came close to accepting.

The Barons returned to the AHL, winning another Calder Cup in 1953 and enjoying continued success until financial struggles forced a move to Florida in the early '70s. Cleveland would have to wait until 1976 for another shot at the NHL, and most hockey fans forgot all about the day the NHL announced to the world that its Original Six would become an Original Seven.

4

HOCKEY'S FIRST SUPERSTARS

The Rocket and Mr. Hockey dominate the decade

HEADING INTO THE 1950S, HOCKEY FANS KNEW THERE were two things you could count on when it came to the Detroit Red Wings. First, they were going to make the playoffs—they hadn't missed since 1938. And second, once they got to the postseason, they probably weren't winning the Cup. They'd won just once in the last twelve seasons, despite making six trips to the final. Two of those had come in the last two years, and Detroit had been swept by the Maple Leafs each time. The Red Wings were good. They just were never good enough.

As the 1949–50 season wore on, a third fact was established about the Detroit Red Wings: You should keep your eye on that Gordie Howe kid. This was good advice for both fans and players, although for different reasons. If you were a fan, you wanted to watch Howe because you didn't want to miss a goal. And if you were playing against him, you had to keep an eye on him because otherwise, you might come out of the game with large swaths of your face in the wrong place.

Born on March 31, 1928, Howe grew up in Saskatoon, the sixth of nine children in his family's Depression-era home. He was a big kid who spent his summers working construction with his dad, and he arrived in the NHL ready and willing to play a physical game. He made his debut as an eighteen-year-old in 1946, and in 1948–49 he put up thirty-seven points in forty games to earn second-team all-star honours. But that 1949–50 season was the breakout. Howe scored thirty-five goals, more than double his career best, while posting sixty-eight points over seventy games. That still only earned him a second-team all-star nod—Rocket Richard had held the first-team spot for six straight years—but it marked his first appearance among the league's top ten scorers. Howe ranked third that year, trailing only linemates Sid Abel and Ted Lindsay. That powerful trio drove the Red Wings to a franchise-record eighty-eight points and first place overall. They took the longest possible route through the play-offs, winning both series in overtime of the seventh game. But win they did, as Howe and the Red Wings rewrote history by seeing their names engraved on the Stanley Cup.

It wouldn't be their last championship. Though Abel was exiting his prime, Howe and Lindsay were just coming into theirs. They had support from another breakout star, twenty-two-year-old defencemen Red Kelly. And while Cup-winning goaltender Harry Lumley was dispatched to the Black Hawks in an off-season trade,* the Wings were confident that their twenty-year-old backup with just seven games of NHL experience under his belt could take over. They turned out to be right; Terry Sawchuk, who'd make eleven all-star game appearances and win four Vézinas before hanging up his skates, was pretty good.

That group would dominate the decade's first half. Howe won four straight Art Ross Trophies as the league's leading scorer from 1951 through 1954, taking home two Hart Trophies along the way. Lindsay was a first-team all-star each of those years, as was Kelly. Sawchuk won the Calder as top rookie in 1951 and followed that with his first two Vézinas—back to back. The 1950–51 Wings became the first team to top 100 points; Detroit would finish in first place overall every season until 1955, winning three more Cups in the process. Two of those came under the leadership of team president Marguerite Norris, who'd taken on the role after the death of her father, James. Norris led the team to three first-place finishes and two championships, becoming the first woman to have

---

*   The deal was massive, featuring nine players, and would hold the record as the NHL's largest until the Leafs and Flames pulled off the ten-player Doug Gilmour trade in 1992.

her name inscribed on the Stanley Cup. The Wings' reign ended in 1954–55, with a championship that would be the franchise's last for more than forty years. But the joy the victory should have brought would be overshadowed by one of the ugliest nights in NHL history.

Howe and the Red Wings were establishing themselves as the league's best team, but Maurice "The Rocket" Richard was still the game's signature player. Even in his thirties, he had a knack for finding the net, and he led the league in goals in both 1953–54 and 1954–55, giving him five goal-scoring titles for his career and cementing the reputation that would eventually see a trophy, handed out to league's leading goal scorer, named after him. Richard had been a first- or second-team all-star every season since 1944, had won a Hart Trophy and three Stanley Cups, and was well established as the face of the Canadiens franchise and a genuine cultural icon among French-Canadians. But in that 1954–55 season, the thirty-three-year-old Richard was chasing one of the few honours he'd never earned: the points-scoring title. As the season ticked away, the race for the Art Ross Trophy came down to Richard and two teammates, Bernie "Boom Boom" Geoffrion and Jean Béliveau. While the other two were popular with fans, Richard was on another level, and there was little doubt as to who the Canadiens faithful were rooting for.

On March 13, 1955, Montreal went into Boston to face the Bruins. The game turned ugly in the third period, when Boston's Hal Laycoe clubbed Richard with his stick, opening up a gash that would require five stiches. Richard went wild, repeatedly swinging his stick at Laycoe in retaliation. Worse, the Canadiens star landed two punches on linesman Cliff Thompson, leaving the official with a cut and a black eye. Attacking an opposing player, even with a stick, wasn't an especially unusual occurrence in the NHL of the mid-'50s, and Richard's actions would have likely resulted in a fine and short suspension if he'd stopped there. But striking an official was another matter entirely. Richard and the Canadiens claimed that the combination of Laycoe's high stick to the head and the blood running into his eyes had left the Rocket disoriented and unaware that he was hitting the wrong guy. They asked Clarence Campbell for lenience.

Campbell wasn't having it. After a March 16 hearing, the league president issued a 1,200-word ruling in which he suspended Richard for the remainder of the season, including the playoffs.* Around the hockey world, there was general support for Campbell's ruling, with some going so far as to argue that he'd gone easy on Richard, who in another sport could have been facing a lifetime ban. But the decision was greeted with shock in Montreal, where it was viewed as yet another example of the league's English-speaking power brokers having it in for a francophone hero. Richard had been wrong, Canadiens fans might acknowledge, but the league would never come down on Gordie Howe or Ted Kennedy to the same degree.

With Montreal already simmering, Campbell announced that he would be at the Forum for the March 17 game against the Red Wings. The situation was a powder keg, with protests outside the building and death threats called in to the president's office. Campbell took his seat after the game had begun, and was immediately booed and pelted with garbage. One fan managed to get around security and offer Campbell a hand-shake, only to sucker-punch the president when he accepted; shortly after, a tear gas canister was set off in the stands. The order came down to cancel the game and evacuate the arena, with the Red Wings declared the winners by forfeit.

With thousands of furious Canadiens fans now spilling onto the streets, the situation escalated to a full-scale riot. The crowd smashed store windows, overturned cars and set fires. Roughly one hundred fans were arrested, and damage was estimated at one hundred thousand dollars. The Richard Riot, as it would become known, raged well into the night. The next day, the Rocket himself appeared on television to accept his suspension and urge fans to do the same. Geoffrion passed his team-mate to secure the scoring title on the season's final day. When he did, Montreal fans booed him.

Beyond the hundred thousand dollars in damage, the Richard suspension may also have cost the Canadiens the 1955 Stanley Cup. Their forfeit loss on the night of the riot ended up dropping them out of first

---

* Richard's reported reaction to the news: "You're kidding. Now tell me the truth."

place overall, as they finished two points behind Detroit on the season. That gave the Red Wings home-ice advantage throughout the playoffs, and they'd go on to defeat the Rocket-less Canadiens in a final that went the full seven, with the respective home teams winning every game.

At the end of the 1954–55 season, Canadiens general manager Frank Selke made a coaching switch, parting ways with Dick Irvin and handing the reins over to former star Toe Blake. Blake inherited a roster stacked with future Hall of Famers, including Geoffrion, Béliveau, Richard and his brother Henri, Doug Harvey and Dickie Moore, with Jacques Plante in net. (Plante was still playing without a mask. He'd begin donning one during practice a year later, but didn't begin regularly wearing it in games until 1959. Other goalies slowly followed his lead, but as late as 1974 fans could spot goaltenders playing barefaced.) It was one of the most formidable lineups ever assembled, and Blake's coaching turned out to be the final piece of the dynasty puzzle. For the first and only time in league history, a team won five straight Stanley Cups. It's hard to overstate how dominant the Canadiens were; they finished in first place every year but one, and never once faced an elimination game in a playoff series. They were so good that the NHL was forced to change its rules to adapt to them. The league began ending power plays after the team with the man advantage scored a goal because the Habs were netting two or three on a single penalty.

Of course, there's a common objection raised whenever you laud the success of those Canadiens teams. You've probably heard some variation of it yourself, and maybe even used it on an especially annoying Montreal fan. It goes something like this: Sure, the Canadiens built some great teams, but they only did so thanks to a major advantage over everyone else in the league—they had first dibs on all the great French players of the era. Basically, the Canadiens only lapped the field because the league gave them a big head start.

It's a comforting thought for fans of other teams who are tired of listening to the legions of devotees of *Les Glorieux* brag about all their Stanley Cups. There's just one problem: It's not true.

Well, not *completely* true. There was indeed a rule that gave the Canadiens first shot at Quebec-based players. Two rules, in fact—one that was in place through much of the 1920s and '30s, and another that was brought in along with the amateur draft in 1963. But most fans who love to cite "territorial rights" have it wrong in a couple of key respects. The first is that other teams had geographical claims of their own. More importantly, the rule that came in with the '63 draft only gave the Canadiens first crack at players whose rights *hadn't already been secured by other teams*. That ruled out most of the top young talent in the world, and it's why Quebec-born stars like Jean Ratelle, Dave Keon and Bernie Parent were available to the New York Rangers, Toronto Maple Leafs and Boston Bruins, respectively. The best player ever acquired by Montreal through its "priority" rights was probably Réjean Houle, in 1969. The franchise's greatest French-Canadian players, from Plante to the Richard brothers to Yvan Cournoyer, Guy Lafleur and Patrick Roy, were all acquired through traditional scouting, drafting and development. All except one, that is, although his arrival had nothing to do with territorial rights.

Montreal brass first spotted Jean Béliveau when he was just fifteen years old. They acquired his professional rights, but the standout from Victoriaville settled in with the Quebec Aces, an amateur team in the Quebec Senior Hockey League. Béliveau seemed perfectly happy in the QSHL, reportedly earning more money there than all but a handful of NHL stars were pulling down at the time. He made a few brief appearances for the Canadiens, but turned down the team's overtures to join them permanently. Eventually, as the (possibly apocryphal) legend goes, Selke got tired of waiting and came up with a novel way of forcing the young star's hand: He bought the rights to the QSHL and formally converted the entire league to a professional outfit. Since the Canadiens held Béliveau's pro rights, he couldn't re-sign with the Aces. When Selke came calling with a generous contract offer, Béliveau had little choice but to accept, finally joining the franchise in 1953 on a full-time basis, at the age of twenty-two.

While the Canadiens were dominating the standings through the late '50s, an equally important story was playing out in Boston. In January 1958, the Bruins responded to a string of injuries by calling up a young winger from the AHL. That player was Willie O'Ree, and though his first stint in the league lasted just two games, he'd make history by becoming the first black player in the NHL.

The milestone came eleven years after Jackie Robinson had broken the colour barrier in Major League Baseball, and well after the NBA and NFL had integrated. O'Ree wasn't actually the first visible minority to play in the NHL; that was Chinese-Canadian winger Larry Kwong, who played a single game for the Rangers in 1948. Nor was O'Ree the first black player worthy of NHL attention; among others, Herb Carnegie had dominated the Quebec senior league,* and Art Dorrington had signed a contract with the Rangers in 1950.

But neither Dorrington or Carnegie was given a shot at the NHL, and it was years before O'Ree received his. Despite a successful career in the minor leagues, O'Ree had been targeted with slurs and insults virtually everywhere he played, and it was no different once he reached the NHL; in one incident, O'Ree recalled Chicago's Eric Nesterenko butt-ending him in the mouth, touching off a bench-clearing brawl. O'Ree headed back to the minors after that first short run in Boston, but he returned to the Bruins in 1960–61, scoring four goals and fourteen points in what would be his only full season in the NHL. The league wouldn't see its second black player until 1974, when winger Mike Marson joined the Washington Capitals.

O'Ree was honoured with the Order of Canada in 2010, and the league recognized the fiftieth anniversary of his debut with a ceremony in Boston in 2008. As of the class of 2017, he had yet to be inducted into the Hockey Hall of Fame.

Maurice Richard retired in 1960, at the age of thirty-eight and after the Canadiens had captured their fifth straight Cup. He left with 544 career goals, the first player to pass the five-hundred-goal mark. Within two years he'd be joined by Howe, the man to whom he'd passed the torch as

---

* For several years, he played alongside Jean Béliveau.

the league's marquee player. While no one could have known it at the time, the third man to hit five hundred goals* was just beginning his NHL journey as Richard bowed out. In Chicago, a twenty-one-year-old winger named Bobby Hull had just led the league with thirty-nine goals in his third season, more than doubling his career total. He was playing with a rookie centre named Stan Mikita, who'd also get to five hundred. So would a big, twenty-two-year-old left winger in Toronto named Frank Mahovlich, who'd scored just eighteen goals in his fourth season but was about to break through with a forty-eight-goal campaign. That's the nature of the NHL: a standard is set, and then someone new comes along to chase it. Richard and Howe paved the way for Hull, Mikita, Mahovlich and the rest, just as those stars would eventually give way to future generations.

Today, there are forty-five members of the five-hundred-goal club, but in 1960 there was only one—and he had just said goodbye.

---

* He would reach the milestone on February 21, 1970.

BROADWAY BULLIES

How the Rangers teased away their shot at an icon

GORDIE HOWE PLAYED AN ASTOUNDING TWENTY-FIVE years for the Detroit Red Wings, easily the longest tenure by any player with a single team. He retired in 1971, having just turned forty-three, and then made a comeback two years later with the Houston Aeros of the World Hockey Association. That match made sense—it gave the fledgling WHA a big name to sell while also giving Howe a chance to play with his sons Marty and Mark—but it was jarring for hockey fans. Gordie Howe in anything other than a Red Wings jersey? It seemed plain wrong.

Well, if you think the sight of a silver-haired Howe in Aeros blue (or, later, Whalers green) must've been odd, try to imagine him in his prime, wearing the red, white and blue of the New York Rangers. It nearly happened.

The Rangers were the first NHL team to see something in Howe. Specifically, it was scout Fred McCorry who spotted a fifteen-year-old Howe in Saskatoon back in 1943 and convinced him to come to the Rangers' training camp. In those days, it wasn't unheard of for teams to sign players that young, locking in their rights well before they would ever skate in the NHL. The invitation represented a fantastic opportunity for Howe, but it made for a difficult experience. While we remember Howe as one of the most fearsome players ever to take the ice, he was shy and introverted as a teenager, and he struggled with being away from home. To make matters worse, the Rangers' veterans decided to give the new kid a hard time. They made fun of him for not knowing how to put his equipment on properly (he'd never owned a full set) and stole his food when it was mealtime. Howe was miserable, and eventually he decided he'd had enough. The future Mr. Hockey walked away from camp and headed back home to Saskatoon.

From the sounds of it, nobody in the Rangers organization even bothered to try to stop him.

Later that winter, Red Wings scout Fred Pinckney got a look at Howe and invited him to Detroit's off-season camp in Windsor, Ontario. This time, the veterans left the kid well enough alone, and Detroit coach Jack Adams liked what he saw. The Red Wings offered Howe a contract and he agreed.

How does hockey history change if those 1943 Rangers ease up on a nervous teenager? It makes for another one of those great "what if?" arguments—although in this case, it's probably one that Red Wings fans would rather not think about. Ironically, Howe's younger brother Vic had a brief NHL career of his own in the 1950s, scoring three goals in thirty-three games spread across three seasons . . . all of them with the New York Rangers.

5

THE CUP HEADS NORTH

The Maple Leafs and Canadiens spend a decade trading titles
while building the sport's greatest rivalry

EVEN WITHOUT THE ROCKET, THE MONTREAL CANADIENS continued their dominance during the 1960–61 season. Boom Boom Geoffrion hit the fifty-goal mark while earning both the Art Ross and his only Hart Trophy, and the Habs went 41–19–10 to narrowly edge out Toronto for first place. But the 1961 postseason turned out to be one of the most unpredictable in recent memory, with both of the league's top teams falling victim to first-round upsets. The Leafs were knocked out in five by a sixty-six-point Red Wings squad, while the Canadiens had their run of consecutive playoff series wins ended at the hands of the seventy-five-point Black Hawks. That set up an unlikely final, with Chicago capturing its first Stanley Cup in twenty-three years.

It was an unexpected start to the new decade. It would also be an outlier, as the rest of the 1960s would see the Stanley Cup passed back and forth between just two teams.

The rivalry between the Toronto Maple Leafs and Montreal Canadiens had essentially begun in the league's earliest days. It was an irresistible combination—the most successful teams from Canada's two largest cities, representing the two halves of the country's culture. The Canadiens became the team of choice for Canada's francophone population, while the Maple Leafs represented the nation's English speakers.* The two teams met in the playoffs in the league's very first season, with Toronto winning a total-goals series on the way to capturing its first Stanley Cup. They wouldn't face each other in the postseason again until 1925—a Montreal win—and then somehow avoided another playoff meeting until 1944. It was 1947 before they squared off in the Stanley Cup final. The Maple Leafs won in '47 and again in 1950, before the Canadiens took back-to-back Cup meetings in 1959 and 1960. So by the start of the 1961–62 season, the Toronto–Montreal rivalry was, to say the least, well established. But it was about to go into overdrive.

Despite a ninety-eight-point season from Montreal, the 1962 Stanley Cup would end up in Toronto. The Canadiens had overcome the loss of reigning Norris Trophy winner Doug Harvey, who'd headed to New York to take over as player-coach of the Rangers, as well as a preseason injury to Jean Béliveau that forced him to miss several weeks. But they were stunned in the opening round by the Black Hawks once again, clearing the path for the second-place Maple Leafs.

That Toronto roster was split between well-established veterans like Red Kelly, George Armstrong, Tim Horton and Johnny Bower, and the next generation, represented by Dave Keon and Frank Mahovlich.** It was an odd mix, but it worked, and the Maple Leafs would go on to repeat as champions in 1963 and 1964, beating the Canadiens in the semifinals both years. The win in 1964 would be especially memorable, coming on the strength of a game six overtime goal scored by defenceman Bobby Baun, who was playing with a broken leg.

But as the league settled into the 1964–65 season, it became apparent that the Maple Leafs dynasty was slowing. The team would end the year in fourth place, due largely to an aging roster that had become even older with the off-season acquisition of thirty-six-year-old netminder Terry

---

*   Not entirely, of course—there are plenty of fans across the country who embraced the "other" side, and were more than happy to tell you all about it.

**   Also making a brief appearance on that 1961–62 Leafs team was a twenty-one-year-old Gerry Cheevers. The future Hall of Famer appeared in just two games, and wouldn't resurface in the NHL again until the Bruins claimed him in the 1965 intra-league draft.

Sawchuk. The Leafs ran into Montreal in the opening round for the third straight year,* and this time it was the Canadiens who emerged with the victory.

The league's best regular-season team was a resurgent Red Wings squad,** but they were eliminated by a third-place Black Hawks team that boasted the league's MVP (Bobby Hull) and scoring champ (Stan Mikita). In the 1965 final, the Habs claimed the Cup in yet another series in which the home team won all seven games. The league introduced the Conn Smythe Trophy for playoff MVP that year, and Jean Béliveau became the new award's first winner.

In 1966, the Canadiens swept the Maple Leafs in yet another first-round matchup. That set up a Cup-final meeting with the fourth-place Red Wings, a team still led by the ageless Gordie Howe. Months earlier, Howe had scored in Montreal to become the first member of the league's six-hundred-goal club. But this time the Canadiens kept him off the scoreboard, mostly; Detroit took the first two games in Montreal before the Habs roared back to finish the series in six. The victory came with some controversy, as the overtime winner appeared to have been directed in with a swipe of Henri Richard's glove. In the days before instant replay, the Red Wings' complaints fell on deaf ears, and the goal counted.

By this point in history, hockey fans knew that expansion was right around the corner, with the league having announced the addition of six new teams in February. The 1966–67 season, then, would mark the end of an era, as the Original Six prepared to give way to a modern age. The season would also coincide with Canada's centennial, the country's celebration of the one-hundredth anniversary of Confederation. It seemed all but inevitable that the Maple Leafs and Canadiens, owners of the last five Stanley Cups between them, would be destined to face off yet again.

---

* For reasons that nobody seems quite clear on anymore, the NHL set up its first-round matchups in those days so that the first-place team played the third, while the second-place team played the fourth, instead of the first-versus-fourth/second-versus-third format you might expect.

** Buoyed by the surprise comeback of Ted Lindsay after four years of retirement.

One obstacle in the way of that Toronto–Montreal matchup that year came in the form of the Black Hawks. The iconic duo of Hull and Mikita had been joined by a big scoring centre named Phil Esposito, and unsurprisingly, that loaded Chicago lineup led the league in scoring by more than fifty goals. The Hawks finished the season in first, seventeen points ahead of second-place Montreal.

But as was often the case in the 1960s, the regular-season standings meant little once the playoffs began. The Hawks drew a Maple Leafs team that hadn't yet rid itself of the popular perception that its players were too old to seriously contend for another title; the roster featured seven regulars who were thirty-six or older, and the goaltending duo of Sawchuk and Bower alone sported a combined age of seventy-nine. But Sawchuk stood on his head against the Hawks, and the veteran Leafs sent Chicago home in six games.

The other semifinal pitted the Canadiens against a rare postseason sight: the New York Rangers. New York had made the playoffs just once since 1958 and hadn't won a round since 1950. The Rangers were heavy underdogs against Montreal, although the series brought some intrigue in the form of Geoffrion playing out his first year in New York after fourteen seasons with the Canadiens. Any thoughts of a dramatic upset were quashed quickly, though, as the Habs swept the series.

That set up the matchup the country had been hoping for, with the Canadiens and Maple Leafs meeting in the Cup final for the first time since 1960. Montreal went in as the favourite, and opened the series with a convincing 6–2 win on home ice. But the Maple Leafs fought back with a Bower shutout in game two, then took a series lead with a double-overtime win in Toronto. Another 6–2 Montreal win evened the series, but the Maple Leafs shut down the Canadiens the rest of the way to take the Cup in six games, with George Armstrong sealing the series win with an empty-netter in the final minute.

It seemed somehow fitting that the Original Six era would end with a group of old-timers claiming the Stanley Cup. In hindsight, of course, the 1967 final would become especially noteworthy as the last championship the Maple Leafs would win for a half century and counting. It would also hold added weight as the last great battle in the Leafs–Canadiens rivalry, which faded over time. The two teams wouldn't meet in the playoffs again until a pair of matchups in 1978 and 1979—postseason meetings that to this day remain the rivalry's last—and the 1980s would see them in separate conferences, which significantly reduced the chance of a meeting in the playoffs.

Thankfully, the two teams have been back in the same division since 1998, although they've still somehow managed to avoid each other in the postseason. The building still buzzes whenever the two rivals face off, and attending at least one Toronto–Montreal game should be on every hockey fan's bucket list. But for now, at least, the days of the two teams trading Stanley Cups are long past.

The Maple Leafs' Cup win came on May 2, leaving the league with just over a month to prepare for the impending expansion draft. The league imposed a roster freeze that would come into effect on May 15, and hours before it arrived, the Bruins and Black Hawks delivered a bombshell in the form of a monster trade. The deal saw Chicago add Gilles Marotte, Pit Martin and Jack Norris in exchange for Phil Esposito. Martin was a respected centre coming off his first twenty-goal season and Norris was a goaltending prospect, but the key to the deal for the Hawks was Marotte, a twenty-two-year-old blueliner who'd finished third in Calder Trophy voting in 1966 and had already established a reputation as a big hitter in his two seasons in Boston. All in all, it wasn't a bad haul for a team still stinging from that playoff disappointment. But sending Esposito the other way looked like a steep price at the time, and it ended up being astronomically high.

Playing centre on a line with Hull, Esposito had just finished the season seventh in league scoring, but management apparently decided to scapegoat him for the playoff loss. The Hawks also threw in a pair of young wingers in Ken Hodge and Fred Stanfield. At the time of the deal, the Bruins had long been a league laughingstock. They'd missed the playoffs for eight straight years, finishing dead last six times in that span, and hadn't won the Stanley Cup since 1941. But the trade, along with the recent debut of eighteen-year-old defenceman Bobby Orr, sparked a franchise turnaround. Esposito went on to become one of the highest-scoring forwards in league history, while Hodge topped the forty-goal mark three times in Boston and Stanfield became a dependable middle-six forward. Meanwhile, Marotte never lived up to expectations, lasting just two full seasons in Chicago before being dealt to the Los Angeles Kings. The Hawks barely made the playoffs in 1968 and finished dead last in the East Division in 1969.

It wouldn't be the last blockbuster of Esposito's career, but it was the one that would have the biggest effect on the NHL. Fans who had their eyes on one sea change—expansion—might not have realized that they'd just seen another. Just as the league was preparing to double in size, Esposito and his new Bruins teammates were getting set to expand the record books.

SUPERSTAR FOR SALE

The richest trade in sports history gets done . . . and then undone

THE PHIL ESPOSITO TRADE WAS A BLOCKBUSTER THAT shook the fortunes of two franchises. But it was, at its heart, a hockey trade— one that saw two teams trying to get the best of the other in a direct exchange of talent. A big deal, sure, but otherwise straightforward stuff.

The same can't be said for another 1960s blockbuster, one that came in 1962 and also featured a bona fide superstar in his prime. At the time, it was, quite literally, the richest trade in sports history. But despite the deal being splashed across the front pages of sports sections around the continent, many of today's fans have never heard of it, because it was yanked off the table at the last moment.

It all starts, as so many regrettable hockey stories tend to, with Harold Ballard.

Part of the Maple Leafs' management group since 1957, Ballard had bought into ownership in 1961. By the eve of the 1962–63 season, the Leafs were the defending champions, and they were built around winger Frank Mahovlich, one of the league's marquee players. The Big M was coming off his second straight all-star season and at age twenty-four was just entering his prime. The Maple Leafs had their franchise player for the next decade. And so, naturally, Ballard decided to sell him.

In defence of Harold Ballard—this is the first time in history those words have ever been strung together by anyone other than an attorney—he was offered one hell of a price. The deal was laid out on October 5, 1962, as Ballard and Black Hawks owner James Norris enjoyed a few drinks together. Okay, maybe more than a few—as legendary *Toronto Star* columnist Milt Dunnell delightfully put it, both men "had been fortified by the gargle." It was

Norris who made the proposition. He would cut Ballard a cheque for a million dollars in exchange for Mahovlich's rights.

It was a stunning offer, and one that at the time probably represented an overpayment. No pro athlete had ever been sold for anything approaching such a figure, and it was hard to justify spending anywhere near that much on one man—in those days, an NHL team might struggle to bring in much more than a million dollars in an entire season. But Norris didn't seem to care; he envisioned bringing together the game's two top wingers, Mahovlich and Bobby Hull, on the same roster. It would be, as the Associated Press wrote at the time, "the most potent 1-2 punch in hockey history."

Ballard agreed to the offer, and word quickly began to spread that a deal had been struck. As Dunnell described it, one of the first to hear of the impending sale was Norris's brother, Bruce, who owned the Red Wings.* He didn't like the sound of the arrangement, so he reached out to Maple Leaf icon Conn Smythe. The Major no longer owned a controlling interest in the team, but his son Stafford held a big chunk of stock. When Conn was finally able to get in touch with Stafford, the father quickly let the son know that he didn't approve. Less than twenty-four hours after the late-night agreement, both sides were facing pressure to back out of the deal.

But there was a new problem: Reporters had heard about the proposal, and the *Chicago Tribune* was going to press with a front-page headline about the Hawks' acquisition of Mahovlich. Media around North America soon picked up the story too.

The next day, Norris wrote the cheque and had it delivered to Ballard at Maple Leaf Gardens. But Stafford Smythe was there to turn it down. Chicago GM Tommy Ivan told reporters, "As far as we are concerned, the deal stands." But the younger Smythe stood by his refusal to accept the money. "We never rolled a drunk yet," was his reported explanation, "and we don't have to start now."

The Maple Leafs had taken the high road . . . for a few days. The team's board of directors apparently had second thoughts shortly after the deal had been publicly struck down and reached out to see if Norris was still interested.

---

* Yes, the Red Wings and Black Hawks were once owned by brothers. There's a reason the league had a Norris Division.

But by then the Hawks' owner had changed his mind. Mahovlich would win three more Stanley Cups in Toronto, and go into the history books as one of the greatest Leafs of all time.

Today, the current generation of GMs constantly inform us that it's just too hard to pull off big trades. Nonsense, old-time fans might think. All they need is a chequebook, some creativity and a bit of the gargle.

6

EXPANSION ARRIVES

The NHL doubles in size and unveils a curious new division format

BY THE MID-1960S, THE NHL'S SMALL SIZE INCREASINGLY stood out from the other major North American sports. In 1965, Major League Baseball had twenty teams; the NFL had fourteen in addition to the American Football League's eight; and even the NBA had nine (with five more on the way over the next two years). The NHL, meanwhile, was still churning along with its Original Six. That was just fine for some of the league's power brokers, who were content with what had become a reasonably steady and predictable business, but to most observers it was clear that the sands were shifting in the sports world, with TV contracts starting to offer a real impact on the bottom line. Attracting broadcasters with just six teams—and only four in the United States—was a daunting task. And so, in February of 1965, Clarence Campbell gave the NHL Board of Governors one month to come up with a formal plan for an expansion process.

Initially, Campbell seemed to straddle both sides of the issue, pushing the owners to move forward while also suggesting publicly that he personally opposed the addition of new teams. In one Associated Press report, he spoke with apparent hesitancy, saying, "Our problem is inordinate prosperity. I believe expansion can only be justified by economics and . . . a major television contract."

That fence-sitting didn't last long. On March 11, 1965, Campbell announced that the league would add teams. And not just one or two—Campbell wanted to double in size to twelve teams, all in one shot, if possible. As *Detroit Free Press* columnist Jack Berry put it at the time, "It won't be an expansion, it will be an explosion." And further, Campbell let it be known that the majority of new franchises would be based in the US, with early reports suggesting that among Canadian cities, only Vancouver had a realistic shot at a team.

The league's ambitious plan for American growth faced at least one problem right out of the gate: There were only two NHL-sized rinks in the entire country that didn't already have teams—one in St. Louis and the other in Los Angeles. Oakland had a facility under construction, and Baltimore and Pittsburgh had rinks that could feasibly be expanded, but those options would take time, and the league couldn't even be sure that any of those five cities wanted a team. Realistically, for expansion to happen the way Campbell laid it out, the NHL would need to wait years while rinks were built around the United States.

Meanwhile, traditionalists argued that things were just fine as they were. Canadian fans voiced outrage that the league seemed to be treating their country as an afterthought during the whole process.* And other Campbell critics pointed out that the league's quality of play would suffer with the addition of roughly 120 new players. Campbell didn't help matters on that last front when he openly acknowledged the logic of the argument, telling Berry "you can't gloss over the facts."**

To address the question of competitive balance between the established clubs and the newcomers, the league proposed a creative solution: All six expansion teams would be placed in the same division and play most of their games against each other, giving the new teams a chance to compete on equal footing while the traditional powerhouses did the same. That seemed like a reasonably fair compromise, especially since it was assumed that the league would use a crossover format once

---

*   Modern fans can let me know if any of this is sounding familiar.

**   An editorial cartoon in the *Detroit Free Press* in 1966 showed a flummoxed Campbell in front of a crib full of six crying babies, while holding a near-empty bottle labelled PLAYER TALENT. "Oops," says the cartoon Campbell, "I'll have to feed them with an eye-dropper."

the playoffs arrived to ensure that the best teams still played for the Stanley Cup.

As the process wore on, several cities emerged as clear favourites for new teams, with the prime targets being the pair that wouldn't need to build a rink once they got the green light. Los Angeles seemed an obvious choice; it was America's second-largest market and would be key to any new TV deal the owners could negotiate. That would likely necessitate the creation of a second California team somewhere like Oakland or San Francisco, so that eastern teams wouldn't need to fly all the way to the West Coast for just one game.

St. Louis also showed up early and often in the speculation, based on their Midwestern location and NHL-ready arena, but the River City's bid was missing something important—namely, anyone who actually wanted to own a team there. When the league sought applications from interested parties, nobody from St. Louis stepped forward. That seemed like an issue. But maybe not an insurmountable one, as the city had a powerful advocate in James D. Norris, the owner of the Chicago Black Hawks. Looking out for the league's best interest as usual, Norris pushed hard for St. Louis, on the basis that adding another Midwestern team would help the NHL grow the game in a crucial part of the country and build the league's fan base for decades to come.

Oh, and also he owned the St. Louis Arena. There was that too.

With Norris gunning hard to get an NHL franchise in his building, the league overlooked the lack of applicants and simply awarded St. Louis a conditional franchise in 1966. The condition was that an owner be found by April.* In case that proved impossible, the NHL had a Plan B. The league had received a bid from Zanvyl Krieger, a businessman and philanthropist who already owned baseball's Baltimore Orioles. Krieger's bid had made the short list, and the league made it clear that its rejection was only temporary. If St. Louis couldn't find an owner, Baltimore was the fallback.

---

*   Norris never actually saw the NHL come to St. Louis; he died of a heart attack on February 25, 1966, just days after the league made its announcement.

Ultimately, insurance tycoon Sid Salomon Jr. and his son stepped forward in St. Louis, and the Baltimore bid was officially killed. At the time, it was assumed that the city would get a team eventually, and it did resurface as an expansion possibility in both 1970 and 1972. But the team never came, and the arrival of the Capitals in nearby Washington, DC, in 1974 essentially spelled the end of the market's chances at ever joining the NHL.

With Los Angeles a no-brainer due to economics and Norris stumping for St. Louis, the NHL was left with four spots to fill. In February 1966, the league announced its decision, formally welcoming six new teams for a reported expansion fee of two million dollars each. The four mystery spots went to Philadelphia, Pittsburgh, Minneapolis–St. Paul and San Francisco–Oakland.

The Philadelphia bid included Ed Snider, then a minority owner and executive with the city's NFL team, the Eagles. Snider had already launched plans to build a new arena; ground was broken in June, and the building, which would be called the Spectrum, was ready for the new team's debut roughly fifteen months later. More than thirty years after the one-season run of the Quakers, Philadelphia finally had a real NHL team.

Pennsylvania's second team was landed via a successful bid from Pittsburgh that included Art Rooney, the legendary owner of the NFL's Steelers. Steeltown had initially been seen as a long shot, with reports that a proposal from Buffalo had better support, but Rooney worked his magic, successfully switching crucial votes from the existing owners in his favour late in the process.

American hockey icon Walter Bush and businessman John Driscoll were the key players in Minnesota's bid. Like Pittsburgh, Minnesota had been seen as an underdog. The Twin Cities weren't an especially big market and wouldn't help drive a TV deal, and they didn't have an arena. But the area had a rich history with the sport, and a strong sales job by Driscoll and (especially) Bush eventually won the day. The final spot went to the Bay Area, where millionaire socialite Barry van Gerbig already owned a chunk of the minor-league WHL's San Francisco Seals and had assembled a team of more than fifty investors, including his godfather, Bing Crosby.

The NHL's choices didn't please everyone; fans in Buffalo were badly disappointed, and a bigger issue was brewing north of the border, where Canadians were furious that the country hadn't been granted so much as a single new team. To snub the country that supplied almost all the league's players—and on its hundredth birthday, no less—felt like a mortal insult. Prime Minister Lester Pearson addressed the decision at one point, and some Canadian members of Parliament rose in the House of Commons to ask the government to intervene. Opposition leader John Diefenbaker claimed the NHL's choices would have "a detrimental effect on young Canadians." The fist shaking from the north couldn't dissuade the league though. With six new American teams on the way, the next challenge was to figure out how the expansion draft would work.

On the one hand, each of the NHL's new teams could argue that the major money they'd forked over entitled them to enter the league with a reasonably competitive roster. On the other, existing teams felt that simply letting someone else into the club had been an act of supreme generosity and that the newcomers should be happy with whatever scraps they were thrown. To complicate matters, the 1967 expansion was by far the largest in North America sports history in terms of the ratios involved. With six new teams picking players from six old ones, each of the Original Six franchises would have to part with twenty players each—the equivalent of a full roster.

That wasn't completely unworkable, since back then every team had a deep list of reserves. But still, losing twenty players in one shot is going to have an impact on even the best-stocked franchise. Think back to the nonstop hand-wringing from teams who stood to lose one player in the expansion draft that built the Vegas Golden Knights' roster in 2017, then imagine how teams in 1967 felt.

In the end, the league decided on a system in which each existing team would protect eleven skaters and one goaltender, with exemptions for junior-eligible players. As the draft progressed, the existing teams would be allowed to add new names to their protected lists. That last wrinkle came at the suggestion of Montreal GM Sam Pollock, and it just so happened that it helped the Canadiens keep most of their stacked roster together. The system didn't leave much for the new teams to choose from, with one exception: the goaltenders. With each of the original teams able to protect just one goalie, the newcomers had a shot at some decent names. In fact, each of the first three players chosen in the 1967 expansion draft would wind up in the Hockey Hall of Fame.

The first to go was Terry Sawchuk, taken from the Maple Leafs by the Los Angeles Kings. Sawchuk was already thirty-seven, but he ended up having three more NHL seasons left in him, although only one came in Los Angeles.* The Flyers used the second pick to pluck a twenty-two-year-old off the Bruins' roster. Bernie Parent would spend a few years in Philadelphia before heading to Toronto and later the WHA, but he returned to the Flyers in time to win two Stanley Cups with the Broad Street Bullies of the mid-'70s. The third pick was used on another veteran star, as the Blues grabbed Glenn Hall from the Black Hawks. Hall turned out to be the best pick of the draft in the short term, going on to win a Conn Smythe Trophy and first-team all-star honours over four seasons in St. Louis.

Faced with a choice between protecting thirty-eight-year-old Gump Worsley, dependable veteran Charlie Hodge or a twenty-one-year-old prospect with just nineteen NHL games under his belt, Montreal bucked the trend established by the other existing franchises and went with Worsley. Van Gerbig's California Seals grabbed Hodge with the sixth-overall pick, but the young prospect would end up unselected and remain Montreal property. His name was Rogie Vachon, and he'd go on to be a Hart Trophy finalist twice over the course of a sixteen-season Hall of Fame career.

With the goalies out of the way, there were only a handful of especially attractive players available to the expansion squads. Several big-name

---

* Sawchuk died following the 1969–70 season as the result of injuries sustained weeks earlier in an off-ice fight with teammate Ron Stewart. Sawchuk had taken responsibility for the altercation, and a grand jury ruled the death an accident.

veterans went unselected, including Toronto's George Armstrong and New York's Boom Boom Geoffrion.* And a handful of rookies who'd turn out to be stars were added to their teams' protected lists as the draft wore on, including Wayne Cashman, Serge Savard and Jacques Lemaire. For the most part, the pickings were slim, as the expansion teams' final rosters made clear. Only three skaters taken in the draft—Oakland's Jean-Paul Parisé, Minnesota's Bill Goldsworthy and Philadelphia's Gary Dornhoefer— would go on to manage at least 500 points over the remainder of their NHL careers.

Luckily for the six new teams, the NHL followed through on its plan to lump them all together—thus was born the all-expansion West Division, while the Original Six remained together in the East Division.** The new format had been expected, but the league threw in a twist: Not only would the old and new teams have their own divisions, but those divisions would each send one team to the Stanley Cup final. In theory, this gave the expansion teams a realistic shot at a championship right out of the gate. In practice, it doomed the league to three straight years of lopsided and nearly unwatchable championship series. In each of those three finals, the St. Louis Blues emerged as the West Division representative. And each time, they were swept aside by an established team. The Canadiens did the honours in 1968 and 1969, while the Bruins took a turn in 1970. The Blues didn't manage so much as a win in any of the series, although the 1970 final did at least provide an iconic moment: Bobby Orr's flying over-time winner in game four.

The league finally came to its senses and switched up the format in 1970, introducing a system that made it possible for two Original Six teams to play for the Cup. That was the right move, because the new teams just weren't all that good, with only the Blues topping the .500 mark in any of the first three post-expansion seasons. But even though they may

---

*   The latter was left off the Rangers' protected list, but reportedly was covered by a leaguewide gentleman's agreement that he wouldn't be picked.
**   Yes, Chicago and Detroit are farther west than Pittsburgh and Philadelphia. Trust me, the NHL's sense of geography is going to get far worse than that as we go.

not have been able to truly contend for a Cup, for the most part the new guys didn't embarrass themselves, and fears of plummeting quality of play didn't materialize. After dipping slightly in the first season after expansion, league scoring rates returned to normal over the next two years.

Any idea of normalcy on the offensive end would be blown to pieces soon enough, thanks in part to Orr, the young defenceman who closed out the decade by winning the Art Ross with an unthinkable 120 points. As it turned out, he was just getting started.

EARMUFF IT FOR ME

When ignoring the crowd goes too far

CROWD NOISE CAN BE AN ISSUE IN THE NHL, SO MUCH SO that coaches of visiting teams have been known to devise game plans focused on taking the hometown fans out of the game. Play a slow and steady style, the strategy goes, and make it through the first ten minutes or so without giving up a goal. That should quiet a boisterous crowd down.

Of course, there are more creative solutions available to any coach willing to use them, as NHL fans learned in a game between the Pittsburgh Penguins and St. Louis Blues in 1970.

The Blues hadn't taken long to establish themselves as the best of the 1967 expansion bunch. Under the tutelage of young coach Scotty Bowman, they had already represented the West in back-to-back Stanley Cup finals, and they won the division by nineteen points in 1968–69. Midway through the 1969–70 campaign, they were well on the way to a third division title.

The fans in St. Louis had also wasted no time earning a reputation for occasional rowdiness and frequent noisiness. The Blues played in front of a capacity crowd of over sixteen thousand at the St. Louis Arena many nights, and the building was known to contain some of the league's most vicious hecklers.

The Blues were sporting a perfect 11–0–0 record against West Division foes on their home ice heading into their matchup with the Penguins on January 3, 1970. With St. Louis posing enough of a problem even before he factored in the fans, Pittsburgh coach Red Kelly decided to get creative: He handed out earmuffs in assorted colours to his players and encouraged them to wear them on the bench in an effort to muffle any unpleasant rink noise. Apparently there was nothing in the league's rule book dictating how players were required to dress when not on the ice. According to newspaper reports, about half the team (and Kelly himself) wore the earmuffs at the opening faceoff.

The plan worked perfectly in the sense that the Penguins were unable to hear any of the taunts that were hurled their way. Unfortunately, they also weren't able to hear each other, their coaches, their opponents or any of the other sounds that typically help guide a hockey player through a game. That turned out be a problem, as the Blues scored just twenty-nine seconds into the first period on the way to a 5–0 lead before the opening frame was fifteen minutes old. Many of the Penguins ditched the earmuffs after that first St. Louis goal, but Kelly stuck to his plan—according to reports, he kept his muffs on until the Blues' fourth goal, at which point the furious coach ripped them off and threw them away.

The Blues ended up cruising to a 6–0 blowout win, which spelled the end of the great earmuff experiment. The Penguins never wore the accessories again and, not surprisingly, no other NHL team has employed the strategy since. Kelly and his charges may have heard no evil that night, but they could see plenty every time they looked up at the scoreboard.

7

HERE WE GROW AGAIN

Expansion continues through the 1970s, with decidedly mixed results

THEN NHL'S TWELVE-TEAM ERA LASTED JUST THREE years. By 1970, the league was ready to grow again, and two new franchises were awarded: the Vancouver Canucks and Buffalo Sabres.

The addition of Vancouver had long felt inevitable. The city had been expected to get a team as part of the 1967 expansion, and the NHL's rejection of its application was blamed largely on the Toronto Maple Leafs,* whose president, Stafford Smythe, had been involved in a proposal to build an arena in Vancouver that had fallen through; many fans assumed that he held a grudge. But when the next round of expansion arrived, Vancouver seemed like a lock.

Buffalo had also been a near-miss in 1967, but by 1970 there was a problem. The Buffalo Bills had just joined the NFL as part of the AFL merger, and the city was also adding an NBA team, the Braves. There didn't seem to be room for three big-league teams in a town that hadn't had any just a year before. And indeed, there wasn't—luckily for hockey fans, it was the Braves who were sent packing a few years later.

The addition of the Canucks and Sabres finally spelled the end of the awful playoff format that had doomed the last three Stanley Cup finals. Of course, this was still the NHL, so the new set-up didn't make all that much more sense. The Chicago Black Hawks were shifted to the West Division

---

* As per Canadian national policy.

with the 1967 expansion clubs. This meant a team that had just won the league's best division was now switching over to its worst. You can probably guess how that worked out: the Hawks won the division easily in each of the next three years, earning two trips to the Stanley Cup final in the process. They still lost when they got there, but at least those series were competitive. As far as the West Division was concerned, that counted as progress.

Meanwhile, the Sabres and Canucks were both slotted into the East Division.

Yes, you read that correctly: the best fit for the Vancouver Canucks, according to the NHL brain trust of 1970, was in the league's "eastern" half. Of course, the NHL could have done the sensible thing and put the Canucks in the West, perhaps shifting a team like Philadelphia or Pittsburgh to the East. But no. Even though the league was running a balanced schedule at this point, it wanted the Canucks to be in the same division as the other Canadian teams. And so off to the East they went.

Not surprisingly, neither the Sabres nor Canucks made the playoffs over their first two seasons. The Bruins, Rangers and Canadiens dominated the division, while the Maple Leafs snagged the final playoff spot both times. But while both new teams went through the expected struggles early on, it's fair to say that the franchises each ended up as success stories. After all, both still exist today. And as it would turn out, that would be more than anyone could say about most teams resulting from the decade's other growth spurts.

In 1972, the league added two more teams, including one that would be dominant within a decade: the New York Islanders. It wasn't the first time the league had iced two teams in the same metropolitan area, but it was the first time in modern history, and the Islanders knew they'd have their work cut out for them if they wanted to draw attention away from the established Rangers. So they decided to make a splash in true New York style: by reaching out to the biggest star they could find and offering him the lead role. In this case, that wasn't a player, but a coach. They offered the job to the recently retired Gordie Howe. True, Howe had never coached before, but the Islanders were willing to overlook that minor issue and hand him the reins. Howe declined, and after a couple of years in the Red Wings' front office he'd return to the ice in 1973 to play seven more pro seasons.

The Islanders eventually turned to Earl Ingarfield, who lasted half a season behind the bench before being replaced by Phil Goyette. The team was terrible that first year, finishing dead last with just twelve wins and thirty points—then the worst record by any team in modern NHL history. But that worked out okay, since it earned them the first-overall pick in the 1973 draft, where they chose defenceman Denis Potvin. For their second season, they turned the coaching duties over to Al Arbour. The seeds of a dynasty had been sown.

As for that second team added in '72, it was just slightly less successful than the Islanders. The league placed the Atlanta Flames in the West Division—while leaving Vancouver in the East because, again, geography is hard. The Flames would last for eight years in Georgia's capital and win a grand total of two playoff games before packing up and moving to Calgary in 1980.* *Oh well*, the league no doubt thought to itself, *now we know the NHL product doesn't work in Atlanta. Lesson learned.*

If you're the sort of person who likes to view NHL history in a glass-half-full way, you could look at the 1972 expansion and say that hey, one out of two ain't bad. If you want to view the league's 1974 expansion through a similarly optimistic lens, you'd probably point out that at least nobody got run over by a Zamboni.

Let's start with the Washington Capitals. Much like the Islanders, DC tried to make a splash right out of the gate by hiring a Hall of Famer, in this case offering the GM's job to Milt Schmidt. Unfortunately for the Bruins legend, he took it.

Remember a few pages back, when I mentioned the Islanders' all-time worst season of thirty points? The Caps smashed that record, debuting with what to this day is regularly cited as the worst season by any team in

---

* For you trivia fans, this remains the only time in NHL history that a team switched cities but kept its nickname.

the history of hockey—if not all of pro sports. The 1974–75 Capitals finished with an all-but-impossible record of 8–67–5, good for just twenty-one points. That's a points percentage of .131, which still stands as the worst the league has ever seen. Schmidt fired coach Jim Anderson after fifty-four games, then sent replacement Red Sullivan packing after eighteen more. He finished the season by coaching the last eight games himself, presumably because by that point nobody else would return his calls.

The best anecdote about the '74–75 Capitals involves their road losing streak. The team didn't win an away game through their first month of existence. Then they didn't win one through their second, third or fourth, and soon fans began to wonder if Washington would make it through an entire season without winning a single game on the road.

That was very nearly the case. But on March 28, 1975, they went into Oakland and beat the Golden Seals by a 5–3 final. That improved their road record to 1–37–0, and the team celebrated in a manner befitting the occasion: by grabbing a garbage can and passing it around like the Stanley Cup.

Speaking of garbage getting passed around, let's talk about the league's other addition in 1974, the Kansas City Scouts.

First the good news: The Scouts were better than the Capitals for every year of their existence. Now the bad news: They existed for only two seasons, they were awful in both, and in 1975–76, they closed out the year with one of the worst stretches of hockey ever played, winning just one of their last forty-four games. That win, it should probably go without saying, came against the Washington Capitals.

The Scouts averaged just over eight thousand fans per game over the course of their brief NHL tenure. They were sold in 1976 and moved to Denver, where they became the Colorado Rockies. It was the NHL's first relocation in over four decades. It would not be the last.

Riding high off the success of the Capitals and Scouts, and with a new four-division alignment in place that jettisoned the East/West divide in favour of groupings based even more loosely on geography, the NHL took a break from its every-two-years expansion pattern, although not exactly on purpose. The league had intended to add another team in time for the 1976–77 season, and in fact it almost did. In June of 1974, the league announced that it had awarded an expansion team to Seattle. But the deal was contingent on the ownership group coming up with the money, and as with the Cleveland Barons decades earlier, that turned out to be a problem.

Seattle was already home to a Western Hockey League team, the Totems, that had an up-and-down history in the market. They were partially owned by Vancouver Canucks investor Coleman Hall, and that created an obvious conflict when the Totems' other owners began angling for an NHL expansion team. The league felt confident enough to award the franchise in 1974, but it quickly became apparent that the money wasn't going to be there, and months after the Totems folded in 1975, the NHL pulled its offer off the table. The Seattle ownership group sued, and the case dragged on for years before the league finally won.

To this day, the Emerald City is always one of the first possibilities mentioned whenever the topic of expansion or relocation is raised, in both the NHL and NBA (the city had had pro basketball from 1967 until 2008, when the SuperSonics moved to Oklahoma City). But for now, Seattle's 1917 Stanley Cup—the first ever won by an American team, and the last Cup of the pre-NHL era—remains its only one.

While the league was focused on reaching into previously untouched corners of the continent in the first half of the '70s, the foundation of its original expansion six-pack was starting to show cracks. Most of the "second six" teams had been reasonably successful; the Flyers had even won Stanley Cups in 1974 and 1975, becoming the first of the era's expansion teams to do so. Granted, they won those titles by punching their opponents in the head until there was nobody left standing, but that was considered legal back then, so everyone was fine with it.

The St. Louis Blues, Pittsburgh Penguins, Los Angeles Kings and Minnesota North Stars all had their struggles, but as the decade wore on they slowly built their fan bases and began to look reasonably stable. The same couldn't be said for the sixth team. The Oakland Seals were a failure almost immediately, and after only one season it looked like they might be sold and moved to Vancouver. The league rejected the move, spawning another lawsuit, and the 1970 expansion birth of the Canucks quashed that idea once and for all.

By 1970 the Seals had been sold to the eccentric Charles Finley, who already owned baseball's Oakland A's. True to form, he didn't waste much time getting creative; the team was rebranded as the California Golden Seals and was soon seen sporting what would become its trademark white skates. The Seals finished dead last in 1970–71, earning the first-overall pick in the 1971 amateur draft. That would've been a good thing, since there was a blue-chip prospect available who'd go on to become one of the greatest players in NHL history. Unfortunately, the Seals had traded away their first-round pick a year earlier, sending it to Sam Pollock in Montreal for immediate help that didn't actually pay off.[*] The Canadiens used that pick to select Guy Lafleur, and the rest was history. It wouldn't be long before the Seals were too.

By 1976, with the team still struggling to establish a foothold in the Bay Area, the league approved its relocation to Cleveland. The Golden Seals left their white skates behind and took on the Barons name, a nod to Cleveland's AHL history (and the NHL near-miss covered in chapter 3). The move was approved in July and finalized in August, leaving the Barons with just weeks to get up and running in their new market. They weren't able to do much promotion, and fans in Cleveland didn't seem all that interested in the newcomers; attendance fell below the levels the team had pulled in Oakland. By February 1977, the Barons were missing payroll and asking the NHL for a bailout. It was initially refused, and at one point the players reportedly threatened to stage a walkout before a game against Colorado. Only a last-minute reprieve from the league and the NHL Players' Association provided enough cash to finish out the year.

---

[*] The Seals got winger Ernie Hicke and the Canadiens' 1970 first-rounder in exchange for their 1971 first-rounder and François Lacombe. They spent the Habs' pick on Chris Oddleifson, who never played a game for them.

The team was sold again in the summer of 1977, with Cleveland natives Gordon Gund and his brother George Gund III stepping in to take on the sinking franchise. That kept the Barons alive for another season, but it would be their last. With the North Stars also struggling, the Gunds cut a deal with the league: They'd take over in Minnesota, the Barons would be partially absorbed into the North Stars franchise, and the NHL's Cleveland experiment would be over after just two years. To this day, the Barons are the last team in major North American pro sports to fold.

The failure of the Barons left the NHL to play the 1978–79 season with seventeen teams. That may have been one fewer than expected, but the league had still nearly tripled in size in just a dozen years. They weren't done, as four more new teams were on the way before the end of the decade. But this time the new franchises wouldn't come via expansion, but by absorbing the competition.

THE WHEEL

The NHL takes a terrible idea for a spin

SO, IT'S 1970 AND YOU'RE THE NHL. YOU'VE JUST ADDED exactly two expansion teams. Everyone agrees that the newcomers should get the top two picks in that year's amateur draft, but it's harder to decide who should pick first: the Buffalo Sabres or Vancouver Canucks.

It's no small choice, as the draft features one surefire prospect who, most scouts agree, should be the cornerstone for a new franchise. That's Gilbert Perreault, the Ontario Hockey Association's reigning MVP, who's coming off a season in which he racked up 51 goals and 121 points in just 54 games. He's the clear-cut number one, and he promises to be an immediate impact player in the NHL. So, again: Who gets him? What's the fairest way to randomly decide between two teams?

Simple, most people would say. Flip a coin.

But you're the NHL. That's too easy. "Let's get weird," you say.

Showing a rare flair for marketing spectacle, the league decided that Perreault's future home would be determined by spinning a giant crown-and-anchor wheel right before the start of the draft—in front of the entire hockey world. The first hurdle: They needed to find a wheel. They eventually did, but that led to a new complication: The wheel they ended up with had thirteen segments, which basic math will reveal didn't exactly divide evenly between two teams. After a round of negotiations, the league, the Sabres and the Canucks emerged with a solution: One team would be assigned spots one through six, while the other would get eight through thirteen. If the first spin landed on seven, everyone involved would be fired and the league would just flip a damn coin. (Okay, that last part wasn't true, although it probably should have been. In fact, a seven would mean a do-over.)

On the day of the draft, the two new teams assembled with the rest of the league, its officials and a bunch of TV cameras in the Grand Salon of the Queen Elizabeth Hotel in Montreal. NHL president Clarence Campbell would do the honours of performing the spin. What could go wrong?

Here's what: The Sabres were given their choice of number ranges and opted for eight to thirteen. (You may wonder how they got the first choice of wheel numbers. By winning a simple coin flip, of course.) The Canucks, then, were left with one through six. Campbell stepped to the front of the room, gave the wheel a spin, and the hockey world held its breath, waiting to learn the fate of the NHL's two newest franchises.

"The number is one!" announced Campbell when the wheel came to rest. The Canucks table erupted in cheers and hugs, the organization celebrating the first of what it hoped would be a long history of clutch wins.

I'll pause here so that older fans can mumble, "Wait, I don't remember Gilbert Perreault ever playing for Vancouver."

In the midst of the Canucks' celebration, Sabres GM Punch Imlach took a second look at the wheel. It hadn't landed on the number one after all; the arrow was actually pointing to eleven. The two digits were laid out on top of each other instead of side by side, which had confused Campbell. When Imlach protested to league officials, they double-checked the wheel and reversed their decision. The Sabres had won the spin, leaving a stunned Canucks front office holding the second-overall pick.

Buffalo drafted Perreault, who went on to play his entire seventeen-year career with the Sabres, establishing franchise records for games played, goals, assists and points that still stand to this day. He was inducted into the Hockey Hall of Fame in 1990, his first year of eligibility. And the number he wore during that illustrious career? Eleven, naturally.

As for the Canucks, they settled on defenceman Dale Tallon, passing over prospects like Reggie Leach and Darryl Sittler. Tallon would last just three seasons in Vancouver before being traded to Chicago; he would go on to a successful career in broadcasting and later in front offices, but his NHL playing days were over before he turned thirty.

What would the history of the Canucks and Sabres have looked like if

Gilbert Perreault had headed to Vancouver? We'll never know. But we almost found out, thanks to a rickety crown-and-anchor wheel, a far-sighted president and a league that just refuses to ever do anything the easy way.

8

THAT '70S SHOW

*Scoring booms, stars switching leagues
and the Flyers bullying their way to the Cup*

WHEN THE NHL WASN'T BUSY ADDING AND SUBTRACTING
teams, it was presenting hockey fans with an evolving product. By the end
of the 1970s, the action on the ice had transformed to such a degree that
fans of the '50s and '60s might have had trouble recognizing the sport.
That was especially true on the offensive side of things. The Original Six
era had featured a fairly consistent level of scoring, with games averaging
from just under five goals to just over six between the end of World War II
and 1970. When the puck dropped for the start of the 1970–71 season,
only one player, Chicago's Bobby Hull, had ever scored more than fifty
goals in a single season. And only four—Hull, Bobby Orr, Phil Esposito
and Gordie Howe—had ever topped 100 points. Those milestones had
become hallowed ground, achievements reserved for truly elite players.

And then the 1970s came along.

Between the 1970–71 and 1979–80 seasons, players combined to
record forty seasons of fifty or more goals, and fifty-two seasons of at
least 100 points. The once-sacred milestones were cleared by the likes
of Blaine Stoughton, Bob MacMillan and Mike Rogers, and leaguewide
scoring rates climbed north of seven goals per game for the first time
since the war years.

Early on, much of that offensive explosion was centred in Boston,
where Orr and Esposito quickly got to work shattering records. Esposito

had already broken Hull and Stan Mikita's Original Six–era single-season record of 97 points in 1968–69, racking up 126. He crushed his own mark in 1970–71, recording a 152-point campaign that would remain unmatched until the 1980s. He did the same for goals, scoring a previously unfathomable 76.

Amazingly, Esposito's record-shattering 1970–71 season wasn't enough to earn him MVP honours on his own team, let alone for the league. That's because while Esposito was rewriting the record book, Orr was redefining the very understanding of how the game could be played. The NHL had seen defencemen who could score before, but never like this. It became common for fans to claim that Orr played the blue line like a forward, but that wasn't quite true—there were barely any forwards who could keep up with him.

By the end 1970–71, Orr had become the first player in NHL history to record more than 100 assists in a season, and he finished the campaign with 139 points, second only to Esposito on the all-time list. He also recorded a ridiculous plus-124 rating for the year. And maybe most important, he permanently rewired the way the hockey world saw the position he played.

The Orr-Esposito Bruins won two of the decade's first three Stanley Cups, taking home the title in 1970 and 1972. The Canadiens earned the honours in 1971 and 1973, making it thirty-nine straight years that an Original Six team had been crowned NHL champion. That streak was about to end.

Orr and Esposito weren't the only ones changing the way the game was played. Hockey had always been a vicious pastime, one featuring crushing hits, bare-knuckle fights and occasional instances of players swinging sticks at each other's skulls. The violence had been controversial even in the game's earliest days, with dire editorials predicting the league's imminent demise if things weren't cleaned up. But the sport's mix of speed, skill and brutality was also a big part of the appeal for many fans.

Even given the rough-and-tumble baseline that was already in place, something seemed to shift in the '70s. Heading into the decade, the single-season record for penalty minutes was Howie Young's 273, set in 1962–63. Only five players had ever topped two hundred in a season. During the decade to come, sixty-six players would join that club.

No other team defined the new era of smash-mouth hockey like Philadelphia's Broad Street Bullies. The Flyers had built skilled but small teams in their early years in the league, but after watching those players get run off the ice by bigger opponents, the franchise decided to change direction. The arrival of Fred Shero behind the bench signalled a new attitude in Philadelphia, and the team quickly earned a reputation for mayhem.

The Bullies' ethos was personified by the team's tough guy, Dave "The Hammer" Schultz. While he wasn't especially big, Schultz quickly made it clear that he was willing to drop the gloves with just about anyone who took liberties with his teammates. And this being the mid-'70s, "taking liberties" could mean anything from cheap shots to clean hits—or even brief eye contact.

Schultz racked up penalty minutes, including a never-to-be-broken record of 472 in 1974–75, and the rest of the Flyers followed his lead. But far from being a one-dimensional goon squad, Philadelphia had the perfect mix of skill and brutality, and no one exemplified it quite like the team's captain, Bobby Clarke.

Fans of the era got used to seeing Clarke flash his trademark toothless grin, often at opponents he'd just finished infuriating. He was unquestionably among the league's most skilled players, winning three Hart Trophies in a four-year span between 1973 and 1976. But despite being on the smaller side, he didn't shy away from the Flyers' physical style, and he could swing a stick with the best of them—often retreating to safety behind Schultz and friends after he'd done so. He could embarrass your goalie and injure your team's best player, occasionally in the same shift.

Many fans hated Clarke and the rest of the Bullies; others saw them as the platonic ideal of what pro hockey should look like. Regardless of how they made you feel, though, there was no arguing with the results. The Flyers took home the Stanley Cup in 1974 and

1975, becoming the first team from the 1967 expansion to win a championship.*

While the Flyers were pushing the boundaries of what the game could look like, a far bigger story was developing. For the first time in its modern history, the NHL faced a legitimate competitor. And it was coming after its star players.

Strictly speaking, the NHL had never been the only game in town. There had always been other professional hockey leagues. But there's a difference between the mere existence of other options and legitimate competition. For most of its history, the NHL had been the undisputed king of the hockey world and the only destination for elite talent.

That changed, at least a little, beginning in 1971. That's when Dennis Murphy and Gary Davidson, two sports promoters best known for launching the American Basketball Association, turned their attention to hockey. Murphy and Davidson announced their intention to launch a new league called the World Hockey Association in time for the 1972–73 season. The plan was to debut twelve teams, with a mix of major markets like New York, Los Angeles and Chicago and smaller ones that didn't already have NHL franchises. And in what amounted to a declaration of war against the NHL, the WHA made it clear that it would pay big money to lure established stars.

That was music to the ears of the NHL's top players, many of whom felt underpaid compared to their peers in other pro sports. The NHL initially tried to fight back in the courts, arguing that its reserve clause** prevented players from jumping leagues. But the WHA challenged that claim and won, paving the way for an all-out bidding war. Things started

---

* The 1975 Cup win came over the Buffalo Sabres in a final that included the infamous "Fog Game," in which unusually humid weather and a lack of air conditioning reduced visibility to near-zero inside Buffalo's Memorial Auditorium, for players and fans alike. Also, Jim Lorentz killed a bat. The '70s were a strange time.

** A clause in each player's contract that stipulated that his professional playing rights remained with the team even after the deal's expiration date. A similar clause in baseball was overturned in the courts in 1975, paving the way for free agency.

slowly, with the WHA snagging a handful of players, including some recognizable names. But the new league eventually established itself as a true competitor to the NHL by way of a bizarre negotiation with one of the game's biggest stars that played out over the 1972 off-season.

By the summer of 1972, Bobby Hull was thirty-three years old and had played fifteen seasons in Chicago. With 604 career goals, he was the second-leading scorer in NHL history, trailing only Gordie Howe. And he wanted to get paid. Contract talks were contentious, as was often the case back then. There had been bad blood between Hull and Hawks management for years, and it seemed to be boiling over, leaving the two sides at an impasse. Still, the idea of Hull signing in another league seemed ridiculous. When the WHA's Winnipeg Jets began to make noise about offering him a deal, it was written off as a publicity stunt by just about everyone—including Hull, who famously quipped that he'd consider going to the Jets for the laughable sum of a million dollars.

Then the Jets presented him with the laughable sum of a million dollars—and more.

Winnipeg's contract offer included a million-dollar signing bonus, and would make Hull the sport's highest-paid player while locking in his services for ten years. Hull took the deal,* jaws dropped across the sports world and the WHA officially became a league worth paying attention to.

More NHL stars would follow in Hull's footsteps, including Bernie Parent and Gerry Cheevers. Other top players were able to leverage the presence of a competitor into better NHL deals, raising the pay scale. The NHL didn't look too kindly on that, and it retaliated by barring league jumpers like Hull from the 1972 Summit Series against the Soviet Union.** But petty recriminations aside, it was clear that a new reality had arrived.

On the ice, the WHA established itself as a reasonable alternative. The quality of play was clearly a notch below the NHL's, but only a notch. The younger league presented a mix of recognizable names and lesser-known

---

* Hull later joked that if he had realized the Jets were serious, he would have said he needed *ten* million.

** According to legend, Team Canada considered sneaking Hull onto the roster anyway, since his NHL contract hadn't technically expired, but eventually abandoned the plan.

players who were able to excel against lesser competition, and the whole thing added up to a perfectly watchable product on most nights. The WHA also differentiated itself through rule changes and innovations the NHL would later copy, including regular-season overtime, scouting Europe for players, and lowering the age for draft eligibility.

Off the ice, things were less rosy. As had been the case with NHL outfits in that league's early days, several WHA teams struggled financially, and franchises began folding or relocating almost immediately. The majority of the league's teams moved at least once, and only the Jets, Edmonton Oilers and New England Whalers made it all the way through the league's eight-year history without interruption. By 1977 the WHA was struggling badly, and merger talks with the NHL were underway. At one point, the NHL considered a plan in which it would absorb six WHA teams and give the newcomers their own division. That idea was voted down by NHL owners, and the WHA carried on as a separate entity, but a merger was beginning to feel inevitable.

The WHA's final seasons saw an influx of talent, including a wiry teenager named Wayne Gretzky whose name may come up once or twice more in this book. But the writing was on the wall. By the end of the 1978–79 season, the league was down to six teams and had to accept a lopsided merger deal. Four teams were folded into the NHL, with the Jets, Whalers, Oilers and Quebec Nordiques being absorbed by way of a complicated expansion/dispersal draft.

After seven seasons, the WHA was dead. But as we'd find out in the '80s, those of its teams that carried on into the NHL would turn out to be kind of important.

With an expansion team riding high as two-time champions, a competing league snapping up players, and new teams showing up almost annually, NHL fans preparing for the start of the 1975–76 season could be forgiven for thinking the days of old-school Original Six dominance had passed.

The Montreal Canadiens had other ideas.

The Habs were only two years removed from their last Stanley Cup, but had won just a single playoff round over that time. With the bruising

Flyers now on top, Montreal's signature mix of speed and skill was start-ing to feel outdated. Sure, it could still work in the regular season—the Canadiens had finished first overall in 1974–75—but the crush and grind of the playoffs were a different matter. Still, the Montreal roster was stacked with talent. Frank Mahovlich had moved on, but names like Yvan Cournoyer, Jacques Lemaire and Serge Savard remained, and younger players like Guy Lafleur and Steve Shutt were just hitting their primes. Montreal also boasted the best goaltender in the world in Ken Dryden, who'd skipped the entire 1973–74 season as part of a contract dispute before returning to the fold.

It was a formidable team, and one that had been built in a decidedly simple way: by having a smart GM who specialized in ripping off dumb teams in trades. The smart GM would be Sam Pollock, who built a monster in Montreal with a signature move. Pollock would find some floundering team desperate for a few more wins in the short term—such teams abounded in the early days of expansion—and offer them some useful spare parts, demanding a first-round pick in return. Often, the pick would be for a draft years down the road, an irresistible oppor-tunity for GMs who weren't even sure their teams would still exist that far in the future. When those teams were inevitably still scuffling along in last place when the bill came due, Pollock would get a top pick and draft a superstar.

The list of players Pollock scored with this ploy is almost laughable: Lafleur, Shutt, Guy Carbonneau, Bob Gainey, Mario Tremblay and even Larry Robinson wound up in Montreal thanks to his wheeling and deal-ing. And the haul could have been better (or worse, depending on your perspective). At one point, Pollock held the California Golden Seals' first pick in 1973 and only missed out on Denis Potvin because the New York Islanders finished worse than the Seals. And after acquiring what turned out to be the first-overall pick in the 1980 draft in 1976, the selection was memorably squandered on Doug Wickenheiser instead of local boy Denis Savard. Put it this way: If Pollock were in your fantasy hockey league and kept pulling off the kinds of deals he executed in the NHL, you'd kick him out. Thankfully for the rest of the league, new Canadiens ownership led to Pollock leaving the job in 1978, and replacement Irving Grundman didn't quite live up to his predecessor's standards.

Still, Pollock's machinations, combined with some old-fashioned scouting and player development, left the Canadiens with a juggernaut. They closed out the 1970s by capturing four straight Stanley Cups, ending the Flyers' reign with a four-game sweep in 1976 and then finishing off the Bruins in 1977 and 1978. The Habs finished first overall in all three seasons, including a 132-point year in 1976–77 that still stands as the all-time record. Those late-'70s teams are often considered the greatest in NHL history.*

The 1978–79 team took a step back in the regular-season standings, posting a meagre 115 points and dropping all the way to second overall, one point back of the Islanders. But they provided what may have been the dynasty's most memorable moment, when a conference final meeting with their archrivals the Bruins went to a seventh game at the Forum. Boston held a late lead, but a penalty for too many men on the ice opened the door for Montreal's comeback, and an eventual overtime winner by Yvon Lambert. The loss was widely blamed on Boston's coach, a dapper fellow by the name of Don Cherry. He was fired, and eventually he went into a career in broadcasting. I hear it's gone well for him.

That win was the Canadiens' fourth straight, and would mark the last for the Pollock-era powerhouse. While the team would remain strong for years to come, their dynasty had ended. Two new ones were about to emerge and dominate the decade to come.

---

* Although not in a list compiled by NHL.com in 2017 based on fan voting. Pollock's Canadiens finished behind the Gretzky-era Edmonton Oilers and Lemieux-era Pittsburgh Penguins. Millennials ruin everything.

THE AUGUST DRAFT

*Confusion over a merger (and one player's threat
of legal action) led to the latest draft ever held*

SINCE THE 1970S BEGAN WITH A STRANGE DRAFT, IT WAS
only fitting that the decade should end with an even stranger one. But how do
you beat a crown-and-anchor wheel and a league president with bad eyesight?
It will not shock you to learn that the NHL found a way.

The 1979 draft is often viewed as the best in league history in terms of the
players it produced. That's not surprising, given that for the first time, the
league allowed teenagers to be eligible. The move was necessary to accommodate incoming WHA players, since that league had allowed eighteen-year-
olds to compete. With the merger already in place, the league was left facing
the possibility that players who had already taken the ice in the WHA would
have to wait two years to join the NHL. That didn't seem to make sense, but
the NHL also wasn't eager to make any permanent changes to the age cutoff.
At one point, it seemed as if they might keep the draft limit at twenty and allow
a special one-time pass for WHA players. That's where Tom McCarthy came in.

McCarthy was an eighteen-year-old winger who'd already built an impressive hockey resumé. Most notably, he'd been the first-overall pick in the 1977
OHA junior draft, going ahead of Wayne Gretzky. By 1979, he was considered
one of the top prospects in the game, and he threatened to take the NHL to
court to get the draft age lowered. Fearing that it would lose the case, and
realizing the WHA merger presented a unique opportunity to rework the rules,
the league settled on a compromise: It would allow nineteen-year-olds to be
drafted, and lower the age to eighteen for WHA players.

That was a big change, one that more than doubled the number of available
players, and it created a cohort of 1979 prospects that included such future

Hall of Famers as Ray Bourque, Mark Messier, Michel Goulet and Mike Gartner.

One name that wasn't eligible: Wayne Gretzky. Although the eighteen-year-old star had been Oilers property in the WHA, the rules of the merger would have placed him back in the draft pool, where he would have been the surefire number one pick. But Gretzky had a personal-services contract with Oilers owner Peter Pocklington that the team argued rendered him ineligible to be drafted. The league eventually relented and ruled Gretzky ineligible, much to the chagrin of the Colorado Rockies, who owned the top pick.*

The 1979 draft was historic in other ways too. It was the last to be conducted in a hotel—the league moved to the now-familiar practice of holding the draft in an arena in 1980.** It was technically the first "entry draft" in league history; in previous years, it had been called the amateur draft. And it was limited to just six rounds; in previous years, the draft continued until all teams chose to pass on a selection, occasionally leading to picks still being made as late as the twenty-fifth round.

Oh, and it was held in August.

If that seems like an odd time, well, it was. It's the only time in league history that the draft was held that late in the summer. In part, the delay had to do with confusion over the eligibility issue—it took the NHL weeks to figure out exactly how it should handle the incoming WHA players, pushing the draft back from its original June date. But there was another issue to deal with: Tom McCarthy hadn't turned nineteen yet. Even after the rules were changed for him, he still wasn't eligible for the draft.

After a tumultuous decade of expansion, bankruptcies, competition and a merger, the NHL didn't seem especially eager to close things out with yet another courtroom battle. The draft was moved to August 9, which just happened to be a few days after McCarthy's nineteenth birthday. He would be eligible, the threats of a lawsuit were dropped, and for one of the rare times in league history, it seemed like everyone was happy.***

---

* The Rockies ended up taking Rob Ramage.

** The draft did make a brief return to a hotel conference room in 2005, thanks to the lockout.

*** After all that, McCarthy ended up being picked tenth overall by the North Stars. Although he was an all-star in 1983, he never lived up to his pre-draft hype and was out of the league for good by 1988.

9

THE HIGH-FLYING '80S

The Islanders, the Oilers and the last great dynasties

WHEN THE 1980s OFFICIALLY ARRIVED, THE NHL LANDSCAPE looked an awful lot like it had for most of the 1970s. On January 1, 1980, the standings showed the Canadiens leading their division, while the Flyers were sitting in first place overall. Those two teams had accounted for the league's last six Stanley Cups, and it seemed they might be headed towards a showdown for a seventh. The Flyers had been especially impressive to start the season, putting together one of the greatest runs in pro sports history. After dropping their second game, Philadelphia didn't lose again until early January. They racked up twenty-five wins and ten ties over that span, good for a thirty-five-game undefeated streak that remains the longest in North American pro sports.

If there was a newcomer on the verge of breaking up the Habs–Flyers dominance in the decade's earliest days, it looked like it could be the Sabres. Buffalo had been one of the league's better teams for years, putting up four straight 100-point seasons between 1975 and 1978 before taking a step back during the 1978–79 campaign. Now they'd lured Scotty Bowman away from the Canadiens* and made him coach and GM, and he

---

* In addition to parting ways with Bowman, the Canadiens also lost Ken Dryden, Yvan Cournoyer and Jacques Lemaire to retirement. Bernie Geoffrion would take over as coach, but he lasted just half a season due to health concerns. The Habs would still manage an impressive 107 points, but their Cup dynasty would end in the second round with a shocking game seven loss on Forum ice to the North Stars.

had the team riding the league's second-best record and looking like it was finally ready to break through and win a Cup.

If you'd decided to wait out your New Year's hangover by continuing to peruse the NHL standings, you would have found other teams that looked like contenders. The Los Angeles Kings were just two points back of the Canadiens for top spot in the Norris Division. The Bruins and North Stars were well back of the Sabres in the Adams, but both were over .500 and looking solid. The Black Hawks and Canucks were battling it out for the Smythe Division lead, while the Rangers were staking a claim to second place behind the Flyers in the Patrick.

And if you were especially bored and decided to keep scanning, you'd eventually make your way past the Pittsburgh Penguins and Toronto Maple Leafs and Quebec Nordiques and even the not-long-for-this-world Atlanta Flames, until finally you hit the league's fourteenth-place team. That unit was chugging along two games under .500, having failed to this point in the season to string together a winning streak longer than two games. This team had plenty of talent and had racked up its share of wins over the years, but this season, nothing seemed to be clicking. You probably would have been tempted to write off the club as not worth worrying about. That, of course, would have turned out to be a mistake, because that team was the New York Islanders. And the 1980s were going to be a pretty interesting decade for them.

The Islanders weren't an out-of-nowhere success story. They had won the Presidents' Trophy in 1978–79 with 116 points before a disappointing second-round loss to the New York Rangers ended their season.* Heading into 1979–80, they would have been a reasonable pick to contend again. But midway through the season, they were stumbling along under .500 and at risk of missing the playoffs, and there was even some talk that time could be running out on head coach Al Arbour. The top line of Mike Bossy,

---

* Earlier that year, a game between the two teams had featured Denis Potvin's hit on Rangers forward Ulf Nilsson. The hit broke the youngster's ankle, Ranger fans never forgot it, and the infamous "Potvin Sucks" chant was born.

Bryan Trottier and Clark Gillies was still among the league's best, but opposing teams had learned that successfully targeting those players could silence the top-heavy Islanders.

Still, the key pieces were there. Denis Potvin was among the league's best defencemen, and Billy Smith was an intimidating presence in goal.* They were too good to be this bad, and they finally proved as much by clawing back to .500 with a January 12 win over the Capitals. As it turned out, that game marked the start of a seven-game win streak, giving them some breathing room in the playoff race and allowing the front office to refocus on patching the few holes in the lineup. Reinforcements came throughout the year, including the addition of Ken Morrow just days after he won a gold medal as part of the "Miracle on Ice" Team USA squad at the 1980 Olympics in Lake Placid. But the biggest move came at the trade deadline, when GM Bill Torrey pulled the trigger on a deal sending Billy Harris and Dave Lewis to the Kings for Butch Goring.

The addition of a dependable second-line centre gave the Islanders a more balanced attack, and the trade is often cited as the turning point for the franchise. The deal came with twelve games left in the season, and the Islanders didn't lose the rest of the way, finishing the year on an 8–0–4 hot streak. That nudged them up to ninety-one points on the season—still well off previous years, but good enough to make them the league's fifth seed heading into the playoffs.

With the influx of WHA teams, the NHL had expanded the playoffs to sixteen teams, seeded one through sixteen with no consideration given to conference, division or geography. The Islanders blew by Goring's old team, the twelfth-place Los Angeles Kings, in round one, then finished off the Boston Bruins in five in the quarter-finals. That set up a tough matchup with the 110-point Sabres, but the Islanders took the first three games of the series before winning in six. By the time a Cup final matchup with the Flyers arrived, the Islanders didn't feel like underdogs anymore. They won that series in six as well, with the Cup-winning goal coming in

---

* In more ways than one. Smith was known to relentlessly hack at opponents. In one notorious incident during the 1980 playoffs, he butt-ended Buffalo's Lindy Ruff in the eye.

overtime from Bob Nystrom. The win came with some controversy, as a missed call on an obvious offside in regulation led to an Islanders goal. To this day, you can ruin a Flyers fan's day by casually dropping a mention of linesman Leon Stickle into any conversation.*

The Islanders had captured the first Stanley Cup in franchise history without ever facing elimination or even trailing in a series. But they were far from done. They rolled through the 1980–81 season, winning the Presidents' Trophy with 110 points, and then cruised through the playoffs on the way to their second straight Cup, this one coming against the over-matched Minnesota North Stars in the final. That was one of the most dominant playoff runs in history, with the Islanders losing just three games in four series. Interestingly, two of the three losses came in the second round against an upstart young team from Edmonton.

The Edmonton Oilers had made NHL headlines before they were even formally part of the NHL. The controversy over Wayne Gretzky's draft status had started before the WHA merger was even official, and Edmonton entered the league facing lingering resentment from some quarters as a result of Peter Pocklington's shady (but admittedly clever) personal-services contract loophole.

Gretzky was expected to be a very good player, but some questioned how he would adapt to the higher calibre of play in the NHL. Any concerns were put to rest quickly as Number 99 dominated immediately. He finished the 1979–80 season tied for the league lead in scoring with Marcel Dionne. That was a stunning performance for a player who was, for all intents and purposes, a teenaged rookie, albeit one who was ruled ineligible for the Calder Trophy because of his WHA experience.

Early on, though, Gretzky didn't have much help in Edmonton, and though he made them a must-see attraction during their first couple of years, the Oilers weren't a very good team. They finished the 1979–80 season with just sixty-nine points and were swept aside by the Flyers in

---

* Thankfully, the league did not react to a single unfortunate missed call by implementing a widely hated offside replay-review system, because that would have been dumb.

their first NHL playoff series. While Gretzky dominated the scoresheet in the regular season, the team's second-leading scorer was Blair MacDonald, who put up ninety-four points. Nobody else even cracked seventy, and the team worked its way through six goaltenders, relying on guys like Eddie Mio and Jim Corsi while finishing with the second-worst goals-against total in the league.

But while it wasn't clear at the time, the seeds of a dynasty had already been planted. The 1979–80 team also featured a rookie forward named Mark Messier. He didn't have Gretzky's immediate impact, finishing with just thirty-three points, but he would quickly develop into an all-star. So would Glenn Anderson, who was drafted along with Messier in 1979 but wouldn't debut until 1980–81. Meanwhile, the 1980 draft saw the team add Jari Kurri and Paul Coffey, and the Oilers followed that by picking goaltender Grant Fuhr in the first round in 1981.

Messier, Anderson, Kurri, Coffey and Fuhr would all eventually join Gretzky in the Hall of Fame, but the early-'80s Oilers were all about the Great One. He followed his record-shattering debut* with 164 points in 1980–81, then upped that to a ridiculous 212 in 1981–82. That would be the first of four 200-point seasons Gretzky would record in the decade.

By his second NHL season Gretzky was already a fixture on sports highlight shows. On January 3, 1981, he made a rare appearance for a reason other than one of his dazzling goals or mind-bending passes. That was the day the unthinkable happened: Somebody hit Wayne Gretzky.

It had become conventional wisdom that catching Gretzky with a hard hit was next to impossible, partly because of his unequalled hockey sense and partly because of the presence of teammates like Dave Semenko and, later, Marty McSorley. But Maple Leafs rookie Bill McCreary apparently missed the memo, as he smoked Gretzky along the blue line that night in Edmonton. The hit was clean, and the Oilers didn't offer much response, perhaps more concerned with the sight of their meal ticket rolling around on the ice in pain. The check quickly became part of hockey lore, although

---

* Heading into the season, the scoring record for a first-year player had been Bryan Trottier's ninety-five points in 1975–76, a mark Gretzky topped by forty-two.

not in an entirely accurate fashion. Despite what you may have been told, it didn't come during the last shift of McCreary's career. He appeared in ten more games.*

By the end of Gretzky's second year in the NHL, the Oilers had yet to finish a season at .500 and had won just a single playoff series. Regular-season success arrived in 1981–82, when Edmonton broke through for 111 points. But that season ended with yet another playoff disappointment, this one thanks to game three of their first-round series with Los Angeles, a game that came to be known as the Miracle on Manchester, in which the Kings stormed back from a 5–0 third-period deficit to beat Edmonton in overtime. Los Angeles would go on to win the series in five games, leading to another round of questions over whether the flashy, record-setting Oilers had what it took to actually win a championship.

Weeks later, the New York Islanders would beat the Vancouver Canucks to win their third straight Stanley Cup, and the narrative had been clearly established: The Oilers were on their way to something special, but the road went through Long Island.

After three seasons of scene setting, hockey fans finally got the main event in 1983, as the Islanders and Oilers met for the first time in the Stanley Cup final. Unlike their second-round matchup in 1981, this series featured both teams near the heights of their powers. Gretzky had racked up yet another Art Ross and Hart Trophy, while Messier, Kurri and Anderson all topped 100 points. Meanwhile, Bossy had recorded his third straight sixty-goal season, and Trottier and Potvin remained near the top of their games.

The Oilers rolled to the final, losing just one game along the way. The Islanders had an only slightly rougher road, and never faced elimination. It was a dream matchup, pitting the reigning dynasty against its heir apparent; youthful exuberance against veteran savvy; the unstoppable force against the immovable object. And after all of that, the series was . . . well, it wasn't very good.

---

* Also, he's not the same Bill McCreary who later became an NHL referee. That's his cousin.

With everyone expecting a shootout, the Islanders went into Edmonton and opened the series by shutting down the Oilers with a 2–0 win. They took the second game by a 6–3 final, then finished off the series back on Long Island with 5–1 and 4–2 wins. Billy Smith drove the Oilers crazy with his stickwork in the series and won the Conn Smythe Trophy. The New Yorkers were champions for a fourth straight year, having outscored Edmonton 17–6 in the sweep. The Islanders hadn't passed the torch; they'd used it to set their opponents on fire.

Take this story with a grain of salt if you want, but according to hockey legend, something very important happened in the aftermath of the sweep. After the Cup-clinching game, several of the Oilers' young stars ended up walking past the victorious Islanders' dressing room. Expecting to see a champagne-soaked celebration, Gretzky, Messier and friends instead saw a subdued and exhausted group of players covered in bandages and ice packs. It was only then, confronted with that vivid scene, that the Oilers finally understood what it took to win a Stanley Cup.

It's a great story. So great, in fact, that it would seem wrong to question whether it ever happened. Both Gretzky and Messier have told some version in the years since, and it's been recounted in plenty of books and history lessons, although the details tend to shift. Was a team that had just won a championship really just hanging around its dressing room with the door wide open for all the world to see? It seems unlikely. But hockey fans love the story, so let's just say it happened.

The inevitable rematch came in 1984, with the Oilers coming off a franchise-record 119-point season. Their road through the playoffs hadn't been an easy one this time, as the Calgary Flames had taken them to a seventh game along the way, but they made it back to the final, where the Islanders were waiting. By that point, the Islanders had run their playoff winning streak to nineteen straight series, a North American pro sports record that's unlikely to ever be broken.

This time, it was the Oilers who kicked off the series with a low-scoring shutout win, taking the opening game 1–0 on home ice. The Islanders roared back with a 6–1 victory in game two, but that would be all the resistance they could muster. The Oilers won the next three games, scoring nineteen goals in the process, and finally ended the Islanders' dynasty in the process of capturing their first Cup.

As the aging Islanders faded from a great team to a merely good one (and, by the end of the decade, an awful one), the Oilers were left as the league's undisputed powerhouse. But a new challenger was ready to emerge, and this one wouldn't come from the other conference. In fact, the Oilers wouldn't even have to look beyond their own province.

THE BLUES TAKE A PASS

A struggling team, a dog food company and a
small Prairie town add up to a draft floor no-show

AS DOMINANT AS WAYNE GRETZKY WAS, THE EDMONTON Oilers dynasty never would have happened if not for the 1979 draft. That's where Edmonton added Mark Messier and Glenn Anderson, as well as long-time defenceman (and future front-office head) Kevin Lowe. Messier and Anderson are already in the Hall of Fame, and Lowe might join them someday, so it's no surprise that the Oilers' 1979 draft is often listed as one of the greatest by a single team ever.*

So, if the '79 Oilers had one of the best classes ever, who had the worst? That honour might also go to the Oilers, who in 1990 somehow managed to pick eleven players who combined to play *zero* NHL games. But while there's not much you could say in defence of that sort of showing, at least they showed up. That likely puts them one up on the 1983 St. Louis Blues.

The 1980s were a reasonably stable time for the NHL, at least compared to what fans had been dealing with in the decade prior. The league stayed at twenty-one teams, and only two moved—the Flames, who went from Atlanta to Calgary in 1980, and the Rockies, who went from Colorado to New Jersey to become the Devils in 1982.

But for much of the 1982–83 season, it looked as though the Blues would be on the move too. The team had been purchased in 1977 by the St. Louis–based Ralston Purina Company—yes, the dog food people—despite the company not showing any particular interest in owning a hockey team. By

---

* As far as trios go, the Oilers' 1979 class might rank behind only the Detroit Red Wings' 1989 haul of Nicklas Lidstrom, Sergei Fedorov and Vladimir Konstantinov.

1981, new management had decided to sell the franchise, and apparently the only condition of sale was that somebody meet the asking price—coming from a viable NHL market was only a nice-to-have. And so, early in 1983, the Blues were sold to a company based in . . . Saskatoon.

Despite being headquartered in a Prairie town with a population of 154,000, the proposed ownership group claimed that it had plans in place for a state-of-the-art eighteen-thousand-seat arena. That was good enough for Ralston Purina and the Blues, who announced the deal in January; St. Louis sports-writer Bob Broeg referred to the planned team as the Saskatoon Whatzits. The sale was finalized, pending NHL approval, in April.

With the team's move to Saskatoon seeming all but assured, general manager Emile Francis bailed to take a job with the Hartford Whalers, and much of the rest of the front office was fired in anticipation of new owner-ship filling the roles. For all intents and purposes, the St. Louis Blues no longer existed.

And then, something unexpected happened: The NHL exercised some common sense. The league's board of governors voted overwhelmingly against the move, reasoning that while the Blues had had some financial challenges in St. Louis, the odds of doing any better in Saskatoon were slim. The final vote was 15–3, with only the Blues, Toronto Maple Leafs and Montreal Canadiens in favour. (The Oilers, Whalers and Quebec Nordiques didn't have votes because they still owed the NHL expansion fees.)

Ralston Purina immediately vowed to fight the decision in court, claiming that special concessions agreed to when the company first purchased the team meant that it didn't need the customary 75 percent approval from the board of governors. To make matters worse, the Puppy Chow people made it clear that they had no intention of continuing to run the team. The Blues' owners basi-cally dumped the franchise at the NHL's doorstep and said, "You deal with it." And this all came to a head just days before the 1983 entry draft.

A handful of Blues scouts made the trip to Montreal at their own expense, but their bosses at Ralston Purina made it clear that their services would not be required. And so, on June 8, the Blues became the only franchise in NHL history to voluntarily decline to participate in the draft. While players like Steve Yzerman, Pat LaFontaine, Cam Neely and Dominik Hasek were being picked,

St. Louis sat on the sidelines, essentially arguing that the franchise need not make any selections because it no longer existed.

And the whole mess was far from over. The NHL countersued, and at one point the Blues franchise was technically terminated. The league eventually found a new owner in Harry Ornest, who assumed control of the franchise—or, from a technical standpoint, a brand new franchise that inherited the name, history and assets of the old one—in time for the 1983–84 season. The team stayed in St. Louis after all, and remains there to this day. Saskatoon is still waiting for its first NHL team.

10

BAD BLOOD

The Battle of Alberta, the Battle of Quebec, and the
Norris Division turn the league into a combat zone

HERE'S WHAT YOU SHOULD REMEMBER ABOUT THE BATTLE
of Alberta: It was darn near the perfect NHL rivalry. It had that irresistible dynamic of an established champion being chased by a hungry
challenger. The Calgary Flames and Edmonton Oilers were in the same
division, so they met frequently during the season and, in most years,
during the playoffs. And the skill level was off the charts, featuring two
rosters packed with all-stars and future Hall of Famers who pushed each
other to be better.

Here's what you probably remember about the Battle of Alberta: Lots
and lots of punching. It was kind of their thing. When the two teams got
together, you could count on seeing something magnificent from Wayne
Gretzky or Theo Fleury or Jari Kurri or Al MacInnis. But you could also
count on seeing something brutal from Dave Semenko or Tim Hunter or
Kevin McClelland or Dave Brown. The chances were good that Mark
Messier would make an impact both ways.

Line brawls were common. Cheap shots were plentiful. Every once in
awhile, the benches would empty. These moments would come early
in the game, to set the tone, or later in the game, to set the *next* tone, and
they were a constant feature of the rivalry. As Oilers defenceman Steve
Smith says in Mark Spector's book, *The Battle of Alberta*: "When you look
back and you think about the Battle of Alberta, every time you went into

that building, you knew you were going to shed some blood. And hopefully you were going to take some with you."*

All of it would no doubt seem strange to anyone who has only become an NHL fan recently and is used to what passes for a rivalry in today's game. Maybe it wouldn't even make *any* sense. After all, these were two of the best teams in the league. Shouldn't they have been focused on winning on the scoreboard, and letting the referees and league officials sort out any transgressions committed by the other side?

Yes, they probably should have. But that wasn't how the NHL game was played back in the 1980s. And the attitude wasn't limited to Alberta.

On April 20, 1984, the USA Network opened its broadcast of game six of the Adams Division final in a delightfully '80s sort of way. There was perky music. There was a *Star Wars*–style scroll to tell the story of the series so far. There were pictures of players that seemed to have been cut out with scissors. And finally, there was a bright blue sky dotted with rounded white clouds, from which the face of Montreal goaltender Steve Penney emerged before floating to the ground. "A Penney from heaven," the announcer informed us. With that intro out of the way, the Montreal Canadiens and Quebec Nordiques took to the ice for one of the most famous games of the decade. By the end of it, nobody was thinking of blue skies and perky music. Instead, they were coming to grips with the fallout of a game that would become known as the Good Friday Massacre.

The 1984 matchup was the second playoff meeting between the two teams, with the Nordiques having won a five-game series in 1982. The Canadiens came into game six leading the series 3–2 and looking to close it out on home ice. The first five meetings had been chippy and occasionally dirty. The only question was whether one team could end it and move on to the next round before things exploded. The answer to that question was "Nope."

The first fight came just twenty-three seconds into the first frame.

---

* Fair warning to Oilers fans: That will not be the only time Smith's name shows up in this chapter.

Quebec's Peter Stastny scored minutes later to give his team a 1–0 lead that they'd carry deep into the second period. With the score tight and tensions high, the two teams stayed on their best behaviour for as long as they could. That turned out to be until just about thirty-seven minutes into the proceedings. Late in the second, things started to deteriorate.

As is often the case with these sort of incidents, answering the question of who to blame for starting the whole mess depends on who you talk to. Montreal fans will point to Dale Hunter running Penney. Quebec fans will counter with Chris Nilan's sucker punch on Randy Moller. But whoever set it off, as the clock ticked down in the second period, a brawl broke out and the benches emptied. That in itself wasn't unusual back then, and for a time you might have believed the Canadiens and Nordiques just needed to blow off a little steam before heading to their dressing rooms for the intermission.

That thought wouldn't have lasted long. Mario Tremblay pummelled Stastny, breaking his nose. The two backup goalies, Clint Malarchuk and Richard Sévigny, somehow ended up paired off and fighting. And then came one of the most infamous punches in league history: Quebec's Louis Sleigher's haymaker to the head of Jean Hamel, who was being held by a linesman.* The Canadiens player was out cold before he hit the ice; he sustained a serious eye injury that would force him to retire months later.

The punch was so brutal that it briefly ended the brawl, with both teams heading off the ice to regroup. Several combatants were kicked out, including Nilan and Sleigher, but in an oversight by referee Bruce Hood and his crew, the teams were sent back out for the third period without anyone informing them of the ejections. Only once the players were on the ice did the penalty announcements start, and by then it was too late. The Habs went after Sleigher, and round two of the brawl commenced. At one point, Dale and Mark Hunter even squared off in a rare brother-versus-brother fight.** By the end of it, eleven players had been ejected,

* Hamel had actually started the season with the Nordiques; at one point, he and Sleigher had been roommates.
** The next would come in 1997, when Wayne and Keith Primeau dropped the gloves.

over 250 minutes in penalties had been handed out, and the game had been delayed by nearly an hour. There was a still a series to finish, which Montreal did with a 5–3 win, but that became an afterthought. The Battle of Quebec had descended to a new level of ugliness.

The two teams would face each other again the following year, with Quebec winning a game seven overtime classic. They'd get two more playoff matchups, both won by Montreal, before the Nordiques moved to Colorado in 1995. Montreal would bid them goodbye with a parting gift: a goaltender who'd play a role in yet another bitter NHL rivalry.

The Battles of Alberta and Quebec were examples of the kind of madness that can break out when two teams hate each other and aren't shy about showing it. But what happens if, instead of two teams with bones to pick, you had five? And then you grouped them all together and had them spend nearly half their regular-season schedules playing each other? Well, as it turns out, you'd have the 1980s Norris Division.

The comparison doesn't entirely hold up, mind you, because the Flames, Oilers, Nordiques and Canadiens were all good. The Norris Division, with rare and short-lived exceptions, was filled with teams that were not. The classic 1980s version of the division—the one featuring the Toronto Maple Leafs, Detroit Red Wings, Chicago Black Hawks, Minnesota North Stars and St. Louis Blues—was formed in 1982, and it was easily the league's weakest for the next decade. The Norris didn't send a single team to the Stanley Cup final until 1991, its champions instead serving as cannon fodder for whichever team emerged from the Smythe Division every year. That wasn't exactly the sign of a great division, but in fairness, there wasn't much shame in losing to the Flames or Oilers. But the Norris Division's true claim to fame was two-fold: Sending absolutely terrible teams to the playoffs, because league rules mandated that every division get four representatives no matter what, and near-constant brawls. Hey, if you can't score goals, make saves or skate backward, you'd better do *something* out there.

From that 1982 realignment onward, the Norris Division basically devolved into a decade-long bar fight on skates, one that featured virtually every notable tough guy of the era. Everyone from Bob Probert to Joey Kocur to Stu "The Grim Reaper" Grimson to Basil McRae to John Kordic to Shane Churla passed through the division at some point, and none of them were there to run the power play.

It's hard to narrow down the best rivalries of the Norris, since each and every possible combination of teams hated each other at least once. Whether it was Jacques Demers trying to fight Herb Brooks, Dave Manson getting a triple game misconduct at Maple Leaf Gardens,* Probert decking Gary Nylund, or John Brophy trying to strangle everyone including his own team, the Norris was never boring. But perhaps the division's finest moment came on March 17, 1991, when the Blackhawks and Blues squared off in Chicago. Going against Norris Division tradition, both teams were actually good and battling it out for the Presidents' Trophy. But that hardly mattered. The wild line brawl that kicked off in the second period, and which culminated in Manson and Scott Stevens skating out to continue their long-running feud at centre ice, would come to be known as the St. Patrick's Day Massacre. Not to be confused, of course, with the aforementioned Good Friday Massacre. The NHL: the only league where somebody mentions a massacre named after a day of religious observance and you have to ask them to be more specific.

Let's pause here to address an issue that observant readers have no doubt picked up on, and which may even have been bothering some of you along the way: the nickname of Chicago's NHL team.

For most of this book, they've been referred to as the Black Hawks. But you may have noticed another spelling that crept in a couple of paragraphs ago: the Blackhawks. The same name, but one word instead of two. "What's the deal?" you may be wondering. "What kind of sloppy editing is this? How hard can it be to get something as simple as a team's name right?"

Well, pretty hard, apparently. At least in the NHL.

---

* Fans may remember that night more for the Gary Leeman–Denis Savard dance-off, which I believe is still ongoing to this day.

The Chicago Blackhawks were originally named after a World War I military division—specifically, the 86th Infantry, which had been nick-named the Blackhawk (or Black Hawk) Division after the legendary leader of the Sauk people, Chief Black Hawk. Team owner Frederic McLaughlin had served in the division, and he named his new team in its honour.

There was one problem: While the paperwork the new team filed in 1926 spelled the name as one word, everywhere else it appeared as two. For sixty years, the team was known as the Chicago Black Hawks—on the marquee outside the arena, on their sweaters, in the newspapers and in the history books. But then, in 1986, the error was discovered. The team real-ized it had been spelling its own name wrong for six decades. And so, with relatively little fanfare, the error was corrected. The Black Hawks have been the Blackhawks ever since—a neat bit of trivia if you're a fan of hockey history, and a minor pain in the neck if you're writing a book about it.

When they weren't pummelling each other, NHL stars of the 1980s did find the time to play a bit of hockey. And that brings us back to the Battle of Alberta.

With the New York Islanders falling back to Earth, the Oilers domi-nated the rest of the decade, winning Stanley Cups in 1984, 1985, 1987 and 1988. Everyone has their own definition of a dynasty, but there's a good case to be made that the Gretzky-era Oilers were the NHL's last. Edmonton probably would have won in 1986 too, joining the Canadiens as the only franchise to capture five straight Cups, were it not for a bizarre loss to—who else?—the Flames.

The two teams met in the Smythe Division final that year and fought through a tough series that went to a seventh game. With the game tied in the third period, the series-deciding moment came on one of the most bizarre plays in NHL history. Oilers defenceman Steve Smith collected the puck behind his own net as the Flames changed lines and made the regrettable decision to try to throw it through the crease to his blueline partner. The puck hit goaltender Grant Fuhr's skate and deflected into the Edmonton net for what would stand up as the winning goal. Flames winger Perry Berezan had executed the dump-in and got credit for the goal, despite already being on the bench when it went in.

Oilers fans have been known to point out that their team scored the winning goal in every series the two teams ever played. But no matter how it happened, the Flames had finally vanquished their archrivals. Calgary would go on to face the Canadiens in that year's final, losing in six games. The Oilers would then resume their dominance. When they won their third championship in 1987, Gretzky gave Smith the first skate with the Cup, which helped start the tradition of the winning team's captain seeking out a deserving teammate to hand off the Cup to.

Record setters that they were, Edmonton's win in the Cup final against the Boston Bruins in 1988 would feature a historical oddity: The Oilers became the only team in NHL history to sweep a series in five games. After winning the first three games, the Oilers went into the old Boston Garden looking to close things out in four. But with the game tied in the second period, a power failure at the rink cut the evening short. The league decided to simply resume the series with game five in Edmonton, which the Oilers won. Presumably there was a plan in place in case the Bruins fought back to force a deciding game, but it's doubtful that much thought went into it. That's how dominant the '80s Oilers were—everyone, including the NHL itself, just assumed they would win.

SPIN THE BOTTLE

*In the 1980s, NHL teams duked it out over pride,
honour and . . . water bottles?*

BY 1985, IT HAD BECOME CLEAR THAT THERE WASN'T much that could stop Wayne Gretzky and the Edmonton Oilers. Already the league's reigning champions, they'd blitzed back to the final, losing just two playoff games along the way. They'd led the league with 401 regular-season goals, scoring at least 400 for the fourth straight year, and boasted a lineup that would claim the Hart, Art Ross and Norris Trophies and even the Lady Byng. They were good.

And then they ran into the one opponent they apparently couldn't handle: Pelle Lindbergh's water bottle.

A water bottle atop the net is now standard issue around the league, to the point that it's hard to imagine what a goaltender would do without one. How would they cope with allowing a goal if they couldn't instinctively turn around for a cool beverage? Why, they might have to acknowledge the red light flashing behind them or the puck sitting inside their net.

That was the dilemma all goaltenders faced until the 1985 playoffs, when the Philadelphia Flyers became the first team to regularly leave a water bottle on top of the net. It was a smart move—that year's playoffs went later than any postseason ever had, and the buildings were getting warm. The Flyers didn't want any of their players dehydrated, least of all Lindbergh, their forty-win star who was about to be awarded the Vézina Trophy. Who could object?

Glen Sather, that's who.

The Oilers coach and GM didn't like the idea of any Flyer having access to in-game refreshment. Or at least, he was willing to pretend he didn't like it in the service of a little gamesmanship. And so, according to Sather, he told the league that either the water went or his team would. If the bottle wasn't removed, Sather claimed, the Oilers weren't playing.

"Why should we?" he asked the media, before laying out the slippery slope the league was facing. "Maybe we want a bucket of chicken on our net . . . Maybe hamburgers. I mean, what's the difference? If you have a water bottle out there, let's have lunch."

"Sure, that would be nice," Lindbergh reportedly responded. "Sometimes I get hungry out there."

(I'll pause here while every rec-league goalie reading this stops to wonder why they never thought of sneaking a bucket of chicken onto the ice.)

The whole thing was silly, and was largely treated that way—the *Philadelphia Daily News* ran a story about the situation with the headline SATHER JUST A BOTTLE OF LAUGHS. But the Oilers boss insisted he was serious, and the league eventually acquiesced, handing the bottle a series-long suspension. And the missing water actually did come into play, as Flyers coach Mike Keenan pulled Lindbergh at multiple points because he thought his goalie might be dehydrated. "I can't see any reason why the man with the most equipment has to play sixty minutes and doesn't get a chance to get a drink of water," Keenan told reporters.

Yes, that's right. There were two coaches involved in the series, and *Mike Keenan* was acting like the reasonable one.

In the end, Sather's boys dropped the opening game 4–1 before roaring back to take the series in five. By the end of the series, Keenan had handed starting duties over to Bob Froese, who allowed all eight goals in the Oilers' 8–3 Cup-clinching win. There was no word on whether he got thirsty during all those post-goal stoppages.

11

THE EUROPEAN INVASION

The NHL opens its doors to the world

AT THE BEGINNING OF THE 1980S, NHL HOCKEY WAS STILL very much a Canadian game. The teams were mostly based in the US, with two-thirds of the league's franchises located there, but the players overwhelmingly came from north of the border. Canada had supplied almost all of the league's players during the Original Six era—peaking at 98.6 percent in 1956–57, according to QuantHockey.com—and beyond. There had been the occasional case of a European-born player reaching the league, such as 1935 rookie of the year Dave "Sweeney" Schriner, who'd been born in Russia, or Slovakian-born Black Hawks legend Stan Mikita. But like Schriner and Mikita, the majority of those European-born players had moved to North America at a young age.

Those league demographics began to change in the 1970s, as NHL teams started to look to Europe for untapped talent. At first, that meant Sweden and Finland, two countries whose players could travel somewhat freely to North America, unlike Soviet and Czechoslovakian players living behind the Iron Curtain. The first European-trained player to appear in the NHL was a Swedish winger named Ulf Sterner, who debuted for the Rangers during the 1964–65 season; he lasted just four games and didn't record a point.

Other European players trickled into the league in the years that followed Sterner's brief stint, but none achieved stardom. The big breakthrough came in 1972, with an unexpected team leading the way. The

100

Toronto Maple Leafs were owned by Harold Ballard, who seemed adamant about wanting nothing to do with European players. But with
Ballard in jail on a nine-year sentence for fraud (of which he'd only
serve a third), the Leafs sent scout Gerry McNamara to Sweden to get
a look at winger Inge Hammarstrom. While there, McNamara laid eyes
on defenceman Borje Salming and eventually convinced him to come
to Toronto. Salming made his NHL debut in 1973 and was an instant
star, finishing in the top five in Norris Trophy voting in each of his first
seven seasons.*

    With Salming paving the way as the first European-trained player to
dominate in North America, other NHL teams quickly went searching
for international talent of their own. They were also joined by teams
from the fledgling WHA, who were desperately looking for players. By
the late '70s, it was no longer unusual to see a European player or two
dotting North American rosters, or to see standouts like Salming, Anders
Hedberg and Ulf Nilsson on league leaderboards. Other European stars
would follow throughout the 1980s, including Jari Kurri, Thomas Steen
and Pelle Lindbergh.**

    The success of European players opened the eyes of many Canadian
and American fans, albeit slowly. Meanwhile, it also caught the attention
of other star players around the world, who started to see a place on an
NHL roster as a realistic goal. But for some of those players, the journey
to North America would be a difficult one.

For a player from the Soviet Union or Czechoslovakia, playing in the
NHL was not supposed to be an option. While both countries had thriv-
ing hockey programmes, there was simply no official path to North
America. Indeed, an entire era of Eastern Bloc stars faced a stark choice:
Play where you're told or risk everything and try to defect.

---

*   While he has become the forgotten man in the story, Hammarstrom accompanied
Salming to Toronto and was a consistent twenty-goal man in the NHL.
**   Lindbergh's story is a tragic one. He became the first European goalie to win the Vézina
in 1985, only to die in a drunk-driving crash mere months later. Fans posthumously voted
him as a starter in the 1986 All-Star Game.

The first major stars to choose the latter option were the Stastny brothers. Peter, Anton and Marian Stastny were coming off a star turn in the 1980 Winter Olympics, where they'd played on a line for the Czechoslovakian team. Peter had been the tournament's second-leading scorer, with fourteen points in six games. Later that year, when the Czech team travelled to Austria for a tournament, officials from the Quebec Nordiques helped Anton, Peter and Peter's pregnant wife, Darina, make their escape to Vienna. The entire plot, as detailed in Tal Pinchevsky's book *Breakaway*, reads like a spy movie and includes a car chase and near-misses with men in black.

Marian stayed behind with his family and was quickly suspended from the national team in a move seen as retribution for his brothers' actions. (As Anton told *The New York Times* in 1981, the Czech authorities would "do black things, very black things, to make us go back.") Marian found himself without a job, abandoned by friends while his family members faced threats. He would make his own escape in 1981, joining his brothers on the Nordiques roster for the 1981–82 season. By the time all three Stastny brothers were reunited in Quebec, Peter was already an established NHL star, becoming the first rookie to break the 100-point barrier. Other Czech players would follow, including Petr Svoboda in 1984, Michal Pivonka in 1986 and Petr Nedved in 1989.

Soviet stars were slow to follow their Czech counterparts, despite interest from NHL teams. The Montreal Canadiens drafted national team goaltender Vladislav Tretiak in 1983 and tried to get him to North America, but Soviet officials wouldn't allow it. Likewise, Viacheslav Fetisov's attempt to join the New Jersey Devils in the mid-'80s was denied. Only one Soviet player, winger Sergei Priakin in 1989, was granted permission to come to the NHL, largely because he was not a key member of the national team. Priakin played two games for the Calgary Flames during the 1988–89 season and forty-six over the course of a three-year NHL career. He scored three goals.

The first Soviet defection didn't come until the spring of 1989, when twenty-year-old winger Alexander Mogilny vanished after the World Championships in Sweden. Mogilny contacted the Buffalo Sabres, who'd drafted him in the fifth round the previous year, and informed them that he was ready to play in America. His defection gave other Soviet stars a plausible threat to use to demand their release from the national programme. That list included Igor Larionov and Sergei Makarov, and Fetisov renewed his years-old request. All three veterans were allowed to come to the NHL for the start of the 1989–90 season—suiting up for the Devils, Canucks and Flames, respectively—and Sergei Fedorov would follow in 1990, defecting to join the Detroit Red Wings.

By 1991, the Soviet Union had crumbled and the Iron Curtain was no more. The trickle of European stars became a flood, and the face of the NHL changed forever.

Even as European players became a common sight around NHL rinks, they had to battle misconceptions and stereotypes. Most centred around their toughness, or supposed lack thereof. It was said they didn't fight, they hid behind visors, and they hacked and slashed and cheap-shotted the more honourable North American players. Ballard famously claimed that Hammarstrom could go into the corner with a dozen eggs in his pockets without breaking a single one. Never mind that a typical Swedish player hailed from a far different background than a Soviet star; to many NHL fans, they were all Euros, and Euros were all the same.

There was certainly some truth to the idea that European hockey differed from the North American version—especially when it came to hitting and fighting. One of the most memorable games of the '70s was a 1976 exhibition clash between the Broad Street Bullies and the Soviet Red Army squad. The Flyers' aggression proved to be so far over the top that at one point the Soviets simply left the ice, prompting Bob Cole's infamous call: "They're going home!" (The Soviets eventually returned to complete the game, which ended in a 4–1 Flyers win.)

Other times, though, the Soviets gave as good as they got, such as during the "Punch-up in Piestany" that marred the 1987 World Junior Championships. That wild brawl between the Soviets and Canadians spun completely out of control, with officials abandoning the ice and even shutting off the arena lights. Predictably, Canadian fans pivoted seamlessly from claiming that the Soviets didn't have the guts to fight to blaming them for starting the brawl.

The media didn't help matters. Don Cherry was notorious for relentlessly criticizing European players during his weekly "Coach's Corner" segment on *Hockey Night in Canada*. He mocked Mats Naslund's height, ripped Ulf Samuelsson for reckless play and reportedly called Tomas Sandstrom "a backstabbing chicken Swede who deserved what he got" after Doug Gilmour broke his arm with a slash in the first months of the 1992–93 season. Those comments were often met with criticism from sportswriters, but viewers ate them up.

Whether old-school types like Cherry accepted it or not, the tide was turning. In 1989, Mats Sundin became the first European-trained player to be taken with the first-overall pick in the entry draft, and by 1994 Fedorov had become the first to win the Hart Trophy. Stars like Jaromir Jagr, Teemu Selanne and Pavel Bure* put up monster numbers in the early '90s, while goalie Dominik Hasek and defenceman Nicklas Lidstrom established themselves among the very best to ever play their positions.

And for the most part, fans loved it. Old prejudices were, if not quite forgotten, at least set aside as the new generation of elite international players took over. Combine their arrival with the emergence of legitimate American stars like Jeremy Roenick and Brian Leetch, and filling the NHL's rosters became more than a one-country production. The league itself had expanded over the decades; it only made sense that the number of countries stocking the pool of players should too.

Today, Canadians make up slightly less than half the league's population, and every team features players from around the world. Newer fans probably can't conceive of an NHL where seeking out the best players on the planet regardless of their country of origin would be seen as controversial. But it's worth remembering the trail that had to be blazed before we could get here, and the men who walked it. As well as the cloak-and-dagger drama— and conviction of Harold Ballard—that helped make it happen.

---

* The Vancouver Canucks pulled a fast one by picking Bure in the sixth round of the 1989 draft; the rest of the league had mistakenly thought he wasn't eligible until 1990.

THE GREATEST JAPANESE PLAYER WHO NEVER WAS

The 1974 Sabres take the whole international thing a little too far

EVEN TODAY, HOCKEY TENDS TO BE DOMINATED BY NORTH Americans and Europeans. But there are exceptions. The game is played around the world, and the NHL has welcomed players born in many nations not traditionally known as hotbeds for the sport. Former players Claude Vilgrain, Olaf Kolzig and André Deveaux were born in Haiti, South Africa and the Bahamas, respectively. And goaltender Yutaka Fukufuji became the first Japanese player to start an NHL game when he manned the crease for the LA Kings in a matchup against the Atlanta Thrashers in 2007.

Fukufuji's debut made for a nice enough story, but he was no Taro Tsujimoto. Then again, nobody ever was—including Taro Tsujimoto.

As the 1974 amateur draft rolled into its eleventh round, Buffalo Sabres GM Punch Imlach informed the gathering that he was using the 183rd-overall pick on Tsujimoto, a slick-skating centre who starred for the Tokyo Katanas of the Japanese Ice Hockey League. The pick raised eyebrows, but was dutifully recorded in the record book. The Sabres, it seemed to everyone in attendance, had gone above and beyond in their international scouting and found a potential gem. There was just one problem: Taro Tsujimoto didn't exist.

As it turns out, Imlach was frustrated at how long the draft was taking. Still mired in the days when the proceedings lasted as long as any team kept taking players, the 1974 draft eventually dragged on for twenty-five rounds because the New York Rangers and Washington Capitals wouldn't stop making picks well after everyone else just wanted to go home.

When things first started to lag, Imlach figured he'd have a little fun. He made up Tsujimoto's name,* and background, and even the Japanese star's current team, the Tokyo Katanas. In hindsight, maybe the team name should have tipped people off—a *katana* is a Japanese sabre, after all. But it didn't, and Imlach and the Sabres were committed enough to stick with the gag. The team even released a 1974–75 roster that listed Tsujimoto among the forwards. Weeks after the draft, reporters covering the team wanted to know when the foreign sensation would arrive.

Buffalo finally admitted the hoax as training camp neared. The NHL didn't find it all that funny, and has since stricken the pick from the official record.

---

* With an assist, apparently, by Sabres PR director and noted prankster Paul Wieland, who borrowed the name from a local gift store.

12

THE TRADE

*The biggest deal in sports history changes
the game on both sides of the border*

FOR MOST HOCKEY FANS, AUGUST 9, 1988, STARTED LIKE
any other day late in the off-season. We were stuck in that summer dead
zone, well after the playoffs and draft but still a month away from the
opening of training camps. Even a diehard hockey lover was probably
more focused on baseball season, or the upcoming Summer Olympics, or
just getting some sun while the getting was good. And none of us had any
idea that the landscape of the entire sport we loved was about to change.

That we were all so completely in the dark might seem strange to
modern fans. You kids today with your around-the-clock sports cover-
age on specialty TV and radio, websites churning out a constant stream
of content, and a nonstop Twitter firehose of rumour and speculation—
you live in a sports world where nothing ever really comes as a surprise.
These days, even the true bombshells have almost always been fore-
shadowed, and the gradual trickle of details and quasi-scoops that
accompanies major news has dulled our ability to be truly stunned by
anything sports-related.

But not back in 1988, when one trade could stop you in your tracks like
a shovel to the face.

If you were a fan back then, you remember where you were when you
heard that the Edmonton Oilers had traded Wayne Gretzky. Maybe
the news came over the airwaves, on a breaking CBC bulletin or "we

interrupt this programme" radio announcement. More likely, it came from a breathless friend or family member, one whom you probably didn't believe at first. Come on . . . Gretzky? To the Kings? Get out of here!

But, of course, it was true. And though the trade felt almost unfathomably huge in the moment, it turned out to be an even bigger deal than any of us comprehended.

As stunning as the deal was to fans, it didn't come out of nowhere. Occasional rumours about a Gretzky trade had been poking around for years, usually tied to the question of whether the Edmonton Oilers could afford to keep him. Those rumours were fun—hey, maybe he'd wind up playing for your favourite team—but they always felt more like wishful thinking for fans outside of Edmonton.

By the summer of 1988, though, the writing was on the wall—even if most of us couldn't read it. Oilers owner Peter Pocklington was facing challenges involving his non-hockey businesses, and he was worried that Gretzky might leave as a free agent when his contract expired. The team had quietly begun exploring a move during the 1987–88 season. In his autobiography, Gretzky says that he found out he was being shopped the day after the Oilers won the 1988 Stanley Cup final. Ironically, that Cup victory was the one that launched the tradition of the winners gathering for a team photo. In previous years, the ice had been too crowded for teams to celebrate properly, so on this occasion the Oilers asked arena security to give them some space. The photo seemed like a nice keepsake at the time; it ended up signifying the end of an era.

Three teams emerged as possible destinations for the Great One: Los Angeles, Detroit and Vancouver. Depending on who's telling the story, the Canucks were the early frontrunners, but they eventually balked at Pocklington's exorbitant demands. Bruce McNall and the Kings had no such concerns; they were willing to meet Pocklington's asking price of fifteen million dollars (US).[*]

---

[*] Pocklington later claimed that the Kings had approached him with a similar offer as far back as 1985.

The other pieces of the deal came together relatively quickly. McNall and Pocklington worked together directly, with Oilers GM Glen Sather involved only at the margins while making it very clear, both privately and publicly, that he didn't support the move. The Oilers would include Marty McSorley and Mike Krushelnyski in the trade, while the Kings would surrender three first-round draft picks, Jimmy Carson and Martin Gélinas.

Viewed purely as a hockey transaction, the deal was ridiculously lopsided. The Kings were getting the best player in the history of the sport, plus two very useful veterans. Meanwhile, the Oilers were getting three draft picks spread over five years, choices that figured to be well down the first round. Sure enough, of the three players eventually drafted with the picks, only Martin Rucinsky had any sort of NHL success. Gélinas was a top prospect, having gone seventh overall in that year's draft, but he never had much impact in Edmonton.

The key to the deal, at least among assets that didn't have dollar signs in front of them, was Carson. He was a legitimate young star, a former second-overall pick who'd just turned twenty and was already coming off a fifty-five-goal season. That total had tied the NHL record for goals scored by a teenager, set by (who else?) Gretzky himself seven years earlier. Carson didn't disappoint in Edmonton, racking up 100 points in his first season. But that would also turn out to be his last; he would walk out on the team four games into the 1989–90 season, forcing a trade to Detroit.

In the end, of course, Pocklington's decision was all about the cash, and if anything, the move we all know as "The Trade" should probably be referred to as "The Sale."

The deal was finalized over the course of several days in late July and early August. Gretzky was in the loop by this point, talking frequently with McNall. A new contract was negotiated, and arrangements were made for dual announcements in Edmonton and Los Angeles. The deal would become official on August 9.

Meanwhile, most of the rest of the hockey world remained in the dark. A handful of Edmonton media members were sniffing around, and rumours of a move had been dutifully reported. But those were largely dismissed as typical off-season fantasy talk. Even Gretzky's teammates didn't realize what was about to happen; Mark Messier wasn't informed until Pocklington called him the night before the announcement. As you might imagine, Messier made it very clear to the owner that he felt the deal was a mistake.

While the whole thing feels inevitable in hindsight, there were moments when the trade could have fallen apart. In one version of the story, Sather made an eleventh-hour plea to Gretzky to reconsider, with the Oilers GM promising that he would quit before signing off on a trade that his star player didn't want. At another point shortly before the announcement, Pocklington and Gretzky disappeared to meet in private, leaving McNall thinking that the deal was about to be submarined. But Gretzky had made up his mind: Things had gone too far, and there was no turning back. He was going to be an LA King.

The trade was formally unveiled with a press conference in Edmonton, one at which Gretzky cried while memorably referencing his former teammate by saying, "I promised Mess I wouldn't do this" through the tears. That was about as far as he got, as he'd eventually get up and take a seat away from the microphones as he fought to control his emotions.

Pocklington had no such trouble, and his performance at the press conference was widely criticized. Despite initiating the move based on financial difficulties related to his various other businesses, the Oilers owner laid the blame squarely at Gretzky's feet. He seemed to target Gretzky's recent marriage to actress Janet Jones as an inciting factor; the couple had their first child on the way, and Pocklington framed the move to LA as one that Gretzky had demanded. There was little truth to that, but it hardly mattered; Jones instantly became a despised figure in Canada.

She wasn't alone. Pocklington took much of the backlash, with Oilers fans burning him in effigy. Much of Canada seemed to go into shock, behaving as if the trade hadn't happened or perhaps could be undone. Nelson Riis, an MP from Kamloops, British Columbia, even stood up in Parliament to demand that the government block the move, reasoning that Gretzky was a national treasure who should be forced to remain in the country. The majority of Canadians probably didn't disagree.

Predictably, the reaction in Los Angeles was markedly different. Gretzky left Edmonton that same morning and headed directly for LA and a second press conference. This time, there would be no tears,* only optimism about an uncharted future.

In the short term, that future included sellout crowds, magazine covers and celebrities lining the rink in LA. Gretzky made the rounds of the late-night talk shows, got his own Saturday morning cartoon show and even made a legendarily awkward appearance as the host of *Saturday Night Live*. Almost overnight, the Kings were the hottest team in the league, if not in all of North American pro sports.

That future also, perhaps inevitably, featured a showdown between the Oilers and Kings in the 1989 playoffs. Gretzky had led the Kings to a ninety-one-point season, a twenty-three-point improvement year over year that pushed the team to second place in the Smythe Division. Meanwhile, the Oilers dropped fifteen points to finish with eighty-four on the year and claim the third spot. That meant an opening-round matchup between the team everyone was talking about and the one that, you could be forgiven for forgetting, was still the defending Stanley Cup champion.

The Oilers jumped out to a 3–1 series lead, but Gretzky and the Kings roared back to force a seventh game in LA. Gretzky opened the scoring less than a minute in, assisted on the winner and had three points on the night as the Kings took a 6–3 win. The Oilers' reign was over.

Six months later, on October 15, 1989, Gretzky broke Gordie Howe's all-time scoring record with a dramatic game-tying goal in the dying seconds. The opponent, of course, was the Oilers. The location was Edmonton. This time, it's fair to say that nobody in the hockey world was caught off guard.

Three decades later, we're still feeling the impact of The Trade. It's not hyperbole to say that almost everything about today's NHL was

---

* Later, Pocklington would infamously suggest that Gretzky's display of emotion in front of the Edmonton media had been an act, calling them "crocodile tears."

influenced in some way by the events of that August morning. As sports-writer Stephen Brunt would later put it, "It was a complete reset of the NHL in one day."

For the teams involved, of course, the impact was seismic. It signalled the end of the Kings as a harmless West Coast novelty, sent out in their silly yellow-and-purple uniforms to serve as cannon fodder for the conference's real contenders. Gretzky never did bring the Cup to LA, although he came close. But he did bring credibility, and that trickled down a generation to this decade's Kings and their pair of championships.

The deal also spelled the end of the Oilers as an unshakable power-house, although not as soon as we all thought. When the Kings won that playoff showdown in 1989, it was easy to write Edmonton off for good. Instead, they stormed back to win one last Cup in 1990, restoring their dynasty and elevating Messier to the top of the league's star chart. But it would be a temporary respite; by 1992, Messier had forced a trade of his own and the Oilers' glory days were all but done. They'd miss the playoffs four straight seasons starting in 1993, and win just two rounds in the years before a surprise run to the final in 2006.

Effects were also felt far outside LA and Edmonton. San Jose and Anaheim are both markets that would have been seen as unlikely NHL homes until Gretzky proved that hockey could thrive in California. Much of the league's sunbelt expansion can be linked to the deal; markets like Tampa, Miami, Phoenix and even Las Vegas largely owe their existence to The Trade.

Gretzky's arrival in California, and the subsequent PR blitz, also helped drag the league into the modern era of marketing. While the NHL still struggles to put its players front and centre, in the 1990s they at least started trying to act like an entertainment business, and ideas like outdoor games and creative additions to all-star weekends followed.

The deal impacted the league's players too, driving home the point that NHL hockey was a business and they could be treated like assets. If the game's greatest superstar could essentially be sold off for a pile of cash, then star players had value beyond what most of their penny-pinching owners were willing to admit. The trade didn't necessarily cause the spiralling salaries that marked the decades to come, but appeals to players to be loyal soldiers got a lot tougher once Pocklington reaped his windfall.

And then there are the fans. For many, even outside Edmonton, the day remains a bitter memory. As the saying now goes, if Wayne Gretzky can be traded, then anyone can. And if a team that just won four of five titles can be forced to dump its best player because the owner needs the cash, then any team could face the same fate.

With the Oilers temporarily out of the way as contenders, the Calgary Flames finally won their Cup, knocking off Gretzky's Kings and then beating the Montreal Canadiens in a rematch of the 1986 final. The season's enduring image was of longtime veteran Lanny McDonald clutching his first Cup at the age of thirty-six, having played what would turn out to be the last game of his career.

The 1980s had come to an end. And while the Stanley Cup remained firmly stashed away in Alberta, Gretzky's footprint in the southern US meant that hockey's horizons were ready to broaden. After more than a decade as a twenty-one-team league, the NHL was primed for another round of expansion.

THE BIGGEST TRADE PROPOSAL EVER MADE

Think the Gretzky trade was huge? Pocklington and the Oilers
nearly pulled off a far bigger one.

THE WAYNE GRETZKY TRADE IS THE MOST IMPORTANT transaction in the history of the NHL. There really isn't even a close second. In pulling the trigger on a deal that sent the greatest player ever to lace up a pair of skates packing, Peter Pocklington had traded the Franchise. How do you top that?

There's only one way, and that's by trading, well . . . the franchise. Literally. We're talking the entire team.

If that sounds crazy, that's because it is completely and inarguably crazy. But according to Pocklington himself, he and Maple Leafs owner Harold Ballard once talked about a deal that would have seen the two owners swap teams in the early '80s.* The Oilers (as in, all of them) would head to Toronto, with the Maple Leafs (again, every one of them) going to Edmonton. The owners would swap cities as well. And to make up for the difference in market size, Pocklington would send Ballard a fifty-million-dollar cash payment. The end result would have seen Pocklington at the helm of the Toronto Oilers, while Ballard and his fifty million dollars would have owned the Edmonton Maple Leafs.

The idea sounds like something that would get you banned from your fantasy league, but Pocklington insists the offer was genuine. What's more, he says the two men shook hands on it but Ballard eventually backed out, apparently after receiving a windfall from elsewhere. That was enough for the

---

* Pocklington makes this claim in his 2009 book, the delightfully titled *I'd Trade Him Again*.

cantankerous Leafs owner to pull the plug on the deal. You know things are getting crazy when Harold Ballard is the agent of reason.

We'll never know what would have happened if the two owners had actually gone ahead and presented the deal to the league for approval. You'd like to think that they would have been smacked upside the head and told to settle down. But this being the NHL, you never know. Maybe Toronto fans would have spent the early '80s cheering on Gretzky, Messier, Coffey and Fuhr, while Edmonton fans would have had to make due with Rick Vaive and . . . well, just Rick Vaive, really. Maybe Allan Bester and Bill Derlago* too.

Instead, everyone stayed put and fans didn't hear about the proposed deal until years later. The Maple Leafs continued to struggle through a decade of losing, controversy and misery (that last bit occasionally eased after Wendel Clark arrived and started punching opponents' skulls into the upper rows at Maple Leaf Gardens). And the Oilers became the sport's dominant force, right up until their owner couldn't afford to keep them together anymore.

---

*   Or, as every young Leafs fan knew him, Builder Lego.

13

EXPANDING HORIZONS

*A Canadian upset, a sure thing that wasn't, and a Stanley Cup
finalist picking players in an expansion draft*

AS THE 1990S ARRIVED, FOR THE FIRST TIME SINCE THE
Original Six era the NHL had made it an entire decade without expanding. Atlanta and Colorado had moved to Calgary and New Jersey,
respectively, but the league still featured the same lineup of twenty-one
franchises that had been kicking around since the 1979 merger with the
World Hockey Association, and it hadn't gone through a traditional
expansion since 1974. An entire generation of hockey fans had never
seen the NHL grow.

Early in the new decade, it was clear that the status quo was about to
change. Interest in the league was at an all-time high, with some reports
indicating that as many as thirty cities hoped to welcome the NHL to
town. And that meant the league could demand an expansion fee of
fifty million dollars per franchise. With those sorts of numbers at stake,
support among the league's existing owners for expansion was over-
whelming. In February 1990, the board of governors announced an
ambitious plan aimed at adding seven teams over the next ten years.
According to a Canadian Press report, the board voted 20–1 in favour
of expansion, with only the Toronto Maple Leafs dissenting.

The big question, as always, was where the new teams would wind up.
Most assumed that the focus would be on the southern US, as the league
attempted to capitalize on Gretzky's success in Los Angeles. Florida

seemed like a sure thing; not only did the state not have a team, but the nearest franchise was in Washington, DC. Miami and St. Petersburg soon emerged as frontrunners.

Another early favourite was Hamilton, Ontario, which already had one of the better arenas in the world in the five-year-old Copps Coliseum. As always, the city faced a hurdle in getting any approval past the Maple Leafs and Buffalo Sabres, who were both reluctant to give up a chunk of what they considered their exclusive territories. But with an arena and strong local interest, Hamilton seemed like Canada's best bet for an eighth team. The other usual suspects surfaced as well. Seattle was mentioned often and loudly; a group from Phoenix tossed its hat in the ring; and there were suggestions in the media that the NHL wanted a team in Texas, with Houston as the leading contender.

And then there was a possibility that seemed almost perfect: a city with an NHL-ready arena, a track record of supporting pro hockey and a solid ownership group already in place. Other bids could boast one or two of those elements, but only one seemed to check every box. All that was left were the formalities. The NHL was going to put a team in Milwaukee.

But before they could get to all of that, the league had to deal with the small matter of welcoming its twenty-second franchise, which had already been awarded to San Jose. The Sharks would be joining the league for the 1991–92 season as an expansion team—sort of.

Look, by now you know that nothing the NHL does is ever simple.

The Sharks' origin story dates back to 1976, when George and Gordon Gund moved the California Golden Seals to Cleveland. The Barons lasted just two seasons in Ohio before folding, and what was left of the roster was absorbed into the struggling Minnesota North Stars, with the Gunds taking over ownership of that franchise.

By 1990 the Gund brothers wanted to return to California, and their original scheme for getting there involved moving the North Stars to the Bay Area. That plan kicked into high gear in February, when city officials in Bloomington, Minnesota, decided against providing fifteen million dollars in arena upgrades to the twenty-three-year-old Met Center. With the NHL already working towards a fresh round of expansion that could include California, the Gunds wanted to make their move before someone else could snap up the market.

The league didn't like this idea. When you're in the process of trying to convince prospective owners to cough up fifty million dollars for an expansion team, the last thing you want is for one of your existing teams to pick up and move into a promising market, especially if they're pleading financial distress along the way. Eventually, a compromise was brokered. Howard Baldwin, who'd been part of the Hartford Whalers organization and a key figure behind the WHA merger, stepped up with an offer to buy the North Stars and keep them in Minnesota, freeing the Gunds to buy a new team in the Bay Area. But while the new franchise would be considered an expansion team and pay the league that fifty-million-dollar fee, the Gunds would also get to take the entire North Stars front office with them to California. And in the 1991 off-season, the new team would be stocked through a complicated process that saw them claim sixteen players from the North Stars ahead of an expansion draft that both San Jose *and* Minnesota would take part in.

That's right. The Minnesota North Stars—a team that had existed since 1967—would get to pick players in an expansion draft in 1991. If that wasn't strange enough, with the agreement in place, the Stars then proceeded to shock the hockey world by going on one of the all-time great Cinderella playoff runs. The sixty-eight-point underdogs beat the league's top two teams, the Chicago Blackhawks and St. Louis Blues, and then knocked off the defending-champion Edmonton Oilers before finally falling to Mario Lemieux and the Pittsburgh Penguins in six games in the Stanley Cup final.

The last game of the final was played on May 25, 1991. Just five days later, the North Stars were picking players in an expansion draft. Never let it be said that the NHL is predictable.

The draft itself was fairly unremarkable; as with most expansion pools, there weren't many good players available. It's probably best remembered for the last pick. The North Stars were left with only the putrid Quebec Nordiques roster to choose from and decided they'd rather pass. But since passing wasn't allowed, they took Guy Lafleur, who'd already announced his intention to retire.* Being selected meant Lafleur couldn't take the front-office job he'd been promised in Quebec. The two teams then worked out a trade to send Lafleur back to the Nordiques in exchange for the rights to Alan Haworth, who hadn't even been in the league since 1988.

In October 1990, with the NHL pushing towards a decision on two expansion teams by the end of the year, the Milwaukee group dropped a stunner: They were out. Lloyd Pettit, who'd been spearheading the effort along with his wife, Jane, and investors, had simply decided that an NHL franchise wasn't worth it.

Pettit's logic was sound. As a longtime hockey broadcaster and former owner of the Milwaukee Admirals of the International Hockey League, he knew a thing or two about hockey—including the fact that the league's notoriously stingy approach to expansion meant his team wouldn't be very good out of the gate. If he was going to hand over fifty million dollars (and potentially a bit more to the Blackhawks as compensation for infringing on their market), Pettit needed to know he'd eventually make money on the deal. He simply didn't see how that was ever going to happen. NHL president John Ziegler told reporters that "we do not agree with some of the [Milwaukee group's] reasons or conclusions," but that hardly mattered. The Pettits had donated much of the money for the city's arena, so having someone else come along to bid for a team seemed unlikely. Just like that, one of the league's top choices was out of the running.

Milwaukee wasn't the only city leaving the process; the Phoenix group had dropped out in August, and other bids had serious questions around their financing. By the time the NHL Board of Governors met to make a final decision in December, the smart money was on Hamilton and either

---

* This was Lafleur's second retirement from the NHL. He'd previously hung up the skates in 1985, was inducted into the Hall of Fame in 1988, and then returned later that year to play for the New York Rangers and then the Nordiques. That meant that he was simultaneously an active player and a Hockey Hall of Famer. The same would later be true of Mario Lemieux.

Miami or a St. Petersburg, Florida, bid led by future Carolina Hurricanes owner Peter Karmanos.

Then came a curveball: After a process that surprisingly lasted just a few hours, the NHL turned down all the favourites and instead announced that they had awarded teams to a group from nearby Tampa Bay and one from Ottawa. Both were solid bids, but had been considered underdogs. Ziegler's announcement was met with a mix of surprised gasps, stunned silence and boisterous cheers.

The Ottawa bid, led by Bruce Firestone, had gained steam late in the process. While the city didn't have an arena, Ottawa did have a history with the league dating back to the original Senators, not to mention a decent-sized existing fan base for NHL hockey. A cynic might note that they were also one of the only bids willing to guarantee the entire fifty-million-dollar fee.

The winning Tampa bid was led by Phil Esposito, who compared his group's victory to Team Canada's comeback win over the Soviets in the 1972 Summit Series. Esposito's efforts had been bolstered by a late infusion of capital from Japanese investors, which apparently impressed the NHL enough to overlook this market's similar lack of an arena. Both the Senators and Lightning would begin their NHL tenures playing out of buildings that seated fewer than eleven thousand fans; the Lightning would later spend a few years in a cavernous domed baseball park.

Meanwhile, Hamilton fans and city officials were stunned and infuriated by the decision, and quickly found a scapegoat: the Sabres, who were rumoured to have torpedoed the bid in an effort to protect their territory. (The Sabres denied that charge, even penning an open letter that ran in *The Hamilton Spectator*.)

And with that, the league had reached its short-term goal of twenty-four teams. For now, at least, the league was done with expansion. Or so we thought.

The 1990 expansion drama had lasted for most of the year, with cities dropping in and out of the running and plenty of time for fans to get caught up in the horse race. Even though the final decision had been made quickly, the overall impression the NHL had left on fans was that there was a long-term plan in place and it was being followed. And then, two short years later, they chucked that impression out the window.

On December 10, 1992, the league announced that two more teams were on the way. There had been no bidding process, no lengthy debates, and certainly no year-long drama. This time, two new teams just dropped out of the blue. And by the way, they'd be hitting the ice in just ten months' time.

Why the rush? Ownership. When you're working with groups that are scrambling to find cash, you can afford to play it cool. Make them sweat a bit. But when the Walt Disney Company comes calling, you get the deal done. Disney had expressed an interest in backing a team in Orange County that they could name after their *Mighty Ducks* series of kids' movies, and the league was too busy nodding to ask many questions. Someone who must have asked one or two was Bruce McNall, owner of the Kings. McNall received half of the Mighty Ducks' expansion fee as compensation for agreeing to let them set up shop nearby.

The other new team would be in Miami, where the deep-pocketed Wayne Huizenga had come calling. Huizenga had made his name in the garbage disposal business* and owned Blockbuster Video, as well as MLB's Florida Marlins and a piece of the NFL's Miami Dolphins.

The decision to expand yet again had apparently come together over a matter of days and still managed to earn the unanimous approval of the board. Just like that, the NHL had added five teams in under three years. It was time to take a break and let the new teams settle in. A short break, as it turned out, but still a break. By the time the NHL made its next expansion decisions, there'd be a new sheriff in town.

---

* Insert your own Panthers punchline here.

DRAFT DODGERS

The Washington Capitals almost find an expansion loophole

ESTABLISHED TEAMS ALWAYS HAVE A CONFLICTED relationship with expansion. On the one hand, their owners love that the new guys have to cut a big, fat cheque that they get a share of. But the GMs can't stand losing someone—anyone—in an expansion draft.

In the early '90s, teams went through three such drafts, supplying players for six teams along the way. In 1991, they had to stock both the San Jose Sharks and Minnesota North Stars, thanks to that complicated quasi-expansion deal with the Gund brothers. That one was relatively painless. The New York Islanders lost a decent goalie in Jeff Hackett, and the Toronto Maple Leafs managed to lose their captain* because they're the Maple Leafs, but otherwise the draft didn't really hurt anyone except the defending conference-champion North Stars.

In hindsight, it's possible that the most important choice made that day involved a player who wasn't chosen. The North Stars had a prospect named Mike Craig whom they didn't have room to protect but didn't want to lose, so they cut a deal with the Sharks: Leave Craig alone, and we'll give you our 1991 second-round pick and our first-rounder in 1992. San Jose used the first-round pick on Andrei Nazarov, who had a decent career, and turned the second-rounder into Sandis Ozolinsh, who would become one of the franchise's first true stars. Not a bad return for not picking a guy who didn't turn out to be all that good anyway.

The 1992 draft to stock Ottawa and Tampa Bay featured truly slim pickings

---

* Veteran defenceman Rob Ramage was picked by the North Stars. The Leafs then handed the *C* to Wendel Clark.

for the newcomers, as a combined $100 million in expansion fees earned the Senators and Lightning a shot at Brian Bradley and not much else. That draft is best remembered as one of the earliest indications that the Ottawa franchise didn't quite have its act together. According to a report in *Sports Illustrated*, the Senators front office arrived at the draft with their picks loaded onto a laptop computer. But they hadn't brought a battery, and the nearest electrical outlet wasn't working, so they had to wing it. And on three separate occasions, they picked players who weren't actually eligible.*

While the Senators and Lightning didn't find much in the way of players, you could hardly blame them; the league allowed each existing team to protect fourteen skaters and two goalies in '92, as long as they exposed players who had NHL experience. That last part turned out to be tricky, because the league left open a loophole that led to some fun.

In 1992 the Washington Capitals had three goalies with NHL experience on their roster. They wanted to keep Don Beaupre and Jim Hrivnak, which was fine, because they had two slots. They also hoped to hang on to prospect Olaf Kolzig. That would have been fine too, because his meagre pro experience would have made him exempt, except the Capitals didn't have anyone else in the organization with NHL experience, which meant they had no choice but to expose Kolzig, who'd played a grand total of two NHL games—unless, of course, they could find another experienced goaltender before the draft.

And so, days before the draft, Capitals GM David Poile signed Bernie Wolfe to a contract. Wolfe had plenty of NHL experience, having previously played four seasons in Washington. The Capitals could expose him, keep Kolzig, and everything would be fine.

There was just one problem: Wolfe was forty years old, and his last NHL action had come in 1979.

You see, the NHL had only specified that players needed to have NHL experience. They didn't say anything about *when* that experience needed to

---

* In fairness to the Senators, and despite what you may have heard, they did not draft a dead player. That distinction belongs to the Ottawa Rough Riders of the Canadian Football League, in 1995.

have been obtained. So, the Capitals' signing of Wolfe, who hadn't played in thirteen years, technically fulfilled the requirement.

Not surprisingly, the Senators and Lightning objected to Poile's move* and the NHL refused to rubber-stamp the Caps' deal with Wolfe. Rather than fight the league over the issue, the Capitals signed veteran Steve Weeks the next day. That met the league's experience requirement, and the Capitals kept Kolzig, Wolfe got to enjoy a one-day NHL comeback, and everyone went home happy.

By the 1993 expansion draft, the league had closed the experience loophole. They'd also tightened the requirements for the established teams, largely because the Sharks, Senators and (to a lesser extent) Lightning had all been embarrassingly bad out of the gate. That led to the Mighty Ducks and Panthers ending up with better teams; Florida in particular hit a home run with goaltender John Vanbiesbrouck, who'd get them all the way to the Stanley Cup final within three years.

But while the Ducks and Panthers did relatively well, in hindsight they both missed out on a pick that could have changed the next decade of NHL history. The Sabres used their goalie spot to protect Grant Fuhr, as you'd expect— Fuhr was a slam-dunk Hall of Famer whom they'd given up fifty-goal scorer Dave Andreychuk and more to acquire from Toronto a few months earlier. And besides, the other goalie on their roster was some weird European who'd been in the league for three years, had a lifetime save percentage under .900 and was already twenty-eight. Who'd ever take that guy?

Nobody did, which turned out to be a lucky break for the Sabres. That unprotected goalie was Dominik Hasek, and he'd win the first of six career Vézina Trophies the very next year. Today, he's considered quite possibly the best ever at the position. In 1993, he was there for the taking for either Florida or Anaheim, and both passed.

---

* According to *The Washington Post*, Phil Esposito reacted to the news by shouting, "What the hell is this? I'm not paying fifty million dollars for Bernie Wolfe. He wasn't any good when I played against him."

14

THE HALL OF PRESIDENTS

A league is only as strong as its leaders

DID YOU LIKE HOW I LEFT YOU HANGING AT THE END OF chapter 13, with the suspense of there being "a new sheriff in town"? That's what we in the business call a cliffhanger, and you probably can't wait to read on and figure out his identity.

Spoiler alert: It's Gary Bettman.

Okay, fine, you'd probably figured that part out. And if so, you already know that Bettman ends up being one of the most important (and controversial) figures in the history of the league, not to mention the most influential of the next quarter century of league history. His name is going to pop up a few more times in the remaining pages, is what I'm saying.

But before we can fully appreciate the job that Bettman is stepping into, we need to go back and look at the others who paved the way for him. Before the NHL created the role of commissioner, it had a president. It was the league's most important job, and over a seventy-five-year period, only a small handful of men were charged with doing it. Here's another spoiler: Some of them ended up being more productive than others.

The league's first president was Frank Calder, who had a reputation as a guy who was always open to different ways of approaching any problem. By which I mean, you could go along with what he wanted, or you could get the hell out of his league.

That sort of approach wouldn't fly now, but it may have been necessary in the earliest days of the NHL. Calder didn't mess around, and he
wasn't much for forgiving his enemies—remember those letters of apology that striking Hamilton Bulldog players had to write before they were
allowed back into the league?—but he knew how to get things done.

Calder was born in England and spent his childhood there, growing
up with sports like soccer and rugby. When he arrived in Canada as a
young man, he became a teacher, and later worked as the sports editor of
a Montreal newspaper. That led to a role as secretary of the NHA, and
when that league folded to make way for the new NHL, Calder was a
near-unanimous choice for the top job.

He guided the fledgling league through those tenuous first few decades,
occasionally angering owners along the way but never facing any serious
challenge to his rule. He spent a quarter of a century on the job, but
by 1943 his health was becoming an issue. A sixty-five-year-old Calder
reportedly collapsed at a league meeting that year, leading to a suggestion
that longtime New York Americans defenceman, coach and executive
Red Dutton take over. That was meant to be a temporary solution until
Calder's health allowed him to return to the job, but that day never came;
he passed away shortly after.

Calder's death left Dutton in charge, initially on an interim basis. He
seemed like a natural choice for the job; he'd played and coached in the
league, and had earned the respect of the various owners while building
the Americans into a viable franchise. There was just one problem: Dutton
didn't seem to particularly want to be league president, even on an interim
basis. He initially agreed to take it on the condition that the owners would
promise to reinstate the Americans at the end of the war. He tried to quit
after only a year, but was convinced to return, and shortly afterwards was
named the league's permanent president.

"Permanent" turned out be relative; by 1946, Dutton was beginning
to suspect that the owners weren't being all that sincere when it came to
the promise to revive the Americans. He'd arranged funding for a new
arena in Brooklyn, and when he presented his plan to the owners, he was
informed that they were reneging on their commitment. He stormed out

of the meeting and resigned. According to one version of the story, he told the owners to "stick your franchise up your ass" on the way out. You have to hand it to him—the man knew how to quit a job.

While Dutton's exit wasn't exactly on friendly terms, he did leave the league with a recommendation for a successor: his recently appointed assistant, Clarence Campbell. Campbell had broken into the league a decade earlier as a referee, a job he held for three seasons before departing to serve in the military.* When he returned to North America in 1946, he was offered a role at the league office as Dutton's right-hand man. He'd been on the job less than a year when Dutton's sudden resignation left the league scrambling, and he was in the right place at the right time to take control.

As it turned out, he'd be a near-perfect fit. Campbell would go on to serve as league president for more than thirty years, guiding the NHL from the early years of the Original Six all the way through the first decade of expansion. Today, he's probably best remembered for his role in the Richard Riot, but he also oversaw the creation of the All-Star Game, the players' pension fund and the amateur draft—not to mention hanging around for the emergence of direct competition in the form of the WHA.

By the time Campbell stepped down in June 1977, the NHL had tripled in size from a six-team operation to one that spanned most of North America. He'd already been inducted into the Hockey Hall of Fame (in 1966) and had one of the league's two conferences named after him. That latter honour was rescinded when Bettman arrived and decided that naming divisions and conferences after people was too confusing.** But to this day, the trophy that Western Conference champions make a big show of refusing to touch is called the Clarence S. Campbell Bowl.

Campbell was seventy-one when he retired after thirty-one years on the job, and he was in poor health and facing accusations of bribing a

---

* His military career saw him achieve the rank of lieutenant-colonel; it's been said that he also prosecuted Nazis at Nuremberg, although that's been disputed.

** You know, as opposed to straightforward names like the "Metropolitan Division."

Canadian senator in what came to be known as the Sky Shops case.* To fill the shoes of a legend, the NHL turned to a forty-three-year-old lawyer from Detroit.

John Ziegler was an interesting choice. He wasn't an outsider by any means; he'd worked with the Red Wings for years and served a year as chairman of the league's board of governors. But he wasn't some long-time league employee, either, and for a group as notoriously old-boys-ish as the NHL, he was an unusual choice to follow the legendary Campbell. It probably spoke to the challenges facing the league at the time that they looked to a lawyer instead of a hockey lifer—and an American lawyer at that.

All that said, Ziegler's early years were reasonably successful. He couldn't save the Cleveland Barons, who were too far gone by the time he took over. But the NHL's most pressing concern in 1977 was the WHA and the possibility of an eventual merger, and Ziegler stickhandled that issue about as well as could have been expected.

It wouldn't be the last challenge he'd face. In 1979, Ziegler had to deal with the fallout after an infamous brawl at Madison Square Garden. After New York Rangers fan John Kaptain reportedly leaned over the low glass to take a swing at the Bruins' Stan Jonathan, Boston players climbed into the stands to go after him. The wild scene that ensued was highlighted by Bruins defenceman Mike Milbury, who located Kaptain, pulled one of his shoes off and beat him over the head with it. It was, to put it mildly, not a good look for the league. Four fans were arrested, and Ziegler suspended Terry O'Reilly—the first Bruin over the glass—for eight games, and Milbury for six.

Ziegler also had to deal with pro sports' emerging drug issues. Rangers winger Don Murdoch was among the first high-profile cases to hit the NHL, and he was suspended for the entire 1978–79 season after being caught at a Toronto airport with several grams of cocaine in his socks.

---

* He'd eventually be convicted, but served no time. The case wasn't related to Campbell's role with the NHL.

(Ziegler later reduced the ban to forty games.) The president attempted to institute the league's first drug-testing policy in 1986, only to have it rejected by the NHL Players' Association. And he'd suspend Hall of Fame goaltender Grant Fuhr for a full season in 1990 for past drug use. (Fuhr's sentence was also later reduced.)

Perhaps Ziegler's most complicated scandal came in 1986, when Pat Quinn agreed to become the new coach and GM of the Vancouver Canucks, accepting a one-hundred-thousand-dollar signing bonus along the way. That wasn't especially unusual, except for one small detail: Quinn was still the coach of the LA Kings at the time. Quinn—a lawyer who knew his way around a rule book—argued that his contract with the Kings had never actually been filed with the league office, but Ziegler was furious, viewing the incident as an obvious conflict of interest. He issued a twenty-one-page ruling in which he hit both teams with the maximum allowable fine—well over six figures each. Quinn was allowed to become the Canucks' GM beginning in the off-season, and he went on to add players like Trevor Linden, Kirk McLean and Pavel Bure to the team, but he was banned from coaching until 1990.

But of course, the story of John Ziegler's presidency wouldn't be complete without diving into an incident that really needs its own section. It involves donuts, replacement officials, bright yellow sweaters and one disappearing league president.

Game three of the 1988 Wales Conference final seemed like a typical match. Granted, the presence of the Devils was unusual—the team was making its first playoff appearance ever.* But New Jersey's 6–1 loss on home ice to the favoured Bruins had been otherwise unremarkable when the final horn sounded.

It wouldn't stay that way for long. As the game ended, Devils coach Jim Schoenfeld raced to confront referee Don Koharski in the hallway. Schoenfeld verbally attacked Koharski, blocked his path and even, the

---

* The Devils' struggles had led Wayne Gretzky to call them "a Mickey Mouse organization" after he went into New Jersey and racked up eight points in a 1983 game.

referee would claim, shoved him. Schoenfeld immediately denied that
last charge, but didn't help his cause by continuing to berate Koharski.
"You fell, you fat pig," he yelled, before adding what would become the
infamous kicker: "Have another donut."*

The NHL acted quickly, with vice-president Brian O'Neill announcing on the day of game four that Schoenfeld would be suspended. The
Devils asked if they could appeal and were told that the suspension could
only be overturned by the league president. And getting him to weigh in
was going to be a problem. Nobody knew where Ziegler was.

That left the Devils scrambling. Their rookie GM, Lou Lamoriello,
apparently spent hours trying to track Ziegler down, to no avail. So, with
game four just hours away, Lamoriello found a New Jersey Superior
Court judge and got a temporary restraining order to prevent the league
from enforcing the suspension against his coach. Schoenfeld would be
behind the bench after all.

The fun was only beginning. The scheduled referee for that night's
game was Dave Newell, who also happened to be the head of the officials'
union. When he heard what the Devils had done, he and linesmen Ray
Scapinello and Gord Broseker delivered a message of their own to the
league: If Schoenfeld is coaching tonight, we're out—find some other
officials. While this drama was playing out behind the scenes, some nineteen thousand fans were sitting in the stands, wondering why the game
hadn't started. The players had been pulled off the ice during warm-ups;
most of them had no idea what was going on. And through it all, there was
still no sign of Ziegler.

To this day, the president's whereabouts during the crisis are a matter
of some conjecture. Some theories have him on vacation; others suggest a
family emergency. *Sports Illustrated* even ran a piece headlined WHERE
ARE YOU, JOHN? In it, writer E.M. Swift urged Ziegler to resign, writing
that he'd reduced hockey to "a leaderless joke."

---

* Note the wording; Schoenfeld did not actually say, "Have another donut, you fat
pig," which is how most fans have come to remember it. His line is basically the NHL's
version of "Play it again, Sam."

With Ziegler AWOL, it was left to the supervisor of officials, John McCauley, and the chairman of the board of governors, Bill Wirtz, to figure out a solution. Wirtz issued an order: Play the game, one way or another. The search for replacement officials was on, with McCauley eventually assembling a ragtag group of amateur hockey officials: Paul McInnis, Vin Godleski and Jim Sullivan. They took to the ice in borrowed skates and sweaters, with the linesmen wearing bright yellow practice jerseys that looked like raincoats, which led to the game being dubbed Yellow Sunday. With a befuddled hockey world watching, the replacements nearly collided with each other during the warm-up.*

After all of that, the crew did a reasonably good job in a 3–1 Devils win. Ziegler finally resurfaced on the day of game five, giving the Devils a chance to make their appeal. After a four-hour hearing, the president upheld Schoenfeld's original suspension. The crisis was over.

Asked if he would be in attendance at that night's game, Ziegler said that he'd have to miss it to write up his official decision. As *Asbury Park Press* reporter Bob Jordan wrote the next day, Ziegler "probably would have helped the league's image by showing up at a hockey game for a change."

Ziegler was inducted into the Hall of Fame in 1987. Thirty years later, visitors to the Hall's website would have found an interesting sentence in his official bio: "Ziegler stepped down as NHL president in 1992 and was succeeded by Gary Bettman, a former executive in the National Basketball Association."

As much as many might wish it were so, that isn't quite accurate—there was one more president to come after Ziegler left. That would be Gil Stein, the league's longtime general counsel, who on June 22, 1992, became the fifth and final president in NHL history.

---

* Believe it or not, things could have been even stranger. In 2017, *Hockey Night in Canada*'s Ron MacLean casually informed viewers that he had been asked to officiate the game that night. MacLean, a longtime amateur hockey referee who was there to host the CBC's broadcast, said that he briefly considered the offer before realizing it wouldn't be a good idea.

Stein's time as league president would last less than a year; Bettman officially became the league's first commissioner on February 1, 1993. But Stein's brief reign still managed to spark controversy, even after it had ended.

In March of 1993, the Hockey Hall of Fame announced that Stein would be inducted into its builder category. The news prompted an uproar among fans and media, many of whom noted that the freshly departed league president had appointed many of the same Hall voters that had just elected him. He'd also changed the voting rules, lowering the bar for builders to a simple majority. The whole thing stunk of a last-ditch desperation move by an outgoing president looking to ensure his legacy. The stench was strong enough that Stein withdrew his nomination. To this day, the Hall has yet to recognize his seven-month stint as the head of the league. It's fair to say that Stein will not go down as the most popular president in NHL history. But he remains the most recent, no matter what the Hall of Fame's website would have you believe.

REFEREE YOUR OWN STINKING GAME

What happens if the officials don't show up?
The NHL rule book has it covered.

IF YOU THOUGHT THE WHOLE "HAVE ANOTHER DONUT" situation was weird, well . . . you're right—it was one of the more bizarre moments in NHL history. And if you've made it this far, you know that's saying something.

But believe it or not, things could have got even weirder. Sure, those 1988 replacement officials in their yellow "raincoats" made for an odd sight, but at least they had some officiating experience. What happens if the assigned officials can't (or won't) work an NHL game and the league doesn't have any qualified replacements on hand?

Luckily for us, the rule book has it covered. And it makes one thing clear: The game must go on. So, who gets to step in and officiate? The players do.

It's right there in black and white—rule 31.11, to be precise. That section dictates the steps to follow if (in a delightful turn of phrase) officials aren't available "through misadventure or sickness." And the last resort is that the players have to call the game themselves, one from each team.

You're probably shaking your head and muttering about how crazy that sounds, even though it would obviously never happen in real life.

And now you're realizing that there's another page to go in this chapter.

And now you're thinking, "No . . . they couldn't have."

They did.

On January 15, 1983, the Hartford Whalers were hosting the New Jersey Devils. A brutal snowstorm was sweeping the area, and referee Ron Fournier and linesman Ron Asselstine failed to arrive for the game. Unlike the 1988 playoff matchup, there were no league officials around to rule on the mess, nor could any capable replacements be found in the half-empty building. It was left to a third Ron—linesman Ron Foyt, who had managed to make it to the arena—to sort things out. And so, with minutes to go before the game, Foyt invoked rule 31.11 and informed each team that while he'd be referee-ing, they'd need to supply one player each to serve as his linesmen. The Whalers offered up Mickey Volcan, while the Devils assigned Garry Howatt.

Howatt was an especially inspired choice, since he was New Jersey's enforcer and had played for Hartford the year before. In 2013, while recalling the game for NHL.com, Howatt admitted that he "was hoping for a fight to break out so I could get in there."

He had no such luck. There weren't any scraps, although Volcan did get to toss future Hall of Famer Ron Francis out of a faceoff. Fournier and Asselstine made it to the rink by the start of the second period, and Howatt and Volcan were thanked for their services and sent back to the press box. Volcan went on to officiate amateur hockey after his playing days.

It remains the only time in NHL history that players had to serve as emer-gency officials, and now that we find ourselves in the era of cell phones and quicker communications, it's fair to say that it will remain that way. But it did happen. And rule 31.11 remains in the rule book to this day—just in case.

15

A TALE OF THREE CENTRES

A new dynasty is born, an old one is dismantled,
and the next big thing makes a delayed debut

THE NHL IN 1990 FELT LIKE A LEAGUE ON THE BRINK OF some major shifts. There were still just twenty-one teams, but plans were already in place to grow that number. A franchise hadn't moved in eight years, but there were rumblings that a few might be eyeing greener pastures. Wayne Gretzky was settled in LA, but the game's inroads into the southern US were only beginning. And while the Edmonton Oilers were back on top as Stanley Cup champions, the underpinnings of their dynasty were already showing serious cracks.

The league was about to be transformed. We just weren't sure into what.

The 1990 draft ended up providing a good metaphor for what was to come. The first round included two of the greatest players ever, but they were hidden in plain sight and easy to miss if you were looking in the wrong direction. While most of the hockey world was debating top prospects like Owen Nolan, Petr Nedved and Keith Primeau, the Pittsburgh Penguins grabbed a lanky Czech winger named Jaromir Jagr with the fifth-overall pick. Meanwhile, the Calgary Flames needed a goaltender, so they traded up to the eleventh spot to grab the one considered the best on the board, Trevor Kidd. He ended up being a solid NHLer, but the Flames sent their twentieth-overall pick to the New Jersey Devils in the deal, and they used it on a goalie of their own: Martin Brodeur.

Just like that, two teams had laid the groundwork for future champion-ships. But as would be the case with so much of what was to come in the decade, it would take time before most of us realized the importance of what we'd just seen.

In Jagr's case, it didn't take long for the impact to be felt. He made his debut for the Penguins immediately, spending the entire 1990–91 season in Pittsburgh. He recorded fifty-seven points, finishing well back in Calder Trophy voting, and certainly didn't dominate. But he didn't have to, because he'd arrived on a team that was already stacked with offen-sive talent.

The Penguins were coming off a pedestrian season that had seen them earn that fifth-overall pick with seventy-two points. That 1989–90 team had missed the playoffs, fired its coach and appointed a new GM, and it looked like it still had plenty of work to do before contending for a Cup.

And so, Craig Patrick rolled up his sleeves. In one of the greatest stretches of GM work the league has ever seen, Patrick added five future Hall of Famers to the Penguins lineup in less than ten months. His off-season included drafting Jagr, trading for forward Joey Mullen and signing centre Bryan Trottier. In December, he traded for defence-man Larry Murphy. And in March, he pulled off what may stand as the greatest trade-deadline move the league has ever seen, prying centre Ron Francis out of Hartford in a six-player deal.

The Francis trade is often cited as the biggest deadline heist in league history, and it's certainly true that it was a disaster for the Whalers. But remember how it looked at the time: Francis was a well-respected player, but he'd had just one 100-point season in his career and the Whalers had stripped him of his captaincy in December. Meanwhile, the key player heading to Hartford, John Cullen, was coming off a 110-point season and had already racked up ninety-four more in sixty-five games when the deal went down. Even so, the move was largely viewed as a win for the Penguins, and Whalers fans were heartbroken to see Francis leave. But at the time, you could at least understand what Hartford was try-ing to do.

Francis clicked almost immediately in Pittsburgh, becoming the final piece of the puzzle that already included defenceman Paul Coffey and forward Mark Recchi. But of course, even taken together, those Hall of Famers couldn't outshine the player the Penguins had built the franchise around.

It's almost impossible to describe Mario Lemieux to younger fans. You start to tell a story about something you saw him do and you just run out or words, trailing off and then shaking your head. So, let me put it as simply as possible: Lemieux was quite possibly the most skilled hockey player to ever grace NHL ice. Yes, more skilled than Gretzky. Yes, more skilled than Orr. He was that good. By the time he'd been in the league for a few years, Lemieux had become one of those players who, like Orr and Gretzky and a small handful of others, could no longer ever truly surprise you. Oh, he had an eight-point night? Makes sense. Scored five goals, five different ways? Of course he did. Four goals in one period of a playoff game? Why not? Split the defence and deked out the goaltender while wearing a forward like a backpack? Yeah, that sounds about right.

Lemieux had put up almost inconceivable numbers in the Quebec Major Junior Hockey League, posting 282 points in seventy games as an eighteen-year-old. The Penguins were widely accused of tanking the 1983–84 season to get him, managing just thirty-eight points to finish behind the Devils in last place overall. And let's be honest: They absolutely did tank. The bigger question is probably why half the league wasn't gunning for rock bottom right along with them.

The relationship got off to a rocky start, with Lemieux refusing to wear his Penguins jersey at the draft, but the two sides made up in time for the big centre to take the league by storm. He scored on his very first NHL shift, and went on to record 100 points on the season and run away with the Calder.

By the end of his second season, Lemieux had won the Lester B. Pearson Award—since renamed the Ted Lindsay Award—as the players' choice for MVP. Shortly after his third season, he scored one of the most famous goals of all time to win the 1987 Canada Cup. By the end of his fourth, he'd broken Gretzky's string of seven straight Art Ross Trophy wins and eight straight Hart Trophies. And after his fifth, he'd scored 199 points in a season, the most ever by anyone other than Gretzky.*

But by 1991, Lemieux was also battling the health issues that would largely define his career. Back problems cost him twenty-one games in 1989–90, and he played just twenty-six games in 1990–91. He was unstoppable when he *was* on the ice—he had forty-five points in those twenty-six games—but for the first time, it looked like something could slow him down.

Lemieux's extended absence was a big part of the reason why those 1990–91 Penguins, as stacked as they were, managed just eighty-eight points. That was still good enough for first place in a weak Patrick Division, but the Pens didn't go into the playoffs as Cup favourites. They nearly made an early exit, falling behind the Devils three games to two before winning two straight to take the series. But they got rolling after that, knocking out the Capitals in five and the top-seeded Bruins in six.**

Waiting for them in the final were the Cinderella North Stars, a sixty-eight-point regular-season weakling who'd somehow transformed into a playoff powerhouse. Minnesota put up a fight, including taking game one in Pittsburgh, but a healthy Lemieux and the Penguins were too much. They won the series in six games, highlighted by an epic Lemieux solo effort in game two that was punctuated by Bob Cole's immortal call: "Look at Lemieux! Oh, my goodness! What a move, what a goal! Lemieux. . . . Oh, baby!"

Seven years after entering the league, Lemieux finally had his Stanley Cup. And he was just in time, because the league's next big thing was about to arrive. Emphasis on the "big."

---

* All told, Gretzky and Lemieux combined for thirteen seasons of 160 points or more; nobody else has hit the mark even once.

** This was the series in which Ulf Samuelsson delivered his infamous knee-on-knee hit on Cam Neely. That hit was dirty, and many fans incorrectly remember it as ending Neely's career. But it was a different (and cleaner) Samuelsson hit in the same series that caused the leg injury that forced Neely to miss most of the next two seasons, and the Bruins star's early retirement was actually caused by unrelated hip issues.

There are no guarantees in hockey. On the ice, the game moves too fast, the puck bounces too unpredictably and the slightest hesitation changes everything. Off the ice, good ideas go bad, good men break their word and good markets run into economic realities beyond their control. The NHL is a league of probabilities and favourites and likely outcomes, but nothing is ever a sure thing.

Except Eric Lindros. In 1991, Eric Lindros was just about the surest sure thing the league had ever seen.

Lindros was earning headlines before he'd even joined the junior ranks, dominating minor hockey in Toronto. Scouts raved about him. He boasted a skill level rarely seen in a teenage prospect, and he combined it with a dominant physical game. This kid was a superstar who could be his own enforcer, a guy who could skate around you or through you. This was Mario Lemieux fused with Bob Probert. At the low end, we were looking at the next Mark Messier. At the high end, maybe Gordie Howe. Maybe better than that. The sky was the limit.

He was a lock to be the NHL's poster child for the next decade or two. And in hindsight, he was. Just not for the reasons we all expected.

Many fans first heard about Lindros in 1989, when the fifteen-year-old was picked first overall in the Ontario Hockey League draft by the Sault Ste. Marie Greyhounds. He refused to report, eventually forcing a trade to the Oshawa Generals and establishing a precedent that would be repeated very soon. Lindros dominated the OHL and quickly emerged as the consensus top pick for the 1991 draft.

In fact, Lindros was considered such a can't-miss prospect that the NHL adjusted its rules for him. With the expansion San Jose Sharks coming into the league in 1991, many assumed that they'd be granted the first pick, as other expansion teams had. Instead, the league ruled that San Jose would get the *second* choice, and that the last-place team among established franchises would get the top pick. Coming in the days before the draft lottery, that set up an odd race to the bottom between the two worst teams in the standings, the Quebec Nordiques and the Toronto Maple Leafs.

There was just one problem: The Maple Leafs didn't own their first-round pick anymore, having traded it to the Devils for veteran defence-man Tom Kurvers in 1989.* The two teams eventually settled on a nice little bit of not-especially-subtle collusion, with the Nordiques trading three veterans to the Maple Leafs for draft picks and a prospect. The Leafs got slightly better, the Nordiques got slightly worse, and everyone was happy. The Nordiques had "earned" the top pick, and Lindros would head to Quebec to start his NHL career. Or so we thought.

Instead, Lindros made it clear that he had no interest in playing for the Nordiques. He claimed it was because the franchise was a mess, which it was—this was the third straight year the team had finished dead last. But fans in Quebec assumed it was actually because Lindros didn't want to play in a French-speaking market. The holdout became a Canadian national controversy.

Unlike the Greyhounds, the Nordiques refused to immediately trade their new star. So, Lindros went back to junior for another season. He also played for Team Canada twice, at the 1991 Canada Cup and the 1992 Olympics. At the former, he announced his arrival by crushing Ulf Samuelsson into the boards at Maple Leaf Gardens, breaking the big Swede's shoulder.

Through it all, he remained adamant: He would never play for the Nordiques. And so, the NHL's next big star put his career on hold. Meanwhile, the player he was most often compared to was making a move of his own.

In the aftermath of The Trade, Mark Messier hadn't just stepped out of Wayne Gretzky's shadow in Edmonton; he'd burst out, announcing his arrival as a legitimate NHL star during a 1989–90 season in which he'd led the Oilers to another Cup while also winning his first Hart Trophy.**

Following that season, Messier asked the Oilers for a new contract.

---

* To make matters worse, Kurvers wasn't even on the Leafs' roster by the end of the 1990–91 season.

** In the closest vote ever at the time, he edged out Ray Bourque by just two points, 227–225.

GM Glen Sather refused, explaining that the team simply couldn't afford it. There were reports during the 1990–91 season that Messier might be traded, with the Philadelphia Flyers rumoured to be making a serious push. Messier went on to endure an injury-riddled season, appearing in fifty-three games and scoring just twelve times. The Oilers went to the Campbell Conference final, but had their reign ended by the North Stars.

By the eve of the 1991–92 season, it was clear that the Oilers dynasty was all but over. The team had already parted ways with Gretzky and Paul Coffey, and a mid-September trade sent Grant Fuhr and Glenn Anderson to Toronto. With opening night approaching, Messier played his trump card, announcing that he was finished in Edmonton. He wanted out, and he was heading home until he was traded.

He got his wish quickly. The day after the season started, the Oilers sent Messier to the New York Rangers for Bernie Nicholls, Steven Rice and Louie DeBrusk.* He was an instant smash on Broadway, leading the Rangers to the Presidents' Trophy and earning his second Hart Trophy.

It all led to a marquee matchup in the second round, with Messier's Rangers facing Lemieux and the defending-champion Penguins. In a series best remembered for Adam Graves breaking Lemieux's wrist with a slash and earning a four-game suspension,** the Penguins fell behind 2–1 through three games before storming back to win the series in six. They wouldn't lose again for the rest of the playoffs, tying an NHL record with eleven straight playoff wins on their way to a second straight Cup.

The early '90s were a golden era of blockbuster trades. In addition to Messier's move to New York and Francis heading to Pittsburgh, we saw Chris Chelios go from Montreal to Chicago for Denis Savard; Dale Hawerchuk head from Winnipeg to Buffalo for Phil Housley; the ten-player deal that sent Doug Gilmour to the Maple Leafs; and the forced swap that sent Scott Stevens from St. Louis to New Jersey for Brendan

---

* Nicholls wasn't any happier about being an Oiler than Messier had been, and he refused to report to Edmonton for two months.

** In true NHL fashion, the league allowed Graves to play an additional game in the series before getting around to handing down its decision.

Shanahan.* But as the 1991–92 season drew to a close, it became apparent that there was one more monster deal to come: the Eric Lindros trade.

Or, as it turned out, *trades*. On June 20, 1992, after letting Lindros sit out a full season, the Nordiques finally traded him. And then traded him again.

The first deal sent Lindros to the Flyers for a package of picks and players. But then Nordiques owner Marcel Aubut cut a second deal, this time with the Rangers. Aubut claimed that the Flyers trade had been agreed to, but never made official; he'd given Philadelphia permission to call the Lindros camp to talk contract, but hadn't put pen to paper. As the mess became public, the NHL assigned the case to arbitrator Larry Bertuzzi.** The hearing took place in Montreal and lasted a week, generating plenty of speculation over just what was being talked about. One rumour suggested that Aubut had actually looped in a third team, the Chicago Blackhawks, to try to get an even better deal. On June 30, Bertuzzi released his ruling: Lindros would be a Flyer, heading to Philadelphia in exchange for Ron Hextall, Mike Ricci, Steve Duchesne, Kerry Huffman, Chris Simon, the rights to Peter Forsberg, two first-round picks and fifteen million dollars.***

The decision was seen as a major win for the Flyers. In hindsight, of course, they're the only one of the three teams that didn't win a Cup over the next few years—and Forsberg went on to arguably become the best player in the deal. There really are no sure things.

But for the time being, the NHL lumbered on towards its 1992–93 season, one that would mark the 100th anniversary of the Stanley Cup. Lemieux was a two-time champion in Pittsburgh, Gretzky was a growing star in Los Angeles, Messier was ready to chase an elusive Cup in New York, and Lindros was set to finally make his debut in Philadelphia.

---

*   The Blues had signed Shanahan as a restricted free agent, only to have an arbitrator send Stevens to the Devils as compensation.

**   The great-uncle of NHLer Todd Bertuzzi.

***   In case you were wondering, the Rangers offer reportedly included Alexei Kovalev, Tony Amonte, Doug Weight, John Vanbiesbrouck, multiple first-round picks and twelve million dollars.

Meanwhile, Doug Gilmour and Pat Burns were ready to start a renaissance in Toronto, Patrick Roy was dominating in Montreal, and a flashy Finnish rookie was finally ready to head to Winnipeg and make his mark.

And of course, another important figure was about to make an appearance, one who would end up having a far bigger impact on the league than anyone could imagine, all without ever lacing up a pair of skates. That new sheriff had arrived.

O CAPTAIN, MY CAPTAIN

The NHL tries its hand at celebrity marketing

IN THE NHL, A TEAM'S CAPTAINCY BORDERS ON THE sacred. The captain isn't just the leader. Often, he's the face of the franchise. When you picture an NHL captain, you think of Gordie Howe, Maurice Richard, Wayne Gretzky, Steve Yzerman, Mark Messier . . .

And Mr. Rogers?

Okay, not quite. But back in 1991, the NHL came up with an odd way to celebrate its seventy-fifth anniversary the following season. They asked each of the twenty-two teams around the league to appoint a celebrity captain. Those celebrities would then join the team for various photo ops, ceremonial puck drops and other marketing appearances. It would be fun, the league probably thought. And in a sense, it was. Some teams took it seriously and found reasonably strong choices to take the job. Others clearly just grabbed the first person they saw wandering by. It's fair to say the resulting mix was eclectic.

The Montreal Canadiens, of course, chose the most famous and important person they could imagine, which is to say a Montreal Canadien: They went with Rocket Richard. The Hartford Whalers chose actress Susan Saint James, who just happened to be married to Dick Ebersol, the president of the league's TV partner, NBC. And the Rangers picked the guy who called their games, Marv Albert. Hey, where are you going to find an A-list celebrity in New York, right?

Other teams put slightly more effort into their picks. Plenty of athletes were selected, including Willie McCovey (by the San Jose Sharks), Kurt Browning (Edmonton Oilers), Jim Kelly (Buffalo Sabres) and Yogi Berra (New Jersey Devils). Oldies-station staples were another popular pick, with Burton

Cummings (Winnipeg Jets), Bobby Rydell (Philadelphia Flyers) and Gordon Lightfoot (Toronto Maple Leafs) making appearances.

Some teams went out and landed legitimate stars, at least by 1991 standards, including John Candy (Los Angeles Kings), John Goodman (St. Louis Blues) and Jim Belushi (Chicago Blackhawks). The New York Islanders went with an inspired choice in Ralph Macchio of *The Karate Kid*. The Detroit Red Wings landed Dave "Cut It Out" Coulier. And he wasn't even the best family-sitcom-star pick in the bunch, as the Bruins scooped up Michael J. Fox.

But then there was the unquestioned best of them all. The defending-champion Pittsburgh Penguins proved to be the class of the league yet again, this time by locking down the services of Fred Rogers. Yes, the kindly children's television star was apparently a hockey fan. (I'm going to assume his favourite player was Senators' Hall of Famer Frank Nighbor.)

The Penguins honoured Mr. Rogers at a pregame ceremony before the 1991 home opener, during which they presented him with a sweater with a captain's *C* on it. Not a Penguins jersey—an actual cardigan, like the ones he wore on his show, which Rogers skated out to accept as Pittsburgh fans gave him a loud ovation. (That's right, skated out. Apparently, he'd done some figure skating in his younger days.)

Sadly, the NHL didn't revisit the celebrity captain concept when the league's 100th anniversary rolled around. We'll have to hold on to the memories—and to the hockey cards that several captains were for some reason given in that year's Pro Set Platinum series. Yes, you can own an official Mr. Rogers hockey card. Don't say this weird league never brought anything magical into our lives.

16

THE GREATEST SEASON EVER

An emotional comeback, a ridiculous rookie,
a stunning playoff run and a brand-new boss

IF THE NHL WERE SCRIPTED ENTERTAINMENT, YOU'D SEND the 1992–93 season back to the writers. "Too busy," you'd tell them. "Way too many storylines. This stuff is great, don't get me wrong, but you can't go and cram it all into a single season."*

Luckily for fans, the NHL isn't scripted, and there are no writers to spread the plot points around. And so, in 1992, the league embarked on what would turn out to be the most dramatic and entertaining season ever. And while fitting a century of history into a single book means skimming over a year here and there, it's worth slowing down to appreciate 1992–93, if only as a reminder of how much fun this league can be when everything is working just right.

It all started in August, when a hotshot Finnish rookie named Teemu Selanne made a splash by signing his first NHL contract with . . . wait, the Calgary Flames?

The Winnipeg Jets had grabbed Selanne with the tenth-overall pick in a loaded 1988 draft.** But four years later, he had yet to make the trip over to

---

*   "Plus the dastardly new villain you introduce halfway through is a little over the top."
**   A neat piece of trivia from that draft: Selanne played in the NHL until he was forty-three, and still only finished fourth in his draft class in games played, trailing Mark Recchi, Mike Modano and Rod Brind'Amour.

North America to sign an NHL deal. Under the rules at the time, that made him a restricted free agent in the summer of 1992, allowing him to sign an offer sheet with any team.

It's not as if the Jets weren't trying to bring the Finnish star to the NHL; they'd reportedly offered him a three-year deal worth a total of $1.2 million.* But the Flames, still stinging from a playoff miss and the disastrous Doug Gilmour trade, decided to make a move against their division rivals, inking Selanne to an eye-popping deal worth more than twice what the Jets had offered.

The Jets still held the right to match the offer, though, and GM Mike Smith quickly did. Four years after being drafted, Selanne finally arrived in Winnipeg, carrying an inflated salary to go along with inflated expectations. More than a few fans grumbled about this kid who'd already broken the bank before he'd even so much as laced up his skates in an NHL game. But it's safe to say those bad feelings didn't last. Selanne had his first multi-point game in his debut, scored his first hat trick in game number five, and had a five-point night under his belt before October ended. By December, the talk had turned to whether he could break Mike Bossy's rookie record of fifty-three goals, set in 1977–78. By January, the question was no longer *whether* he'd break the mark, but by how much.

The record-breaking goal came on March 2, 1993, with Selanne converting a long-distance set-up from Tie Domi and marking the historic moment with a memorable glove-flinging celebration.** He'd finish the season with a league-leading seventy-six goals and 132 points, shattering the rookie records.

Selanne's heroics overshadowed the also-delayed debut of Eric Lindros, who burst into the league with an impressive forty-one-goal campaign of his own. Lindros actually finished fourth in Calder voting, behind Selanne (the unanimous winner), Toronto Maple Leaf goalie Félix Potvin, and 102-point Boston Bruins winger Joé Juneau. But while his rookie season was

---

* It wasn't a bad deal; that $400,000 per year would be higher than the NHL's average salary of $368,000.

** Future NHL coach Dallas Eakins goes down in history as the man who fumbled the catch.

hardly a disappointment—and included an impressive two-goal performance in his first game in front of the Quebec City fans he'd refused to
play for—it featured some unfortunate foreshadowing, as Lindros was
limited to just sixty-one games due to injury.

The rookies weren't the only players putting up ridiculous numbers.
While scoring rates were down from the peak of the mid-'80s, they were
still well over seven goals per game. In his first full season in Toronto,
Gilmour transformed from a reliable two-way centre into one of the
league's very best players, posting 127 points. That set the Maple Leafs
franchise record, but actually ranked just seventh in the league scoring
race. Players like Pat LaFontaine (148), Adam Oates (142) and Pierre
Turgeon (132) all established career highs, while Steve Yzerman racked
up 137.

Selanne's seventy-six goals were matched by Buffalo's Alexander
Mogilny, and twelve other players hit the fifty-goal mark (including
sixty-goal seasons from wingers Luc Robitaille and Pavel Bure). And
while the scorers were putting up big numbers, there were some
impressive performances from goaltenders too; Potvin led the league
in goals-against average as a rookie, and Ed Belfour, Curtis Joseph and
Tom Barrasso all had big years.

But in a season stocked with individual triumphs, nobody could match
the story being written by Mario Lemieux. The Penguins star had been
in the midst of yet another unstoppable season when he unexpectedly left
the team in the first week of January. Soon, the devastating news broke
that Lemieux had been diagnosed with Hodgkin's lymphoma, a form of
cancer. While the condition had been caught early and wasn't considered
life-threatening, it would require weeks of radiation treatments that
could end his season.

Instead, after two months of treatment, Lemieux made his dramatic
return on March 2. He then finished the season with a torrid scoring run,
recording three points or more in twelve of his last twenty games to blow
past LaFontaine and reclaim the lead in the points race. He ended with
sixty-nine goals and 160 points, claiming his fourth Art Ross despite missing more than a quarter of his team's games.

After that hectic regular season, it was fair for fans to wonder what the playoffs might serve up as a finale. Things got off to a strong start, with the Buffalo Sabres winning a round for the first time in nearly a decade thanks to Brad May's "May Day" goal against the Bruins.* Meanwhile, the St. Louis Blues stunned the Chicago Blackhawks with a first-round sweep (capped off by an epic Belfour meltdown), while the Maple Leafs got a game-seven overtime goal from tiny Russian rookie Nikolai Borschevsky to upset the Detroit Red Wings. In round two, the underdog New York Islanders stunned the Penguins with David Volek's overtime winner, ending Pittsburgh's two-year reign and ensuring there'd be a new champion.

But as the playoffs wore on, two stars who'd mostly been absent from the regular-season highlight reels emerged as dominant forces. Wayne Gretzky, who'd missed half the season with back problems and finished with fewer than 100 points for the first time in his career, had returned to his old ways and was leading Los Angeles on a run through Canadian playoff hopefuls. Gretzky and the Kings knocked off the Flames, Canucks and Maple Leafs, the latter coming in a classic seventh game that saw Gretzky score three goals at Maple Leaf Gardens in what he'd later call the greatest game of his career. To this day, Toronto fans insist that the series should never have gone to a seventh game, and that Kerry Fraser's missed call on Gretzky's high-stick on Gilmour in overtime of game six cost the Leafs the Cup.**

Waiting for the Kings in the final was yet another Canadian team. The Montreal Canadiens had survived the first three rounds of the playoffs on a long stretch of overtime heroics and some all-world goaltending from Patrick Roy. The three-time Vézina winner had struggled through an uncharacteristically weak 1992–93 season, and after the Canadiens opened the playoffs with two straight losses to the Nordiques, there had even been scattered calls for coach Jacques Demers to turn to André "Red Light"

---

* As called by legendary Sabres play-by-play voice Rick Jeanneret.

** Let the record show that those fans are 100 percent correct. It's in a history book now, so that makes it true.

Racicot in goal. Demers wisely stuck with his star, and Roy was his usual, unbeatable self the rest of the way.

The Kings took game one of the final in Montreal and led game two late, but the series turned on a controversial decision by Demers. Late in the game, the Habs coach called for a stick measurement on Kings defenceman Marty McSorley. The actual measurement was barely needed; the dramatically curved blade was clearly illegal. The resulting power play saw the Canadiens tie the game; Éric Desjardins's overtime winner knotted the series. Two more overtime wins in LA sent the Canadiens home with a chance to end the series in five, and they did exactly that with a 4–1 win to capture their twenty-fourth Stanley Cup.

As the final buzzer sounded and the victorious Canadiens poured onto the ice to celebrate, the most fascinating season in NHL history had officially drawn to a close. And as the overjoyed Forum crowd looked on, a clearly nervous gentleman who'd only been on the job for a few months made his way onto the ice to perform his very first Stanley Cup presentation.

As the John Ziegler era came to a close in 1992 (and with it quickly becoming apparent that Gil Stein was not a long-term option as league president), NHL owners decided that it was time for a new voice at the top of the league. There would be no internal promotions or next-in-line succession plans. The league had tried those before. It was time for an outsider's fresh eyes.

Lists were drawn up and interviews were conducted, with prominent business executives and well-known politicians contacted to gauge their interest. But at some point, somebody got the idea of aiming higher: What if the NHL could somehow lure away NBA commissioner David Stern?

It would have been a remarkable coup for the much smaller league. It was also, as quickly became apparent, a pipe dream. But eventually, an intriguing possibility emerged: NBA senior vice president Gary Bettman.[*]

The idea made sense. Bettman wasn't anyone's definition of a hockey

---

[*] It was apparently Stern himself who made the suggestion, leading to a long-standing conspiracy theory among the anti-Bettman brigade that the NBA commissioner intentionally sabotaged his competition by sending an in-over-his-head executive their way. That's not true—I think.

guy, but with years of experience in the pro sports world, he wouldn't be coming to the NHL as some sort of rookie. He was impressive during his interviews, arguing that hockey presented a bigger opportunity than the owners might have realized. And then there was the key line on his resumé: his role in helping the NBA implement a salary cap. NHL owners had long dreamt of a similar cap in their own sport, but had little notion of how to make it happen. Here was a guy who had been there and done that. Now, exactly how much Bettman actually had to do with the implementation of basketball's cap is a matter of some debate. He was sometimes sold to hockey fans as the guy who'd led the way for the NBA, although other reports suggested he'd merely been a supporting player in getting the details drawn up. Either way, the NHL was impressed, and Kings owner Bruce McNall led the charge to bring Bettman aboard.

On December 12, 1992, just days after their surprising Anaheim-Florida expansion decision, the NHL announced that Gary Bettman would become the league's first commissioner. The board of governors' vote had been unanimous. Newspapers around North America printed a photo of a grinning Bettman, awkwardly wearing an oversized NHL jersey while posing with McNall and Stein, who was still technically the league president.

Bettman officially started in his new role on February 1, 1993, and he immediately set about remaking the league's executive office. He swept out some of the old-timers and increased the size of the business staff. And in a decision that ruffled some feathers among the tradition-first crowd, he pushed for the league to rename its divisions, abandoning Patrick, Norris, Smythe and Adams in favour of simpler, geographic names, while also changing the playoff format to an NBA-like conference system.

Not everyone was on board, especially in Canada, but the initial reception to Bettman's arrival was relatively warm. When he stepped out to present the Stanley Cup to the Canadiens on that spring night in 1993, reading a few lines in French from a tiny piece of paper he held in his hand, nobody in the crowd even booed him.

The greatest season ever played was a massive success in terms of entertainment, but the one that followed, 1993–94, may have been even better from a marketing perspective. There were fewer offensive heroics: only one sixty-goal scorer (Bure) and one player who topped 120 points (Gretzky), while Boston's Cam Neely scored fifty goals in just forty-nine games in an injury-shortened campaign. Sure, scoring dropped by nearly a goal a game, but that was seen as just a temporary blip. And at least some of the drop could be attributed to the next wave of star goaltenders—Dominik Hasek had a breakout season in Buffalo and Martin Brodeur earned the Calder Trophy in New Jersey.

Meanwhile, the Stars put up ninety-seven points after relocating to Dallas, and both the Mighty Ducks of Anaheim and the Florida Panthers were respectable in their debut seasons. It wasn't perfect by any means—Mario Lemieux played just twenty-two games due to fatigue and back problems—but it was still very good. And the playoffs were even better, serving up first-round rivalry matchups between the Habs and Bruins, Islanders and Rangers, and Leafs and Blackhawks. The Sharks won their first playoff series, stunning the Red Wings in seven, and Bure scored a highlight-reel game-seven overtime goal to knock out the Flames.

But the biggest story was the New York Rangers. After missing the playoffs the previous year, they returned to the top of the standings and cruised through the first two rounds in just nine games before running into a tough Devils team in the Eastern Conference final. The two rivals delivered a classic, one that featured Mark Messier's infamous guarantee that the Rangers would come back from a 3–2 deficit to win the series, after which he made good on it with a hat trick in game six. Stéphane Matteau's double-overtime winner in game seven sent the Rangers to the final, where they overcame a scrappy Canucks squad in seven to capture their first Stanley Cup since 1940.

When a more polished Bettman handed the Cup off to a giddy Messier as the Madison Square Garden crowd roared, once again there wasn't a boo to be heard.

The key to the Bettman hiring, even more than his NBA experience or salary cap promises, was his willingness and ability to think big. The NHL, he convinced the owners, could be so much more than they knew.

The potential was there; they just needed a way to tap into it. Now, he'd just handed the Stanley Cup to the most marketable player on his most marketable American team. The new commissioner had barely settled into his new office, and the wheels were already in motion. For once, the NHL looked like a league with a plan.

A *Sports Illustrated* cover line from June 1994 declared that "the NHL's hot and the NBA's not." The accompanying article noted that American media had taken to describing the NBA product as "butt-ugly," while the NHL was considered "hip" and even "sexy." While basketball desperately searched for a new star to replace the recently retired Michael Jordan, the NHL could offer Gretzky, Messier, Lemieux, Lindros and more. And while the NBA product was increasingly sluggish, defensive-minded and even violent, the NHL promised high-scoring fun.

Hockey's television ratings still lagged behind those of football, baseball and basketball in the US, but they were on the rise. Marketing dollars were at an all-time high, with the Mighty Ducks providing a huge boost. NHL logos were starting to show up in mainstream pop culture, everywhere from rap videos to sitcoms to late-night talk shows. And for the first time in a generation, it didn't seem completely crazy to think that the league could someday catch the NBA and become America's third-favourite team sport. Less than two years into Gary Bettman's tenure as commissioner, the NHL was on fire.

Now they just had to keep the momentum going.

In hockey, timing is everything. The passing lane is there, and then suddenly it's not. A textbook bodycheck delivered half a second too late becomes a dirty hit. One moment you've got a wide-open net staring at you, and the next there are three bodies piled in front. Sometimes, it's not about how good your shot is—it's when you decide to take it.

Heading into the 1994–95 season, Gary Bettman decided it was time to take his shot. With the collective-bargaining agreement with the players expiring on October 1, and Major League Baseball on the verge of cancelling the World Series due to a work stoppage, the commissioner made his move for a salary cap. That August, he threw the first punch, unilaterally withdrawing various benefits and insisting that players would need to pay their own expenses related to training camp. Those camps went on as planned, as did the exhibition schedule, but negotiations made little progress. When the calendar rolled over from September to October, Bettman announced that the season would be delayed. For the first time in its history, the NHL was locking out its players.

The bad blood on both sides mounted quickly, with Chris Chelios telling reporters, "If I was Gary Bettman, I'd worry about my family, about my well-being right now." (He later apologized.) Even Gretzky, who usually avoided controversy, publicly rebuked the league's new leadership. For their part, the owners insisted that they were merely asking for a luxury tax, not a hard cap, although that felt like semantics. The players offered small concessions, but nowhere near enough to get the league's attention. Within weeks, chunks of the schedule were being officially wiped out.

The battle dragged on until December, when the scales began to tilt in favour of the players. NHL Players' Association head Bob Goodenow had convinced his charges to stand strong, assuring them that the owners would fold. Now he was being proven right. Bettman had been assured by his owners that they were united behind him, but as the weeks turned into months, several key allies were getting cold feet about the possibility of losing an entire season. The two sides finally reached an agreement in early January, in time to salvage a forty-eight-game schedule.

While the new deal was widely viewed as a victory for the owners at first, it quickly became apparent that the players had won the day. Bettman had failed to get any sort of meaningful cap or tax system, settling instead for a cap on rookie salaries and some tweaks to the arbitration system. The commissioner had learned some hard lessons, ones he'd be sure to act on if and when the next opportunity came around.

The NHL resumed play on January 20, 1995, but by then any tangible momentum from the past two seasons had been squandered. The Rangers had already stumbled through a bizarre off-season that saw Messier hold out and coach Mike Keenan bolt for the St. Louis Blues. Basketball's next Michael Jordan turned out to be Jordan himself, as he ended his brief and bizarre foray into minor-league baseball in March and returned to the league to a hero's welcome. By that point, it was clear that sports fans across America had met the NHL's prolonged absence with a shrug.

Just like that, all that buzz and excitement the league had built up over the previous two seasons had evaporated. And in its place was a new style of hockey that quickly began to spread through the league.

THAT'S USING YOUR HEAD

What happens when you make a rule change
so silly the entire league ignores it?

IF YOU WERE AROUND AT THE TIME, YOU PROBABLY REMEMBER plenty about the 1992–93 season. Selanne's glove toss, Gilmour's spin-o-rama, Lemieux's comeback and Roy's wink all conjure up instant memories for fans of the era.

Here's something you probably don't remember: the NHL's new rule on mandatory helmets.

"Wait," you're probably thinking. "The helmet rule didn't happen in 1992." That came all the way back in 1979, when the league ordered that all new players entering the league would have to wear a helmet. The grandfathered nature of the rule meant that head protection gradually became more common over the years, until Craig MacTavish was the last player left without one by the mid-'90s.

That's all true. But that's not the rule I'm talking about. I'm looking at the NHL's *other* helmet rule—the one that said players could stop wearing them.

This one came in the 1992 off-season, and you can thank Gil Stein for it. The NHL's beleaguered president, already feeling the pressure to make his mark amid rumours that the owners would quickly replace him, decided to get creative with the rule book. One of his brainstorms involved suspensions. Stein decided that, while supplemental discipline was clearly needed to keep players in line, it was unfair for fans to miss seeing their favourite stars just because an ankle had been hacked or a throat cross-checked. And so Stein declared that suspensions for first-time offenders could now be served on off-days, with players paying fines and missing practices but still suiting up for games. That meant that when Doug Gilmour, for example, slashed Tomas

Sandstrom hard enough to break his arm, he was banned for eight . . . days. The incident cost the Leafs star almost thirty thousand dollars in forfeited pay, but he didn't miss a game.

The suspension rule was strange, and it was quickly tossed aside—as was Stein. But at least it had some small impact on the season. The same couldn't be said for another Stein idea. During that 1992 off-season, the president scrapped the mandatory head-protection rule, allowing players who wanted to go bare-headed to ditch their helmets.

Why? Marketing. Stein argued that it was better for fans to be able to see their heroes up close, and he hoped that some of the league's bigger stars might be willing to offer some nice close-ups of their hair flowing in the breeze. There was just one problem: Virtually nobody wanted to go bucket-less. Out of the league's six hundred or so players, only one—Calgary enforcer Greg Smyth—took advantage of the new rule. He tried the old-school approach for a handful of games before deciding it wasn't worth the risk and going back to wearing a helmet. Nobody else even bothered.*

Smyth was an honest player and well respected around the league, but he wasn't exactly the sort of guy the NHL was looking to put its marketing muscle behind. The rule was quietly scrapped, and to this day most fans don't even know it ever existed. So, the next time you're trying to stump a hockey know-it-all at the sports bar, ask them to name the last season when helmets weren't mandatory for the league's skaters. If they immediately answer 1992–93, there's a good chance you're talking to Gil Stein.

---

* At least not during the regular season. Brett Hull went helmetless at the NHL All-Star Game, reasoning that nobody ever gets hit in those contests.

17

THE DEAD PUCK ERA

Why scoring dropped, and why the NHL still can't
figure out what to do about it

WITH THE 1994 LOCKOUT WIPING OUT NEARLY HALF A season, the league failed to produce a 100-point player for the first time since the barrier had first been cracked in 1969, and there were no fifty-goal scorers for the first time since 1970. Nobody even came especially close; Eric Lindros and Jaromir Jagr tied for the points lead with seventy, while Peter Bondra topped the league with thirty-four goals.

Fans weren't especially concerned—"Of course a shortened season would result in reduced numbers," they reasoned. With that temporary bout of labour stoppage unpleasantness behind it, they thought, the NHL was no doubt ready to resume its high-scoring ways. With the big-market New York Rangers on top of the league and new leadership at the NHL office ready to make a heavy marketing push, the sport was well on the way to rebranding itself as a fast-paced, skilled and exciting product.

But while we didn't realize it at the time, those fifty-goal and 100-point milestones had already become endangered species. At the same moment that the NHL's executives were selling speed and scoring, its coaches were pulling the game in the opposite direction. A significant shift in the prevailing style of play was underway, and the timing couldn't have been worse for a league just figuring out how to sell itself to the world.

———

Ask most hockey fans to pinpoint the genesis of the NHL's low-scoring era, and they'll foist the blame squarely on the 1994–95 New Jersey Devils.

Those Devils were a reasonably good team. They finished the season with a respectable 22–18–8 record, good for a tie for second place in the Atlantic Division and ninth place overall. They'd been to the Eastern Conference final a year before, losing that seventh-game double-overtime thriller to the Rangers, and the roster featured three future Hall of Famers in Martin Brodeur, Scott Stevens and Scott Niedermayer.

But the Devils weren't exactly anyone's idea of fun. The forward ranks weren't especially inspiring, with only Stéphane Richer so much as cracking the thirty-point mark. New Jersey finished in the middle of the pack in goal scoring and won their games largely by keeping the puck out of their own net. Brodeur obviously played a big part in that, as did a blue line built around Stevens and Niedermayer. But the Devils had another weapon in the war against offence: the neutral-zone trap.

The 1994–95 Devils didn't invent The Trap. The idea of clogging up the neutral zone between the blue lines had been around since hockey's earliest days, and specific systems had been used by various European teams, most notably the Soviet powerhouses. The Devils weren't even the first NHL team to use the concept; they were just the first to perfect it, thanks to coach Jacques Lemaire, disciplined players and more than a little bit of clutch-and-grab.

The Devils had a relatively easy time slicing through the Eastern Conference playoffs, losing just four games and never facing elimination while knocking off the Boston Bruins, Pittsburgh Penguins and Philadelphia Flyers. It was a nice run, and well deserved for a franchise that had battled its share of ups and downs over the years. Even as the Devils prepared for the final, rumours swirled that the team was about to move to Nashville and that Bettman wasn't doing much to help them stay in New Jersey. (This led to a memorable interview on a live Fox television broadcast in which the commissioner was drowned out by furious Devils fans bombarding him with expletives and helpful suggestions about certain acts he might want to perform on himself.)

New Jersey made for a plucky, if somewhat boring, underdog story. But any hope of a happy ending dimmed when they arrived in the final to find a powerhouse waiting for them. The Detroit Red Wings had finished in first place overall and led the Western Conference in scoring. They featured seven future Hall of Famers, including three up front and four on the blue line. And with players like Steve Yzerman, Paul Coffey and Sergei Fedorov leading the way, the Wings were exactly the sort of speed-and-skill team that was supposed to run circles around the defensive-minded Devils.*

It looked like a mismatch and, inspiring underdog stories aside, nobody gave New Jersey much of a chance. This one felt like a sweep.

And it was—just not the way we all thought it would be. The Devils stunned the Red Wings in four straight to capture their first Stanley Cup. Detroit's talent-packed roster was held in check: Yzerman managed just a single point, Coffey had only two and the Wings never scored more than twice in any game of the series. Upsets are part of what makes sports fun, but this one didn't seem to make sense. The better team hadn't just lost, it had been brushed aside with apparent ease. Hockey people like simple explanations, and the 1995 final sure seemed to provide one: An expensive roster full of superstars had just been shut down by a system.

In reality, the gap between the Devils and Red Wings probably wasn't as wide as we'd all assumed. Because of the lockout, there hadn't been any interconference games that season, so comparing an Eastern team to a Western one was tricky. But there was at least some truth to the idea that the Devils had used a defensive system to shut down a more talented team. And more importantly, when it comes to the copycat NHL, perception often trumps reality. All around the league, teams took note. Suddenly, everyone was looking at the newly crowned Devils and their defence-first approach and wondering: Can we do that?

If the 1994–95 Devils provided the question mark that sparked the NHL's defensive revolution, the 1995–96 Panthers were its exclamation point.

---

* That year's Red Wings also gave up fewer goals than New Jersey, but that part doesn't really fit the narrative, so it's largely ignored.

The Devils were viewed as a team that could win at least a playoff round or two. The Panthers were a third-year franchise that had never made the playoffs. They certainly weren't terrible in the way that other early-'90s expansion teams had been—they'd missed the postseason by just a single point in each of their first two seasons—but the roster was essentially a collection of no-names, featuring star goaltender John Vanbiesbrouck, respected veteran Scott Mellanby, and then a whole lot of guys like Jesse Belanger and Brian Skrudland. The Panthers were okay, maybe a bit better than okay, and when they finished the season with ninety-two points, that felt about right.

Meanwhile, the Pittsburgh Penguins looked like a dynasty ready to reawaken. After his cancer comeback in 1992–93, Mario Lemieux had played just 26 games in 1993–94 and then sat out the entire shortened 1994–95 season to rest and recover. But he returned to play most of a season in 1995–96, racking up 69 goals and 161 points in 70 games to reclaim the scoring title. Jaromir Jagr finished second with 149 points, Ron Francis racked up 119 and the newly acquired Petr Nedved added 99. The Penguins scored 362 goals, leading the league by a mile while winning the Northeast Division.

While Pittsburgh was knocking out the Washington Capitals and the Rangers to reach the Eastern Conference final, the Panthers were writing a Cinderella story with wins over the Bruins and Flyers, and pelting their opponents with rats along the way.* That set up what seemed like a classic David-versus-Goliath matchup, with the expansion newbies facing down an offensive juggernaut.

Instead, much like the previous year's Wings-Devils series, the scrappy underdogs shut down the big-name stars. Lemieux and Jagr were each held to just one goal and the Penguins never scored more than three in a game.**

---

* The story goes that Mellanby had one-timed a live rat in the Panthers dressing room before their home opener, then scored two goals to lead the team to a win. Teammates christened the feat a "rat trick," and fans began tossing plastic rats onto the ice. By the playoffs, the home crowd was littering the ice with thousands of them after Panthers goals.
** Francis missed the series after breaking his foot in round two, which certainly didn't help.

The Panthers fought back from a 3–2 series deficit to force a seventh game, then went into Pittsburgh and earned a smothering 3–1 win to advance to the Cup final.

Never mind that their story went south quickly when they got there, with the Colorado Avalanche sweeping the series; the sight of an expansion team toppling Mario and friends seemed to solidify the NHL's new way of thinking. The Devils had shown that you could shut down a borderline all-star team if you had a superstar goalie, two generational blueliners and a commitment to defence. The Panthers had proven that you didn't even need that much; with a little luck and solid goaltending, even a roster full of grinders could get the job done.

You could almost hear owners around the league calling their GMs and asking, "Why are we spending millions on these big-name goal scorers when there's a cheaper way that works just as well, if not better?"

Why indeed. The 1995–96 season had seen just 6.28 goals per game, the lowest full-season average since 1972. It felt like rock bottom. As it turns out, there was a ways still to go. The league hasn't come close to seeing that much offence in a season in the more than two decades since.

This seems like a good time for a football story.

In 2004, the Indianapolis Colts hosted the New England Patriots in the American Football Conference championship game, with a trip to the Super Bowl on the line. It was a marquee matchup for the NFL, one that pitted two of the league's most marketable quarterbacks against each other in what figured to be a high-scoring grudge match. Instead, the game was a mess. Peyton Manning and the Colts had been the league's second-highest-scoring team, and Manning would be named MVP. But the Patriots shut them down, limiting Manning to just 237 yards through the air and one touchdown pass while picking him off four times.

How they did it is a matter of interpretation. Their defensive backs challenged the Colt receivers with a playing style that Patriots fans would describe as "physical" and "aggressive." Other teams were more likely to use words like "mugging." It wasn't the first time the Pats had employed that sort of style, but given the stakes, the performance was perhaps their most dominant. The Pats had shut down Manning and Company on a huge stage and given the rest of the league a blueprint for doing the same. And so the NFL changed how the rules were called.

Recognizing that offence sells in pro sports, the league took immediate action. It didn't form a committee and ask it to report back in a few years, nor did it make tiny, nearly imperceptible tweaks to the established rule book. No, the NFL made it clear that there would be a radical change in how contact between defenders and receivers was called. Clutch-and-grab tactics would no longer be tolerated, and the game would be opened up for offensive stars to do their thing. Passing offence, which had dipped leaguewide in the 2003 season, quickly rebounded, and marquee stars like Manning, Tom Brady, Aaron Rodgers and Drew Brees spent the next few years rewriting the record book.

That's one way for a pro sports league to handle a reduction in offence. Which brings us back to the NHL.

Faced with falling scoring rates and a pair of high-profile playoff upsets in which defensive-minded teams shut down rosters stacked with offensive talent, the NHL decided to . . . well, to think about doing something. Maybe. If they needed to.

Scoring dropped under six goals per game during the 1996–97 season, then plunged all the way to 5.28 for 1997–98. It would remain under 5.5 for the next six years, hitting a low of 5.14 in 2003–04. A big part of that drop was goaltending; the butterfly style had become common and the athletes who played the position were getting bigger every year. So was their equipment. Where attacking players used to have big sections of net available to target, by the end of the '90s there was precious little to shoot at.

But beyond the goaltenders, it was clear that something important was changing across the league. Everyone was playing some variation of The Trap, and clutching and grabbing—and occasionally, outright tackling—ruled the day. Where there had once been a divide between offence-first coaches and defensive-minded ones, now everyone behind a bench seemed to be focused on keeping the puck out of the net. If you lost 1–0, that was okay, but win 6–5 and you could count on a bag skate the next day.

And through it all, the NHL's most significant rule change was one that reduced scoring even further. The league began using replay review to wave off any goal that featured an attacking player in the crease, even if it was just a toe and hadn't affected the play in any way. Fans were trained to hold off on celebrating goals until they were sure they wouldn't be disallowed. Despite complaints, the league stubbornly stuck by the maddening rule until the 1999 Stanley Cup final, when the Dallas Stars scored the championship-winning goal while Brett Hull's skate was clearly in the crease. Now that the worst-case scenario had come to pass, the rule was never seen again.*

Scoring got a brief boost in 2005–06, when officials were instructed to call the rule book more strictly, but it came largely from an increase in power plays and proved to be temporary. Scoring fell again, and has hovered back around the 5.5-goals-per-game level for the last few years. The league continues to tinker, introducing a new faceoff rule here and slightly smaller goaltending equipment there, but seems powerless to affect any sort of real change. A slashing crackdown for the 2017–18 season seemed to help a bit, but whether its effects will last is something only time will tell.

Today, goalies are massive; defence-first philosophies have been drilled into a generation of players; and shot blocking has been perfected. Many of the goals we do see are the result of flukes and lucky bounces, as players simply fling the puck at the net and hope it deflects in off somebody. It's not unheard of to see an entire season pass without a single fifty-goal scorer. In 2014–15, Dallas Stars winger Jamie Benn won the Art Ross Trophy with just eighty-seven points, a total that would have seen him tie for thirty-fifth in 1992–93. The offensive side of the record book has remained essentially unchanged for two decades, while the goaltending section has been all-but-entirely rewritten. "It's a 3–2 league now," we're

---

* To this day, the league insists that officials got the Hull call right because he followed the puck into the crease and therefore had a right to be there. That may even be true, but it's not how most fans understood the rule, and the lack of any announcement about the play being reviewed led most to assume the league had just bailed on the call to avoid waving off a Cup-winning goal.

constantly told by the experts, referring to final scores. They rarely mean it as a compliment.

To be sure, many fans are perfectly happy with how today's game is played; you can't raise the topic without being subjected to a knowing lecture about the inherent beauty of the 0–0 stalemate. But others, especially those who were around for the era of four-hundred-goal teams and 140-point superstars, can't help but wonder how the world's most exciting game was allowed to get so dull.

So, could the NHL have actually done anything about it? That's tough to say. Certainly, there was an opportunity in the mid-'90s to act decisively to get ahead of the problem, like the NFL did a decade later. Bettman and the NHL talked a good game, constantly assuring fans that they were concerned by the lack of offence and were ready to act, but they consistently chose to tweak and tinker instead of pulling the trigger. It's possible that a more forward-thinking (pun intended) league could have responded by redefining how the game would be played. But today the job is much tougher. Every new draft class is made up of players who weren't even alive before the dead puck era dawned; with years of defence-first coaching drilled into them, they don't know any other way to play. Goaltenders aren't getting any smaller. And now, players who came up and played their entire pro careers with a defensive mindset are graduating into the coaching ranks, ready to teach the next generation how to choke the life out of the game.

We often hear it said that today's players are better than ever before, and that's almost certainly true. We can pine all we want for the high-flying '70s and '80s, but the reality is that much of that generation's eye-popping offensive totals came because opposing players just couldn't keep up. In the days after massive expansion but before the wave of incoming European players and US development programmes, there simply wasn't enough talent to go around. Wayne Gretzky and Bobby Orr would be superstars in any era, but put them up against goalies who struggle to stay upright and third-pairing blueliners who can barely skate backwards, and you get stat lines that look like pinball scores.

Giving offence a boost even back to early-'90s levels would almost surely require radical change. Maybe the league converts to full-time four-on-four someday. Maybe they figure out a way to ban shot blocking, or change how power plays work, or overhaul goalie equipment completely. Maybe they reconfigure all the rinks to a wider European style to create more room on the ice. That last one gets mentioned a lot, although rarely by anyone who's seen how stupefyingly dull those European leagues can be.

There's one approach that would seem like a common-sense solution: Just make the nets bigger. Adding a few inches all around the goal would make for a barely perceptible change for fans while potentially restoring the balance between offence and defence by giving shooters more to aim for. But many fans hate that idea. The league has a long history of fiddling with the blue lines, faceoff circles, goal lines and even the puck itself, often without most fans even noticing. But somehow, bigger nets are apparently the line that can't be crossed.

So, maybe there's nothing left to try. Maybe the experts are right, and hockey—played the way it's meant to be played by the very best players available to play it—really is a 3–2 game, and fans would be better off if we just accepted it. Give the league some credit; they've certainly given us all plenty of time to get used to it.

People still cite that famous *Sports Illustrated* cover about the NHL being hotter than the NBA, but these days it's usually done ironically. The combination of the ill-timed lockout, lack of offence, and the bad luck of four straight years of Stanley Cup final sweeps stalled the league's momentum. Canadian teams struggled with the game's new economics, while in the US television ratings stalled and the sport slipped towards niche status.

By 2000, the *Los Angeles Times* was describing the NHL product like this: "Games are dull and tedious affairs. The season is interminable, an eighty-two-game death march. Goals are ugly." That was a little harsh, granted, but it was hard not to look back wistfully at those heady days after the Rangers' Cup win, when it seemed like the NHL and its new commissioner were on the verge of something big. And then, just maybe, to wonder where it all went wrong.

ESPOSITO'S SMUDGE

The legendary scorer tries a fancy move against the Flyers

MAN, THAT LAST CHAPTER GOT DEPRESSING. SO, LET'S wipe away the misery of the dead puck era with some levity. And fittingly enough, we'll turn to one of the league's all-time leading scorers to provide it.

In a career heavy on superlatives, Phil Esposito was rarely described as an especially creative player—most of his 717 career goals were the result of finding and taking the most direct route to get the puck to the net.*

But as a GM, Esposito was about as creative as they came. He was one of the most prolific traders of all time during his three seasons running the New York Rangers in the '80s, even trading a first-round pick to Quebec for head coach Michel Bergeron. And his stint as the Tampa Bay Lightning's first GM wasn't much different, with Esposito wheeling and dealing through six seasons. But it was a trade he *didn't* make that may have been his most creative move of all.

Heading into the 1997 off-season, Esposito was facing a tough negotiation with restricted free agent Chris Gratton. The team had spent the third-overall pick on the towering centre in 1993, and he'd finally broken through with a thirty-goal season in 1996–97. That was good news for the Lightning, but bad news for Esposito, who had to get his young star signed before some other team came along with an offer sheet. (Back then, offer sheets to restricted

---

* In one of the few examples of the NHL nailing a comedy bit, Ron MacLean did a sketch for the league's awards show in 1997 in which he called Esposito to inform him that the league was now applying its controversial in-the-crease rule retroactively, and that his status as the fourth-leading goal scorer of all time had been affected. "Where am I now?" Phil asks. "Well," a hesitant Ron informs him, "we have you three behind Doug Houda."

free agents were a weapon that teams wielded fairly often, not merely a tool GMs mumbled vaguely about without ever using.)

With negotiations going slowly and rumours of an incoming offer sheet swirling, Esposito turned to the trade market. Everything came to a head on August 12, 1997, when the Philadelphia Flyers announced that they'd signed Gratton to an offer sheet. Too late, Esposito informed them. He'd already traded Gratton to the Chicago Blackhawks. And just like that, the NHL found itself facing yet another arbitration involving a disputed trade, a big young centre and the Flyers.

It quickly became apparent that the Flyers had indeed signed Gratton before Esposito traded him, and had informed the Lightning of that fact as required. But that's where Esposito's creativity came in, as he presented the league with a novel excuse. Yes, he admitted, he'd received the Flyers' fax. But it had been smudged and he couldn't read it properly, so he hadn't actually been informed of anything and was therefore still free to trade Gratton's rights to Chicago.

It was a novel approach. Unfortunately for the Lightning, it didn't work—an arbitrator quickly ruled the trade invalid. The Flyers' offer sheet stood, and Esposito grudgingly worked out a trade that sent Gratton to Philadelphia for Mikael Renberg.

Both Gratton and Renberg were largely busts in their new homes. So, a mere sixteen months after the case of the smudged fax, the two teams essentially undid the deal, agreeing to another trade that sent Gratton back to Tampa and Renberg back to Philadelphia. Maybe we all should have just listened to Phil Esposito in the first place.

18

THE LAST GREAT RIVALRY

The Red Wings and Avalanche trade Cup wins and haymakers

WHAT'S THE BEST RIVALRY IN NHL HISTORY?

This question is a fun way to start a debate with hockey fans, many of whom have strong feelings on the topic. The answers you'll get will often divide along generational lines. Old-school types will default to the Habs and Leafs, which is probably the right answer if you're looking at the entire century of league history. Since the start of the expansion era in 1967, you could probably make a better argument for Montreal and Boston. There's a case to be made for the Battle of either Alberta or Quebec, or maybe Rangers-Islanders or Blackhawks-Blues. More recently, you'd want to mention Pittsburgh and Philadelphia or the three-way Battle of California.

All are strong rivalries, and all have had their moments. But for seven seasons from 1996 through 2003, there was no debate to be had. Over those years, there was only one rivalry worth mentioning: the one between the Detroit Red Wings and Colorado Avalanche. The two teams combined for five Cups, countless line brawls and two legendary goalie fights. It all made for must-see TV every time they took the ice together, because you knew you were either going to see a bunch of guys playing like the future Hall of Famers they were, or a bunch of guys punching each other senseless. There was a good chance you'd see both at the same time.

It was the rivalry that defined the last decade of the pre–salary cap era.

And in hindsight, perhaps the most interesting feature of the Detroit-Colorado enmity was how close it all came to never existing at all.

Before we get to the Avalanche, we need to take a detour to visit Wayne Gretzky.

With the dead puck era taking hold in 1995–96, the Red Wings quickly became the class of the NHL. There was no hangover from their disappointing loss to the Devils in the 1995 final; instead, they shook off a middling October to dominate the league. After a 5–5–2 start, the Wings won twenty-two of their next twenty-four and never lost two straight the rest of the way, all the while racking up an NHL record sixty-two wins. They'd finish the regular season with 131 points, twenty-seven ahead of the league's next best team.

But while the Red Wings looked to be rolling towards a return to the final, Mike Keenan had other ideas. Keenan was in his second year as coach and GM of the St. Louis Blues, and he wasn't in the mood to concede the Western Conference to anyone. So, in February 1996, he went out and traded for the greatest player ever.

The second Gretzky trade didn't quite have the same impact as the first; the Great One was headed towards free agency, and with the Kings struggling both on the ice and on the balance sheet, it had become apparent that a move to a contender was in the cards. The New York Rangers quickly emerged as the frontrunner, which probably made it irresistible for Keenan to one-up his former team. The Blues also had to contend with the NFL's Rams coming to town, so adding a big-name player was a priority.

On February 27, 1996, St. Louis announced that it had acquired Gretzky from LA in exchange for three players and two draft picks.* Gretzky arrived in St. Louis and immediately replaced Shayne Corson as team captain, and in his very first game Keenan played him twenty-seven minutes. The Blues

---

* The full deal was Gretzky for Roman Vopat, Patrice Tardif, Craig Johnson, a first-round draft pick and a fifth-rounder. None of the players or picks amounted to much in Los Angeles.

were only a .500 team, but they were stacked with big names, including Al MacInnis and Chris Pronger as well as two key pieces of Gretzky's Oilers dynasty, Grant Fuhr and Glenn Anderson. They also had the league's top goal scorer in Brett Hull, and the idea of pairing him with the best play-maker ever to lace up skates seemed like a sure thing.

But as we learned with Lindros, that doesn't always mean much. Gretzky's time in the Gateway City didn't really work out as planned. He and Hull never found much chemistry, and the Blues stumbled down the stretch. But they made the playoffs and knocked out the Toronto Maple Leafs in the first round, setting up a showdown with the Red Wings in round two.

Based on the standings, it should have been a mismatch—the Red Wings had finished fifty-one points ahead of St. Louis. But the Blues' veteran-laden roster came together and gave Detroit all it could handle. They took a 3–2 lead through five games, but couldn't finish the series at home. That set up a classic game seven back in Detroit, one that went to sudden death tied 0–0. Early in the second overtime, Gretzky found himself on the receiving end of a sloppy Vladimir Konstantinov turnover at centre ice. Hockey fans had seen Gretzky turn that sort of break into a scoring chance hundreds of times over the years. But this time he flubbed it, misplaying the puck into his own skates. Steve Yzerman stole it, carried the puck to the St. Louis blue line and unleashed one of the greatest laser-beam shots of all-time past Jon Casey. The Blues were out, and Gretzky's time in St. Louis was over. He signed with the Rangers as a free agent that summer, and he would spend the last three years of his career in New York. Even in his late thirties and with scoring down around the league, he still hit the ninety-point mark in two of those seasons—because of course he did.

The Red Wings had survived Gretzky's Blues by the slimmest of mar-gins and headed to the Western Conference final to face the Avalanche in a series that would prove transformational for both teams. All the unfor-gettable moments may feel inevitable in hindsight, but the greatest rivalry the NHL has seen in recent years was one Wayne Gretzky turnover away from never happening at all.

———

The 1996 Western Conference final seemed like a great matchup. The record-breaking Red Wings would get a tough test in the Avalanche, who'd finished second overall with 104 points. It was the first season in Colorado for the former Quebec Nordiques, and they'd become instant contenders thanks to a gift from the hockey gods: the midseason arrival of Patrick Roy.

The trade that brought Roy to Colorado had come in the aftermath of his meltdown against—who else?—the Red Wings. After being left in net for nine goals in front of jeering hometown fans in a December game, a humiliated Roy marched past coach Mario Tremblay and told president Ronald Corey that he was done in Montreal. The Canadiens capitulated quickly, sending Roy and team captain Mike Keane to the Avalanche for wingers Martin Rucinsky and Andrei Kovalenko and goaltender Jocelyn Thibault. It was a robbery for the Avs, not to mention a trade that Montreal would have never agreed to if they'd still been dealing with their archrival Nordiques, and it still stands as one of the worst moves in Canadiens history.

For many fans, Roy's behaviour seemed curious. He'd always been an emotional player, and the Red Wings blowout had clearly stung his pride. But demanding a trade from a team you'd spent a decade with based on one bad game seemed, well, crazy. Surely there was something else going on.

There was, as we'd later find out. Roy and Tremblay hadn't been getting along,[*] and the goalie was unhappy that Corey had replaced coach Jacques Demers and GM Serge Savard with two novices. But as it turns out, there was another key name behind the blowup: Detroit goaltender Mike Vernon.[**] The two goalies had happened to cross paths at a local breakfast spot on the day of the game, and Roy vented about all the pressure he was under from fans and media. Vernon could relate, having been under a similar microscope in Calgary, and he told Roy about what a relief it had been to be traded and get a fresh start. It seemed like an innocuous

———

[*] Fun fact: The two had been roommates during Roy's rookie season.
[**] Vernon told the story in a radio interview with the CBC in 2014.

enough conversation at the time—just two goalies talking shop, grousing about how tough the job can be. Hours later, Vernon watched from the other crease as Roy got lit up by the Red Wings and stormed off the ice. And as he later put it, "I'm like . . . 'Oh no.'"

The Avs went into Detroit and stunned the hosts by taking the first two games. The Red Wings fought back in a must-win game three on the road, earning a 6–4 decision, but then dropped the fourth game. Facing elimination on home ice, Detroit shelled Roy in a 5–2 win to send the series back to Colorado.

But nobody remembers any of that. When it comes to the 1996 series, all we remember is Claude Lemieux. Specifically, we remember Lemieux drilling Detroit's Kris Draper into the boards from behind. The impact broke Draper's jaw, cheekbone and nose, and he underwent surgery to reset most of his face. Lemieux was given a five-minute major and tossed from the game.

At first, there was little fallout from the incident. With their season on the line, the game was simply too important for the Wings to go looking for revenge. The hit came with the Avalanche leading 1–0 in the first period, and the Red Wings scored on the power play to tie the score. But the Avs added three in the second period and closed out a 4–1 win, ending the Red Wings' dream season. Afterwards, Detroit players were furious, especially when Lemieux returned to the ice in a T-shirt for the celebration and handshake line. Dino Ciccarelli told reporters, "I can't believe I shook this guy's friggin' hand . . . that pisses me right off."*

Lemieux was suspended for the first two games of the Stanley Cup final. The ruling, handed down by NHL senior VP Brian Burke, was harsh; even today, the league rarely gives out multigame suspensions during the playoffs, so suspending a thirty-nine-goal scorer for two games of the final was no small sentence. But in hindsight, it was nowhere near enough, and Lemieux returned in time to score a key goal three minutes

---

* He really did say friggin', by the way, making this perhaps the only hockey quote in history where that word was actually uttered and not just substituted by a nervous editor.

into Colorado's victory in game three. The Avs swept the Florida Panthers, capturing the franchise's first Stanley Cup.

Hockey's code is hazy and open to interpretation, but in this case it seemed clear: Payback was coming. The only question was when.

Red Wing fans hoping for vengeance would have to wait. Lemieux was injured for the first two games between the teams the following season, and the third game—in Colorado—passed without incident. That left just one regular-season meeting on the schedule. It's a date that fans of both teams could still tell you off the top of their heads: March 26, 1997.

Against all odds, the problems started with Peter Forsberg and Igor Larionov, two scrappy players who were nonetheless hardly known as troublemakers. But with those two tangled up and drawing the officials' attention, Detroit tough guy Darren McCarty saw his chance. He jumped Lemieux, then pummelled his downed opponent. He even seemed to throw a few knees, and at one point he dragged Lemieux over by the benches so that players from both teams could get a better look.*

From there, things escalated when Roy became involved, skating out to help his teammates. He was intercepted by Detroit's Brendan Shanahan in a spectacular midair collision, and for a moment he seemed content to head back to his net. But then he spotted Vernon, and the two squared off in what probably stands as the most memorable goalie fight of all time.** Vernon earned the win, cutting Roy over the eye in the process, as the Detroit crowd broke the sound barrier and linesmen worked to scrape Lemieux's blood off the ice. The whole thing was a stunning sight for just about everyone who witnessed it, with the possible exception of referee Paul Devorski, who handed out just twenty-two penalty minutes for the entire brawl and didn't eject a single player, including McCarty.

The Red Wings and Avalanche played in different divisions, had no geographical connections and shared no history dating back further than

---

* Lemieux was widely mocked for turtling instead of fighting back. He'd later claim that McCarty's first blindside punch had concussed him.

** Ron Hextall and Félix Potvin might disagree.

a year. Heck, one of the teams had only existed for two seasons. None of that mattered. We officially had ourselves a rivalry.

From that night on, it seemed as if every Detroit-Colorado game brought a free-for-all. Sometimes it was your standard one-on-one fight, or the occasional line brawl. Sometimes it was bigger, like the night in 1998 that saw Roy avenge his loss to Vernon with a decision over netminder Chris Osgood. Sometimes it was best forgotten, like the time Dominik Hasek skated down the ice to challenge Roy, only to wipe out at the last moment and slide harmlessly into the crease.

Fans couldn't get enough. And neither, apparently, could the hockey gods, who served up four more playoff showdowns over the next six seasons. The Wings won a Western Conference final rematch in 1997, on their way to the first of back-to-back Stanley Cup wins. The Avalanche won second-round matchups in both 1999 and 2000. And the Red Wings took a memorable seventh-game victory in 2002, humbling Roy in a 7–0 blowout. That one came after a 2–0 Detroit win in game six that was highlighted by Roy's embarrassing "Statue of Liberty" gaffe in which he gift-wrapped the winning goal for Shanahan while overselling a save.

The rivalry raged for seven seasons, only starting to fade when Roy retired after the 2002–03 season. By that point, the teams had combined to win five Stanley Cups. Both captains, Yzerman and Joe Sakic, rank among the NHL's top ten all-time scorers, and multiple players from each team have been inducted into the Hall of Fame—including five who were on the ice for that famous 1997 brawl.[*]

The rivalry had everything, including a degree of respect. In one of the matchup's best stories, Detroit pest Sean Avery once tried to chirp Sakic, only to be yanked away by teammate Brett Hull. "*You* do not get to talk to Mr. Sakic," Hull informed him.

Will we ever see another rivalry like it? Never say never, but . . . no, let's face it, we never will. With a salary cap in place, it's unlikely that we'll ever see a team stacked with as much talent as the Avalanche and

---

[*]   Roy, Shanahan, Forsberg, Larionov and Nicklas Lidstrom.

Red Wings could offer—let alone two at the same time. And as the game continues to evolve away from violence and self-policing, we can expect that line brawls, goalie fights, premeditated payback and crazed sprints towards midair collisions will become rarer and rarer.

The Red Wings-Avalanche rivalry may not have been the best the league has ever seen. That remains a topic of debate, and there's plenty to be said for some of those old-school matchups from generations gone by. But even if Detroit and Colorado aren't your pick, they'll almost certainly go down in history as the NHL's *last* great rivalry.

And you can thank Patrick Roy, Mike Vernon, Claude Lemieux, Darren McCarty and yes, even Wayne Gretzky for making it happen.

HOW HOLLYWOOD SAVED
THE AVALANCHE

A Harrison Ford blockbuster helps Colorado keep their franchise player

THE TERM "FRANCHISE PLAYER" GETS THROWN AROUND A lot, but in the case of the Colorado Avalanche, Joe Sakic truly *was* the franchise. He was there before the Avalanche even existed, establishing himself as a bona fide star during the Quebec Nordiques days. He was the team's best player when it made the move south, serving as the public face of the franchise as it started the process of winning over a new fan base. He was the one who received the team's first Stanley Cup from Gary Bettman in 1996, and the one who handed off its second to Ray Bourque in an emotional moment in 2001. He never played anywhere else, and when he finally hung up his skates in 2009, it was only a few years before he became the team's general manager. Joe Sakic *is* the Colorado Avalanche.

And that's why it comes as a surprise to many fans to learn about the day he signed a contract with the New York Rangers. Well, an offer sheet, at least.

Just two years after the Avalanche had landed in Colorado, and one year after they'd won the Stanley Cup, Sakic found himself facing restricted free agency in the summer of 1997. The Avs wanted him back, but playing out of the old McNichols Sports Arena, the team was already losing money. In the days before the salary cap, that left teams like Colorado vulnerable to having their stars poached by the league's richer markets.

There weren't many richer than New York. And unfortunately for Colorado, the Rangers had a big hole to fill after Mark Messier bolted town to sign with the Vancouver Canucks.* They targeted Sakic, and early that August they got him to sign a three-year, twenty-one-million-dollar offer sheet. The contract included a fifteen-million-dollar signing bonus to be paid up front, designed to make the deal all but impossible for the cash-strapped Avalanche to match.

Colorado GM Pierre Lacroix told reporters that he didn't know whether or not he'd match the offer, and he sure sounded like a man who was telling the truth. He'd recently signed Peter Forsberg to a big extension and was already paying Patrick Roy plenty. It really did seem as if the Avalanche might have to let Sakic walk, accepting five first-round picks from the Rangers as compensation but crippling a Cup contender in the process.

And that's when Harrison Ford showed up.

The Avalanche were owned by a company called Ascent Entertainment, which was involved in the film industry. Just days before Sakic signed the Rangers' offer, Ford's summer blockbuster *Air Force One* had opened across the country. The film had been bankrolled by an Ascent subsidiary, and its success or failure would have a direct impact on Ascent's bottom line—and, by extension, the Avalanche's ability to pay Sakic.

The film was a hit, opening with a thirty-seven-million-dollar weekend and riding strong reviews and word of mouth to weeks of solid business. By the time a decision was due on Sakic, *Air Force One* had more than recouped its reported eighty-five-million-dollar budget and Ascent could breathe easier about making big commitments elsewhere among its businesses.

And so the Avalanche paid up to keep Sakic. Soon a new arena was built, and the Avalanche's days of being a target for big-market bullies were over. Sakic would lead the team to another Cup in 2001, winning MVP honours in the process, and he'd go on to become one of the few members of the Hockey Hall of Fame to have only played for one franchise. And everyone agreed to never speak of that Rangers contract ever again.

---

* That move ended up being a disaster for both sides, and Messier returned to New York three years later after Vancouver bought him out. To this day, Messier is probably the most hated player in Canucks history.

If *Air Force One* had crashed and burned, there's a good chance that the Avalanche's franchise player would have wound up on Broadway. But both on film and on the ice, Harrison Ford arrived just in time to save the day.

19

INTERNATIONAL INCIDENTS

The NHL heads to the Olympics

THE IDEA WAS NEARLY IRRESISTIBLE FOR HOCKEY FANS: The league would send its best players to the Winter Olympics, where they'd face off for the gold medal and international bragging rights in front of a potentially massive worldwide audience. In fact, the whole thing seemed like a slam dunk—maybe because, as they had done in pursuing a salary cap, the NHL was following pro basketball's lead. The NBA had sent its top stars to the 1992 Summer Games in Barcelona and reaped a windfall of publicity as the US "Dream Team" rolled over all comers. Surely the NHL, with its plucked-from-basketball commissioner leading the way, could do the same. Heck, the hockey version would be even better—instead of one team of superstars crushing all the competition, a best-on-best hockey tournament would feature at least six countries capable of winning gold.

It was an obvious path forward for a league looking to expand its global reach, and by 1995 it was clear that the NHL was pushing in that direction. But there were obstacles for the league to overcome, not least of which was dealing with the NHL Players' Association. Gary Bettman's relationship with the players was already frosty after the contentious negotiations of the year before, and both sides held the right to reopen the collective-bargaining agreement in 1998, raising the possibility of a successful Olympic debut being immediately followed by a momentum-killing work stoppage. In a rare moment of compromise and common sense, the league and players agreed to extend the CBA. One hurdle down.

But if bargaining with the NHLPA was tough, the league was in for a true challenge when it came to navigating the waters of international sports. Both the International Ice Hockey Federation and the International Olympic Committee had turf to protect, after all, and the NHL's potential arrival on the scene raised serious questions over who would control what in the international hockey world. While sending pros to the tournament felt like a no-brainer in North America, some of the European federations pushed back. At one point, IIHF president René Fasel reportedly tried to mollify the Swedish and Finnish federations by promising them a chance to host games in upcoming Canada Cup tournaments. One problem: That contest wasn't run by the IIHF, and Fasel's attempt to give away something that wasn't his to give nearly caused the whole deal to collapse.

Even if it could get all the parties on board, the NHL faced having to put its season on hold to accommodate an Olympic break, a challenge the off-season NBA players hadn't had to deal with. And the 1998 tournament was being held in Nagano, Japan, meaning the games would be played in the middle of the night for North American fans. The NHL's real goal was the 2002 games, which would take place in the United States and which held the possibility of massive North American ratings and media attention. But the league badly wanted to get to Nagano, if only as a test run before the truly big show.

Hockey fans watched the drama unfold through much of 1995. In early October, the announcement came: The NHL was indeed going to Nagano. Bettman had managed to successfully herd all the cats, and for the first time, the league would be sending its very best to the Olympic Games.

The idea of an international best-on-best competition was certainly not a new one. While fans had never seen teams full of NHL professionals compete for gold medals at the Olympics, the league already had a long history of pitting its top players against the world.

The most famous such contest remains the first. In 1972, word spread to Canada that the Soviet federation was interested in a challenge series pitting the world's two top hockey nations against each other. Negotiations followed—with players' union head Alan Eagleson quickly emerging as the main force in getting a deal done—and plans were put in place for an eight-game Summit Series* to be held in September. The showdown would feature the Soviet national team facing an all-star roster of Canadian NHLers. That "NHL" part turned out to be important—as part of the ongoing feud with the World Hockey Association, that league's players were ruled ineligible, meaning top Canadian stars like Gerry Cheevers, Derek Sanderson and (most notably) Bobby Hull couldn't be named to the team. Meanwhile, Bobby Orr was unable to play due to injury, leaving Canada without its best player.

All the same, North American fans expected Canada to easily win or even sweep the series. Predictions of a mismatch faded quickly after game one, a stunning 7–3 Soviet win in Montreal. Team Canada rebounded in Toronto to take the next meeting, but the two teams tied in the third game, and a subsequent 5–3 win by the Soviets gave them a 2–1–1 series lead. That loss ended with the Canadians being booed off the ice by Vancouver fans, and some players lashed out at the lack of support, including an emotional Phil Esposito. With a two-week break as the series headed to the USSR for its second half, Team Canada played exhibition games in Sweden while Canadians from coast to coast panicked over what was shaping up as a potential embarrassment, if not an outright disaster.

Game five started off on a light note, with Esposito taking a pregame pratfall before recovering with a dramatic bow, but ended with another Soviet victory. Game six featured a Canadian win, as well as a controversial moment when Bobby Clarke slashed Valeri Kharlamov in what appeared to be a premeditated attempt to injure the Soviet star.** Canada added another win in the seventh game, tying the series and setting up a winner-take-all finale.

---

* To be technical, while we remember it as "The Summit Series" today, it wasn't actually called that at the time.

** In a 1973 *Sports Illustrated* piece, Clarke comes close to admitting as much. "I realized immediately that someone had to do something about him," Clarke says. "It's not something I was really proud of, but I honestly can't say I was ashamed to do it."

That eighth game would go on to become one of the most memorable in hockey history. The Soviets led 5–3 in the third period, but Canada pushed back to tie the game. Yvan Cournoyer's tying goal nearly sparked a riot; when the goal judge didn't initially signal a score, Eagleson made an attempt to reach the timer's bench. Soviet police got involved, with Canadian players coming to Eagleson's defence and eventually leading him across the ice to the safety of the bench. With the game still tied and the Soviets preparing to claim a series victory based on goal differential, Paul Henderson snuck the puck past Vladislav Tretiak with thirty-four seconds left on the clock. That goal, famously called by Foster Hewitt, was witnessed live by millions across Canada and still stands as perhaps the most significant sporting moment in the country's history.

Team Canada won the series, but the Soviets had served notice that the battle for international hockey supremacy was not a one-country competition. And hockey fans were hooked. The next step would be to build on the success of 1972 with a regular event, this one featuring even more teams.

The Canada Cup would be a new event organized by Eagleson and the NHL (with support from the IIHF). Unlike the two-team Summit Series, it would be a multination tournament featuring a round-robin and a playoff round. The inaugural edition came in 1976 and featured six teams: Canada, the Soviet Union, the United States, Finland, Sweden and Czechoslovakia. The tournament was a success, even though the expected rematch between the Soviets and Canadians didn't materialize; instead, Canada faced Czechoslovakia in the final. The Canadians swept the best-of-three series, highlighted by Darryl Sittler's fake-shot overtime winner to end the tournament. Bobby Orr was named MVP in what ended up being the only best-on-best international experience of his career.

The tournament returned in 1981, and this time it delivered the Canada-Soviet meeting fans had hoped for in a one-game final. But it was an anticlimactic finish, one that saw the Soviets embarrass the Canadians with an 8–1 blowout win. Canada would gain a measure of revenge over their rivals in 1984, although it came in the tournament semifinal; a rare Paul Coffey defensive gem broke up a Soviet two-on-one in overtime, and Canada scored the winner seconds later. They'd go on to sweep Team Sweden in the best-of-three final.

The tournament's best year came in 1987, when Canada and the Soviets met in the three-game final. It was the first multigame series between the two nations' best players since 1972, and what resulted was arguably the greatest display of international hockey ever seen. The teams split the opening two games, with each winning 6–5 in overtime, before Wayne Gretzky's set-up of Mario Lemieux for the winner with just over a minute left in the deciding game delivered the most iconic moment in Canadian hockey since Paul Henderson's series winner.

By the 1991 tournament, political upheaval was spelling the end of the Soviet powerhouse. Instead, fans got a preview of what would become the sport's new dominant rivalry, with the first-ever meeting between Canada and the United States in the final of a best-on-best tournament. The Canadians swept the meeting, earning their third straight Canada Cup win.

Though Canada was dominating the Canada Cup tournament by the early '90s, the nation hadn't had much luck at the Olympics. The Winter Games were still the domain of the Soviets, who captured gold in seven of the nine tournaments from 1956 to 1988. The other two gold medals went to the Americans, who won in 1960 and then again in the infamous Miracle on Ice in 1980.

The Soviets captured a final gold medal in 1992, although they did it as the "Unified Team" due to the fall of the Soviet Union. By then, the Olympics had let in professionals, although the NHL still steadfastly refused to allow any active players to participate.* That meant the best that North American fans could hope for was the occasional sight of big-league

---

* That included future Hall of Famer Glenn Anderson, who tried to get special permission to play for Team Canada in the 1994 tournament and even negotiated an escape clause in his contract with the Toronto Maple Leafs. Despite pressure from Canadian fans that included a cross-country petition, the NHL refused to honour the clause and Anderson wasn't allowed to play.

holdouts like Sean Burke, Eric Lindros and Petr Nedved in Olympic action.

In another development that presaged Nagano, the Olympic tournament added the shootout to decide deadlocked elimination games. The first came in Albertville, France, in 1992, with Canada narrowly edging an underdog German team in the quarter-finals. That would be overshadowed two years later, when Canada and Sweden went to a shootout in the gold-medal game. Future NHL star Peter Forsberg's highlight-reel winner landed him on a Swedish postage stamp and delivered gold for the Tre Kronor.

That would end up being the last gold-medal game played without NHL participation for over two decades. But before the league could get to Nagano, there was one more tournament on the schedule. By 1996, the Canada Cup had been rechristened the World Cup, and the tournament delivered a rematch of the 1991 final between Canada and the US. This time, it was the Americans who took home the title, fighting back to win the last two games of the final in Montreal.

From the NHL's perspective, it was just about the perfect result. After years of straggling behind the world's top hockey programmes, the Americans had finally won a best-on-best tournament. And with a reasonably young roster built around stars like Brett Hull, Brian Leetch and Jeremy Roenick, they looked like a team that could hold on to top spot for a while. For a league that was struggling to maintain a place in American sports headlines, a matchup between Team USA and Canada in the World Cup was good; that same matchup in the Olympics could be a gold mine.

And so, heading to Nagano for its Olympic debut, the league was dead set on putting its best foot forward in front of the world.

The first sign of trouble for Team USA at the Nagano Games came almost immediately, with a disappointing 4–2 loss to Sweden on their tournament's first day.* They followed that with a victory over Belarus, their

---

* A preliminary round had begun days earlier, but the major nations didn't play until the tournament's second week.

group's weakest entry, but dropped a 4–1 decision to Canada to end the round-robin with just a single win.

Team USA's poor showing in the early going wasn't in itself a disaster, since all eight teams made the playoff round. But it served up a tough quarter-final matchup with the Czechs. On paper, the Americans were the better team, and they looked like it, dominating stretches of play while outshooting their opponents 39–18. But Czech goalie Dominik Hasek was fantastic, leading his team to a 4–1 win. It wouldn't be the last game he'd steal.

And just like that, Team USA was done before the medal round. To make matters worse, members of the team trashed their rooms in the Olympic village on the way out. The incident came amid rumours that American players were keeping late hours and making regular appearances at local bars. It all added up to a black eye for the American programme and the NHL, with Bettman trotted out to explain that "such conduct is unacceptable and will not be tolerated."

With one half of its North American contingent humiliated, the league then watched Team Canada fall to Hasek and the Czechs in the semifinals. That game came down to the dreaded shootout, one in which Canadian coach Marc Crawford notoriously left Wayne Gretzky on the bench while sending out defenceman Ray Bourque to take a shot. It may not have mattered; a fantasy lineup of Gretzky, Gordie Howe, Rocket Richard, Bobby Orr and Mario Lemieux might not have been able to beat Hasek that night. A dispirited Canadian squad would go on to lose the bronze-medal game to Finland, returning home without any hardware.

Hasek's performance sent the Czechs through to a gold-medal show-down with a depleted Team Russia, which had made a surprising run despite the refusal of several key players to play for the team. Hasek was unbeatable yet again, and Petr Svoboda's lone goal stood up in a Czech win.

While the Czechs made for an inspiring Olympic underdog story, for the NHL the results were just about the worst-case scenario. The two North American teams had been held off the podium, and a gold-medal opportunity to showcase all that the sport had to offer had instead delivered a dreary 1–0 snoozer. But there were bright spots to be found: The logistics had worked, and the response from players and fans was positive.

The league quickly confirmed its commitment to the 2002 Games in Salt Lake City.

And sure enough, that tournament served up the league's dream matchup: Canada against the US in the Olympic final. The two teams delivered an entertaining game, with Canada earning its first gold medal in fifty years with a 5–2 win. The game set ratings records in Canada, and was the most-watched hockey game in the US since the Miracle on Ice.

The 2002 Games marked a turning point for Canadian hockey. After the disappointments of 1996 and 1998, the country was back on top of the international hockey world. It would stay there in 2004, winning gold in the World Cup's return. Team Sweden won the 2006 Olympic tournament, but Canada reclaimed top spot in 2010 with Sidney Crosby's "Golden Goal" in overtime against the Americans. They'd win again in 2014, as well as at the 2016 World Cup.

This is where the international story gets a little bit murky.

In 2016, with fans already looking ahead to the 2018 games in Pyeongchang, South Korea, word began to spread that the NHL's participation was no sure thing. At first, most fans dismissed the reports—the NHL had been going to the Olympics for a generation; surely it was only bluffing in the hope of getting a better deal.

It wasn't. Early in 2017, Bettman announced that the league wouldn't be taking part in the 2018 Games. The explanation was that the league no longer saw the Olympics as worth the disruption to its schedule. Fans were frustrated, and players were furious—both at Bettman and at their own union for failing to lock Olympic participation into the latest collective-bargaining agreement.

Despite the abrupt ending, there are indications that the league's Olympic absence may be temporary. The 2022 Olympics are scheduled to be held in China, a market the NHL has long had its eye on. Nobody would be surprised to see the sudden concern with schedule disruptions evaporate in time for NHL players to return in 2022.

But for now, the NHL's Olympic story is over. Whether there's a "To be continued . . . " appended to the finale remains to be seen.

THE CASE OF THE DISAPPEARING CANADA CUP

We said you won it; we never said you could keep it

THE 1981 CANADA CUP FINAL REMAINS THE MOST LOPSIDED championship game in major international hockey history. After a scoreless first period, the Soviets jumped out to a 3–1 lead after two periods, then pummelled goaltender Mike Liut and Team Canada with five unanswered goals in the third to take home the trophy.

Well, to *win* the trophy, anyway. Take home? Not so much.

At the end of the game, Alan Eagleson and Canadian prime minister Pierre Trudeau appeared on the ice to present the victorious Soviet team with the Canada Cup trophy. The Soviet players made the (fairly reasonable) assumption that the Cup was theirs to keep, at least until the next tournament. Not so fast, Eagleson decided. Apparently, the trophy was meant to remain in Canada (a detail that hadn't come up in 1976, since Canada had won). After the presentation, Eagleson set out to get the Cup back, claiming that "it belongs to the people of Canada and it's staying here." He enlisted the help of local police to reclaim it from the equipment bag the Soviets had stuffed it into.*

Even among the most diehard Canadian supporters, Eagleson's move reeked of poor sportsmanship. One such fan, a Winnipeg trucking company owner named George Smith, decided to do something about it. Upset over the controversy—as well as Eagleson's claim that Winnipeg fans were cheap because they hadn't sold out one of the tournament's games—Smith kicked

---

* This all apparently happened as the Soviets tried to leave the rink, although in some of the more dramatic versions of the story, the confrontation takes place at the airport as they're preparing to board their flight home.

off a media campaign encouraging Canadians to donate one dollar each to fund a replacement trophy. "We have the dignity of Canada to live up to," Smith explained, and apparently he wasn't the only one who felt that way. His campaign ended up raising thirty-two thousand dollars from around the country, and according to a 2011 *Toronto Sun* article, that total included twenty dollars from a player agent that was accompanied by a note reading, "Screw Eagleson."

That was more than enough to create a realistic replica, but word got back to Eagleson, who wasn't having any of it. He threatened to sic the Mounties on Smith and seize the replacement trophy. Eventually, cooler heads prevailed, and Smith presented the replica to Soviet officials at the country's embassy in Ottawa.

20

SOUTHERN COMFORT

*Relocation and expansion return as the
league's landscape shifts farther south*

THE SECOND HALF OF THE 1990S WAS NOT A GREAT TIME
to be a Canadian hockey fan.

When the country wasn't busy panicking about losing international
tournaments, it was panicking about losing its grip on the NHL. The
percentage of Canadian players had continued to drop as European stars
flooded the league and the American development programme started to
pay dividends. By the late '90s, the league's Canadian content was drifting
down towards the 50-percent mark.

But there was a bigger problem for cranky Canadian fans: The country
was losing its teams.

The first blow came in 1995, when the Quebec Nordiques packed up
for Colorado. The move itself was hardly unexpected; the Nordiques
had struggled at the gate for years, and it was becoming apparent
that the market was going to face enormous challenges in a modern
NHL landscape. (Three straight years of last-place finishes earlier in
the decade hadn't helped.) Team ownership had lobbied for public
funds for a new arena, but the cash-strapped Quebec government had
balked, instead offering financial aid to temporarily boost the team's
bottom line. After a Save the Nordiques rally was held in Quebec City,
Maclean's magazine reported that only three hundred fans bothered to
show up.

But while the move wasn't a surprise, it was still a shock to the system for Canadian hockey fans. They were used to seeing American teams come and go, but the Nordiques were the first Canadian franchise to fail since the Montreal Maroons more than a half century before.

They wouldn't be the last. Even as the Nordiques were finalizing their move to the US, it seemed as if the Winnipeg Jets would be joining them. The Jets were facing many of the same issues, including a small market, an old arena and a government that was reluctant to offer much help. By 1995, owner Barry Shenkarow was ready to sell. Despite Bettman's attempts to assure Winnipeg fans that he was on their side—a message he delivered in person after reportedly arriving in the city under police escort—it was becoming clear that the franchise needed a miracle.

And so, fans tried to give it one. Jets supporters organized a drive to raise enough money to buy the team themselves, with locals selling personal items and writing cheques in an effort to reach the $110 million it would take to keep the team in town. Local businesses chipped in too, and the CBC even found a strip club where dancers were donating a night's tips to the cause.

The effort was inspiring. It was also futile. Bettman's tone changed, and he told fans that "there's realities of business that can't be ignored." That didn't go over especially well in Canada. A *Globe and Mail* editorial accused Bettman of that hockey favourite, "crocodile tears," and of offering up assurances for small-market teams that "were largely hot air." Unlike the Nordiques, the Jets would make it to the 1995–96 season opener, if barely. The writing was on the wall, and by January the league had approved the team's sale and relocation to Arizona.

Quebec and Winnipeg weren't the first franchise relocations of the Bettman era—the Minnesota North Stars had already moved to Dallas, and the Hartford Whalers packed up for Carolina shortly after. But as far as Canadian fans were concerned, the pattern was clear. In less than one year, the country had seen a quarter of its NHL teams move to the United States.

Even as the league struggled to keep its existing teams in place, the lure of new markets had launched another wave of expansion talk. By 1997, there was reported interest from eleven different groups, including three from Houston. Two of those Houston bids were eliminated, and the league also dutifully performed the traditional rejection of a bid from Hamilton, Ontario.

There was also a bizarre long-shot bid by Hampton Roads, Virginia. While the market was tiny in comparison to other contenders, it had a potential owner in George Shinn, owner of the NBA's Charlotte Hornets, as well as plans for a new arena. It had a name—the Rhinos—and a proposed colour scheme of teal and purple. There was even a mascot: a hockey-playing rhinoceros named Rhockey. It was all enough to get the proponents in the door to make a presentation to the NHL that was apparently well received, but the bid was eventually eliminated before things got serious.

The league soon narrowed its list down to six potential targets: Nashville, Atlanta, Columbus, Oklahoma City, St. Paul and the one remaining Houston group. On June 25, 1997, the league made its decision, announcing an ambitious plan to add four new teams by the year 2000.*

First up: Nashville. The city had been on the league's radar for years and had come close to landing a team in 1995, when it seemed like the New Jersey Devils were on the move. There was plenty of smoke to that fire, including a Bettman letter to a New Jersey newspaper in which he made it clear that the team couldn't continue without a new arena. Despite actually being reported as a done deal by a New York radio station, that move never came to pass. Neither did rumours linking Nashville with struggling teams like the Whalers and Florida Panthers.

This time out, the league was ready to award an expansion franchise to owner Craig Leipold. Nashville already had a state-of-the-art arena, and while it certainly wasn't what you'd consider a traditional hockey market, it seemed eager to embrace the sport. The league granted Leipold a franchise for the 1998–99 season, conditional on the team hitting a season-ticket target. It did, and the Predators were born.

---

*   Coincidentally, the news came on the thirty-second anniversary of the announcement of the six-team expansion announcement back in 1965.

The next choice was somewhat controversial, as it saw the league return to a market that had already failed once: Atlanta. But that debacle was nearly two decades in the rear-view mirror, and now the city was the largest TV market in the country without an NHL team. With a new arena on the way, Atlanta had been viewed as a sure thing, and the league granted the city a franchise beginning in the 1999–2000 season.

Also joining the league that year would be Columbus. The market had never had a major pro sports team, and its residents had voted down a proposal to use public funds for an arena. But the ownership group stepped up with private money, and that was good enough for a league that was anxious to return to Ohio—a state that boasts three of the top forty TV markets in the US—after the brief but disastrous foray into Cleveland in the '70s.

The final team was awarded to St. Paul, and would begin play in the 2000–01 season, bringing hockey back to Minnesota less than a decade after the departure of the North Stars. The market itself was a fantastic one for hockey, with a thriving amateur scene and a dedicated fan base. The NHL's economics had been the issue back in 1993, and there was at least some concern over whether all that much had changed in the intervening four years. The Minneapolis *Star Tribune* ran an analysis that reckoned the new team would need to draw seventeen thousand fans a game to make a decent profit and concluded that "this is risky business." As it turned out, the team averaged more than eighteen thousand at the new Xcel Energy Center right out of the gate.

While a return to Minnesota may have represented a risk, at least it was a bona fide hockey market. The rest of the league's choices left traditionalists scratching their heads. Atlanta? Columbus? Nashville, of all places? And all this while existing teams were moving to Colorado, Texas, North Carolina and even Arizona?

Less than a decade after Wayne Gretzky headed to Los Angeles, the NHL's map had been completely redrawn. And not everyone was happy about it. As far as Canadian fans were concerned, the fix was in. Not only had the country failed to land a new team, but it hadn't come especially close. In fact, the league seemed to be trying to get as far away from Canada as possible.

It was an outrage. And it wasn't hard to figure out who to blame: Gary Bettman. If the commissioner was criticized in Canadian media—and he was—it paled in comparison to the hammering he took around the country's water coolers and in its sports bars. Why was this basketball-loving lawyer from New York so hell-bent on ripping the national game away from its home and native land?

It's worth pausing here to ask whether that reputation was warranted. Did Bettman really hate Canada and want to shift as much of the league as possible down south?

There's little question that the expansion and franchise relocations of the Bettman era have been focused almost entirely on growing the league's American footprint. But that hardly seems unreasonable—the league needed to grow, and the United States was the obvious place to do it. Bettman had arrived with hopes of securing a major American TV contract, but had initially been forced to settle for a discounted deal with Fox. Having more markets to offer a potential TV partner seemed like a solid strategy.

But that didn't necessarily have to come at the expense of the existing teams. Bettman didn't do much to save either the Nordiques or the Jets, and by the end he even seemed to be nudging them out the door. There's an argument to be had about whether there was anything he realistically *could* have done, though—remember, he'd only been on the job since 1993 and both franchises were already struggling badly by then. But Canadian fans might have liked to see him at least pretend to be disappointed.

On the other hand, it's easy to forget that the Jets and Nordiques weren't the only Canadian teams on life support during Bettman's first decade. In 1997, Peter Pocklington once again found himself facing hard choices in Edmonton, and this time he didn't have a generational talent he could sell off for cash. He put the team up for sale, with most reports assuming they'd become the next NHL franchise on the move and some suggesting they might head to Nashville, freeing up an expansion slot that would then be handed over to Houston. Later, Pocklington was on the verge of selling the team directly to a Houston group headed by Les Alexander, the owner of the NBA's Rockets. But in the spring of 1998, local investors stepped forward and the city agreed to a sweetheart deal on the Oilers' arena lease; the board of governors approved, Pocklington washed his hands of the team and the Oilers stayed in Edmonton.

The Ottawa Senators found themselves bankrupt early in 2003. Despite sitting in first place in the standings, at one point the team failed to make its payroll. They weren't alone in those pre-lockout days—the Pittsburgh Penguins had gone bankrupt in 1998, and the Buffalo Sabres followed the Senators in 2003—but they seemed like a strong candidate to pack up and head south. Instead, Bettman found an owner in Eugene Melnyk who'd keep the team in town.

How much credit does the commissioner deserve for keeping the Oilers and Senators in Canada? Your mileage may vary. Some would point out that the league didn't want teams moving in the middle of the 1998 expansion process, and that nobody in their right mind was looking to relocate a team in 2003 with labour Armageddon looming. But the point remains that if Bettman really was the anti-Canadian villain he's often made out to be, he could have done an awful lot worse.

By opening night of the 2000–01 season, the NHL was a thirty-team league, with 80 percent of its franchises located in the United States. There were more teams in California than in Alberta or Ontario, more in Florida than in Quebec, and more in relatively new southern US markets than in all of Canada combined. Four northern-based teams had moved south on Bettman's watch, and six of the nine expansion teams added in the decade had been in what could euphemistically be called "non-traditional" markets.

Whether fans liked it or not, the NHL's map had been redrawn. Now the league just had to figure out a way to make it all work.

WHEN COMPENSATION GOES BAD

How an unfortunate loophole led to the Mark Messier era in San Jose

AS THE NEW CENTURY DAWNED, GARY BETTMAN AND THE
league's leadership had plenty to keep them busy. They'd just added four new
franchises, scoring was plummeting, small-market teams were struggling and
the skate-in-the-crease rule had just spoiled their Stanley Cup final. What's
more, battle lines were already being drawn for what was shaping up as an
ugly labour war when the collective-bargaining agreement expired. Everyone
had a lot on their minds.

So, when it came to implementing new ideas, you could understand if they
were just a little bit distracted and not exactly attuned to some of the finer details.

One of those new ideas involved unrestricted free agency. For years, big-
market teams had been picking on their smaller brethren, raiding them for talent
every summer. The league couldn't do much about that, at least until the CBA
expired, but they could at least try to help out those small-market have-nots. So,
the league decided to offer compensatory draft picks to teams that lost UFAs.
Those picks would be based on market size, with struggling teams eligible for
picks as high as the second and third round each time they lost a free agent. It
was a good rule, one that helped even the playing field just a little bit.

There was just one problem, and you may have already spotted it. Nowhere
in the rule did it say anything about the free agent having to have actually
played for the small-market team. He just had to be on the team's roster when
he became a free agent. Eventually, teams figured that out. And when they
did, they started making really weird trades.

The deals went like this: Days—or even hours—before the free-agency
period started, a big-market team with a star UFA would trade him to a smaller
market in exchange for a draft pick. The smaller-market team would let the

player become a free agent and sign elsewhere, at which point it would get a better draft pick from the league as compensation.

The trades were a win-win for both teams. And to make things even sillier, the star free agent would often turn around and re-sign with the big-market team that had just traded him away.

The first major trade to exploit the loophole came on June 29, 2002, when the Dallas Stars sent Ed Belfour to Nashville for a fifth-round pick. The Predators had no interest in actually acquiring Belfour's services, but when he signed with Toronto days later, they got a second-round pick from the league.

The Leafs and Predators hooked up on a similar deal later that year. Tie Domi was sent to Nashville for twenty-four hours, at which point he re-signed in Toronto and the Predators got a free fourth-rounder. The Leafs also sent Curtis Joseph to the Calgary Flames, while the New York Rangers rented Mike Richter to the Oilers. Yes, Mike Richter, who you may remember as playing his entire career with the Rangers, was actually an Edmonton Oiler for a day.

The Rangers did it again in 2003, trading Brian Leetch to the Oilers and Mark Messier to the Sharks. Both players re-signed in New York shortly after, and the trades were largely forgotten. But the Messier deal turned out to be important. The Sharks got a third-round pick from the league, which ended up in the hands of the Vancouver Canucks, who selected Alex Edler. And the Rangers got a fourth-round pick from San Jose, which they used on future captain Ryan Callahan.

But with all due respect to Callahan and Edler, no team emerged as a bigger winner from this whole sham than the team that started it all. Remember that second-round pick the Predators got from the NHL for "losing" Belfour? It ended up being the forty-ninth-overall pick of the 2003 draft. And there, nestled in between the selections of Dmitri Chernykh and Ivan Baranka, the Predators used their freebie on a hard-shooting defenceman named Shea Weber. He turned out to be pretty good.

The 2003 off-season saw the end of the shenanigans; the 2004 lockout and resulting CBA closed the loophole once and for all. But Predators fans still remember it fondly. And maybe somewhere out there, some fan in a Sharks jersey with Number 11 and MESSIER on the back does too.

21

A HISTORY OF VIOLENCE

The debate that's defined a league

THE HIT CAME LATE IN THE SECOND PERIOD, WITH THE Vancouver Canucks and Colorado Avalanche locked in a scoreless tie. It was February 2004, and the game was a showdown between the two best teams in the Northwest Division. But if you happened to be just tuning in at the thirty-nine-minute mark, you hadn't missed much.

That changed with the bounce of a puck between two oncoming players in the neutral zone. Vancouver's Markus Naslund, the team's captain and one of the league's leading scorers, reached out to poke it ahead. Colorado's Steve Moore all but ignored it, instead targeting Naslund for an open-ice hit. The Canucks star saw the impact coming and leaned back to try to avoid it. That evasive action turned what could have been a major collision into more of a glancing blow, but it was a blow that saw Moore catch Naslund in the head as he flew by. The impact twisted Naslund's body and resulted in his face bouncing off the ice; he was cut over the eye and suffered a concussion.

Some saw an elbow, one that was targeting a vulnerable opponent's head. Others saw a clean hit gone bad because an opponent bailed out rather than absorb the contact. The officials didn't see anything worth whistling, and no penalty was called on the play. Canucks coach Marc Crawford was furious, as he made clear after the game. "It just mystifies me why this happens in this league," a red-faced Crawford told reporters. "That was a cheap shot by a young kid on a captain—leading scorer in the league—and we get no call."

The Canucks ended up winning 1–0, but that hardly mattered. Naslund was hurt and would miss several games. And the injury had come at the hands of "a young kid," one who hadn't earned the right to throw that sort of hit, clean or otherwise, in the eyes of a veteran coach. Players and fans alike knew what that meant. Hockey is played by a code, and the code was clear in this case: Payback was required.

In its more than 100 years of existence, the NHL has evolved to the point where it would barely be recognizable to the men who played it back in 1917. The league has grown and shrunk and then grown again. Scoring rates have peaked and plummeted. The strategies, rules and record book have been written and rewritten.

But if there's been one constant, it's the debate over violence in the game. No other sport on the planet so seamlessly combines breathtaking grace with jaw-dropping brutality. And no other sport has generated as many arguments over how much violence is too much. From newspaper columns to talk radio to sports bars around the continent to Saturday night "Coach's Corner," the debate carries on, with no end in sight.

The sport's earliest days featured plenty of brawls and stick-swinging, and multiple players were killed in the chaos, including Alcide Laurin in 1905 and Owen McCourt in 1907. Years later, the fledgling NHL would recognize the need to clean up the game, although there was little in the way of agreement over what exactly that meant.

In those early years, it wasn't unusual for local police to get involved in games, occasionally even wading onto the ice to break up fights. In 1927, the Stanley Cup final between the Boston Bruins and Ottawa Senators featured an ugly brawl that the Montreal *Gazette* described as "a rowdy free-for-all which rivaled gang warfare at its worst." The fight saw Boston's Billy Coutu attack two officials, an action that led to him being the first (and so far only) NHL player ever handed a lifetime ban for an act of violence.*

If that ban was meant to send a strong message, it didn't seem to

---

* Coutu was officially reinstated in 1932, but never played in the NHL again.

resonate, even with Coutu's teammates; in 1931, Eddie Shore reportedly punched an official and was suspended for just one game. Two years later, Shore would be involved in a much more notorious incident when his hit from behind fractured the skull of Toronto star Ace Bailey. Shore would be suspended for sixteen games; Bailey never played again.* A benefit held for Bailey on February 14, 1934, would pave the way for the modern All-Star Game; that same night, the Maple Leafs made Bailey's number 6 the first ever to be retired by an NHL team.

The sport calmed somewhat as the years went on, but the league continued to generate headlines with occasional outbreaks of violence. The brawl that led to the Richard Riot would become the most notable of the Original Six era, but was far from the only case of things getting out of hand. And even the game's biggest stars weren't immune. In 1953, Montreal's Boom Boom Geoffrion was involved in a vicious stick-swinging match with New York Rangers rookie Ron Murphy. Geoffrion delivered a brutal overhand chop to the side of Murphy's face, then punctuated the moment with a José Bautista–like flip of his stick. Murphy was knocked out instantly, falling to the ice face-first, and wouldn't play again that season. Geoffrion was suspended for the team's remaining games against New York.

The attack was considered shockingly out of character for Geoffrion, a player rarely involved in acts of violence. The same couldn't be said for another 1950s star who found himself at the centre of an incident. Gordie Howe was already one of the league's most feared players by 1959. But it was the night of February 1 that year that sealed his reputation as perhaps the toughest player of all time. That was the evening Howe squared off with the league's reigning heavyweight champion, New York's Lou Fontinato. Howe decimated his opponent. As the *Ottawa Citizen* described it in an article subtly headlined HOWE NEW NHL BOXING CHAMPION, the Red Wings star had "let go with an uppercut that dislocated one of

---

* One widely repeated story, which even earned a mention on the Hockey Hall of Fame website, had Bailey's distraught father hopping on a train to Boston with a loaded gun, intending to find Shore and exact revenge, only to have Conn Smythe intercept him and slip sleeping pills into his drink.

Gordie's fingers and left the New Yorker's nose at a grotesque 45-degree angle."

For his part, Fontinato gave the new champ his due, telling reporters that Howe was "not bad, not bad at all." The media immediately looked ahead to a possible rematch a week later, but were disappointed when Fontinato was unable to play. An Associated Press report on "the return match" delivered the disappointing news that "Fontinato apparently still can't breathe properly, hardly surprising in view of the way the 200-pound Howe spread his 193-pound opponent's nose across his face."

The Howe-Fontinato match, and the hockey world's reaction to it, could stand as the poster child for the league's complicated relationship with on-ice violence. Here you had a player, badly injured by fisticuffs that had little to do with the game itself, and fans and media largely stood up and cheered. A little bit of blood was just part of the game, and as long as everyone involved in a scrap was a willing combatant, the rest of us were there to spur them on. Significant suspensions remained relatively rare; when Chicago's Reggie Fleming and Montreal's Gilles Tremblay engaged in a wild stick-swinging incident in 1962—"These were no fractional wedge swings, as in golf, but full driver swipes," reported the *Chicago Tribune*—they both received three-game suspensions and were sent on their way.

For better or worse, the league was comfortable with a certain level of brutality, and was even willing to promote a sense of danger. When the NHL was given a glossy write-up in *Life* magazine in 1968, readers were informed that the league was all about the opportunity to witness "brawny men, armed with clubs, collide in tests of their raw power."

"To stay in the pros," the article made clear, "the NHL player must surrender any conventional ideas he might have about his own personal safety."

That turned out to be truer than the magazine's editors could have imagined. The profile appeared in the February 2, 1968, edition. Days before the finished piece hit newsstands, Minnesota North Stars forward Bill Masterton suffered a head injury in a game against the Oakland Seals. The injury came on a hard but legal hit; like most of the era's players,

Masterton didn't wear a helmet, and he lost consciousness when his head struck the ice.

Masterton was removed from life support two days later, and he remains the only player in league history to die as the direct result of injuries suffered in a game. Today, the league's award for perseverance and dedication to hockey bears his name.

Throughout the league's early decades, the toughest players were often among the best. That made sense: If you were particularly skilled, you could expect to be targeted by the opposition, and you'd better know how to give as good as you got. Players like Geoffrion, Richard and (especially) Howe understood that, and they made sure that a message got around the league: Come after me at your own risk. As Leafs owner Conn Smythe famously put it, "If you can't beat 'em in the alley, you can't beat 'em on the ice."

But there was more than simple message-sending going on. When it came to fighting, every player knew that occasionally dropping the gloves was part of the game. And many of the same skills that made for a good player—size, strength and balance—also translated into the ability to defend oneself with the gloves off.[*]

As the Original Six era gave way to the 1970s, something began to change. Expansion and the WHA thinned the talent pool, and there was more room available on NHL rosters for specialists. That might mean a checking forward or a power-play quarterback. But it also began to mean a role that was euphemistically called the "enforcer," "tough guy" or "policeman." More straightforwardly, the '70s saw the dawn of the designated fighter.

Fontinato was the first player to ever top 200 penalty minutes, in 1955–56. Prior to the 1970s, only Howie Young in 1962–63 had ever topped 220. But by 1973–74, Philadelphia's Dave "The Hammer" Schultz had blown by the 300 PIM mark, finishing the season with 348. The next year, he finished with a ridiculous 472.

---

[*]   Just ask anyone who ever squared off with Larry Robinson.

The Hammer was the league's first five-star enforcer, and he was a key part of the Broad Street Bullies teams that won two straight titles. But he was far from the decade's only feared fighter. In 1975–76, five players finished with over 300 PIM. Names like Steve Durbano, Dave "Tiger" Williams and Dennis Polonich were giving Schultz a run for his money atop the penalty leaderboard. And if other teams were loading up with pugilists, well, your crew had better have a few of its own. The arms race was on.

In 1977, the Hollywood film *Slap Shot* hit the theatres, introducing the concept of "old-time hockey" to a whole new audience.* It was also the year that Boston's John Wensink became a local legend by challenging the entire North Stars bench after a fight. Two years later, Mike Milbury and the Bruins went into the MSG stands. Hockey's reputation as the sport of goons had been thoroughly established.

By contrast, the 1980s were hardly the most violent decade the NHL had served up. But those were the years when the brawl became an art form. The era of the specialized enforcer coincided with the advent of nightly sports shows and VHS tape trading to create an environment in which gloves flying made for great entertainment. Most teams of the day had at least a couple of enforcers, with more available in the minors if needed. The tough guys were typically both their teams' most maligned and most popular players. Often, they were also the smartest, the best at working the media and even the most active in the local community. A few of them could even play a little bit; heavyweight champ Bob Probert once scored twenty-nine goals and sixty-two points in the same 1987–88 season in which he led the league with 398 PIM. Others couldn't do much besides fight. To fans, it hardly mattered. The cult of the tough guy spread quickly.

But as it did, so too did calls for the NHL to get off its hands and do something. High-minded arguments in favour of reducing fighting (if not banning it from the game outright) became a common sight in sports pages. And it wasn't just the media who were insisting on a better way.

---

* In the film, Paul Newman's line about "old-time hockey" is meant to refer to playing the game the old-fashioned way—that is, with skill and honour. Instead, the term became synonymous with Hanson Brothers–style mayhem.

While many fans loved to cheer on a good scrap or five, others were put off by the constant brawling. And probably more importantly, league partners and TV executives whispered about how all the fighting was keeping the NHL from reaching its full potential.

It began to feel inevitable that eventually, somebody somewhere would go too far and the league would have to draw a line. That day came on May 14, 1987, with the Montreal Canadiens hosting the Philadelphia Flyers in game six of the Wales Conference final. The Flyers were looking to end the series and head to the Stanley Cup final against the Oilers, so it was a big game. Except they didn't even make it to the opening faceoff before the trouble started. The two teams went at it during the pregame warm-up.

As is often the case, it all started with Claude Lemieux. The Canadiens winger had a habit of ending the warm-up by shooting a puck into the opposing net. The Flyers, for whatever reason, decided that was unacceptable and sent backup goalie Chico Resch and tough guy Ed Hospodar out to guard their crease. The Canadiens responded by having Shayne Corson serve as Lemieux's bodyguard. A waiting game ensued, and when the two Flyers finally gave up and left, Corson and Lemieux made their way down to the Flyers' zone. But Hospodar and Resch jumped back onto the ice, and the chase was on. Soon, so was the brawl.

The outbreak wasn't exactly a surprise—according to legend, Flyers coach Mike Keenan had dressed extra players for the warm-up because he suspected a brawl—but the NHL's reaction was. After watching the two teams fight for fifteen minutes, the league sent everyone off the ice to get cleaned up, and then started the game without issuing any penalties. It was as if the melee had never happened.

But it had, and the league eventually responded with a key rule change. That summer, it introduced a mandatory ten-game suspension for the first player to leave the bench for the purpose of fighting. For all intents and purposes, the rule spelled the end of the NHL's days of all-out war.[*]

---

[*] This punch-up is not to be confused with another unforgettable Flyers-Canadiens playoff brawl, the one that saw Ron Hextall skate out of his crease to jump Chris Chelios. That one came in 1989 and, owing in part to the new rule, nobody came off the bench to join in the fun.

Fighting was still common, though, and the league's reaction to it remained complicated. On the one hand, by the early '90s there was a growing push to eliminate fighting altogether, and it came from an unlikely source: Bruins president Harry Sinden. The Big Bad Bruins had never been shrinking violets—this was the team of Terry O'Reilly and Don Cherry and Cam Neely—but Sinden felt that the league would never reach beyond niche status if bare-knuckle bouts were part of the show, and he wasn't alone. Meanwhile, others, like Vancouver's Pat Quinn, subscribed to the theory that the threat of violence actually made the game safer, and that the enforcers were integral to keeping the peace. "You have to let the policemen do their jobs, so the game can run in a good and fluid fashion," Quinn said in 1994. "In the old days, if a guy tried to take a knee out, he'd have a stick in the nose the next time around."

The league never seemed all that close to actually banning fighting, although the instigator rule, which saw harsher penalties for the player starting a scrap, was introduced and later strengthened. But even as the NHL inched towards a less violent on-ice product, the mayhem was being marketed heavily elsewhere. From VHS tapes to video games,* fans could purchase products packed with violence, and fights dominated the nightly highlight reels.

The blows weren't even limited to player versus player. In 1991, Kings coach Tom Webster was suspended four games for throwing a punch at Calgary's Doug Gilmour; later that same year, Webster was handed a twelve-game ban for throwing a stick at referee Kerry Fraser. In 1989, a Boston fan jumped on the ice and was smoked into the boards by linesman Ron Asselstine. In 1992, a Nordiques fan did the same, and this time Buffalo tough guy Rob Ray leaned over the bench and pummelled him.

The sport's conflicted view of fighting was driven home in 1992. In February, Probert suffered a rare loss at the hands of young Rangers tough guy Tie Domi. Never one to shy away from a headline, Domi

---

* One example of the league's mixed messaging: It pushed for fighting to be removed from the popular EA Sports series of NHL video games in 1993, much to the outrage of the title's fans. Within a few years, the fights were back—and often marketed as a selling point.

skated off the ice, making a gesture that mimed strapping on a champion-ship belt in front of a roaring MSG crowd. The two teams didn't meet again until December, but in the lead-up to that contest the possibility of a rematch generated headlines around the league. One wire service ran a "tale of the tape" that included sections for each player's reach, best punch and current record, and the New York media described the game as the hottest ticket in town.

Domi and Probert dropped the gloves just over a minute into the game, with the Red Wings enforcer earning the decision and regaining his title. NHL president Gil Stein was reportedly furious, and he consid-ered suspending both players before ultimately settling on fines. Predictably, the media roared. Probert and Domi should "meet over a two-day series of elimination bouts," *The New York Times* sarcastically suggested. "Sell tickets. Sell it to television. Give the winner a trophy like the Stanley Cup. Call it the 'Stein Stein.'" Meanwhile, fans checked their schedules to see when Probert and Domi would cross paths again.

Any hope (or fear) that Gary Bettman would put an NBA-inspired end to the fisticuffs vanished quickly. Instead, the new commissioner focused his attention on dropping the hammer on over-the-top attempts to injure, and he was given an early opportunity to put the league on notice when Washington's Dale Hunter blindsided Pierre Turgeon after a goal during game six of the 1993 Patrick Division semifinal. Bettman reacted with a twenty-one-game suspension, then the longest in the league's modern history, and was widely lauded for it—"Goonery is extinct," enthused *Toronto Star* columnist Jim Proudfoot.

Hunter wouldn't be the last to feel Bettman's wrath. Marty McSorley was suspended for the rest of the season after slashing Donald Brashear in the head in February 2000, a sentence the commissioner later extended into the following season. Given the veteran McSorley's age, it amounted to an unofficial lifetime ban.

But when it came to fighting, Bettman seemed content to accept the status quo. Bench-clearing brawls were a thing of the past, but one-on-one battles remained common, and the occasional line brawl was par for the course. On March 4, 2004, the Flyers and Senators engaged in a cascading series of altercations that established a new league record for penalty minutes in a game. It seemed like it would only be a matter of time until some other game went nuclear and the record was broken. Instead, the league turned out to be just four days from the moment that would change everything.

The code said that Steve Moore had to fight a Canuck.

It didn't matter whether he wanted to or not. It didn't even matter whether his hit on Markus Naslund was clean. Vancouver's best player had been hurt, the Canucks wanted revenge and Moore was honour bound to give them a shot. This was how the sport worked.

And so, on March 8, 2004, in the first game between the two teams in Vancouver since the hit,* Moore did his duty. Six minutes into the opening frame, he dropped the gloves with Vancouver's Matt Cooke. It was the first fight of Moore's career, but he held his own against the more experienced Cooke, earning a draw, if not an outright victory.

The Avalanche seemed to get a lift from seeing their teammate honour the code, scoring seconds after the fight and eventually pumping home five goals by the end of the period. In theory, that should have been the end of it. But the Canucks weren't satisfied, and if Cooke couldn't get the job done, someone else would have to take his shot.

That someone ended up being Todd Bertuzzi, and the shot he took would change the sport.

Midway through the third period, with the Avs leading 8–2, Bertuzzi challenged Moore. When his invitation was declined, the Canucks winger stalked his opponent down the ice before delivering a sucker punch from behind to the side of Moore's head. Moore collapsed to the ice, with Bertuzzi falling directly on top of him. Players from both teams rushed to join the pile.

Initially, the crowd cheered what seemed like it would be a typical line brawl between rivals. But it quickly became apparent that something had

---

* The Canucks and Avalanche had played on March 3 in Colorado with Bettman in attendance. The game went off without incident.

gone terribly wrong; Moore lay on the ice, not moving, as trainers rushed to his side. He'd suffered three fractured vertebrae and a concussion, and he would leave the ice on a stretcher. While we didn't know it at the time, Bertuzzi's attack had ended Moore's career.

It was the worst-case scenario for hockey's vaunted code—or close to it. Payback had been delivered, and this time it hadn't just resulted in a black eye or some wounded pride. A twenty-five-year-old's career had been ended by a blow he never saw coming. And while Bertuzzi was vilified around the world for the sucker punch, the ugly truth was that he hadn't done anything all that different from what Schultz or Probert or Domi would have been expected to do in the same situation. It was probably inevitable that a scene like this would play out someday, and maybe we were lucky that the fallout wasn't even worse. The league reacted quickly by suspending Bertuzzi for the season. British Columbia's attorney general charged him with assault that June, and Moore filed lawsuits against Bertuzzi in 2005 and 2006. But the impact spread far wider than two players or two teams. In the days and weeks after the incident, the hockey world seemed as though it had finally began to accept reality: We can't do this anymore.

Fighting didn't end in 2004, and there have been plenty of line brawls since. Many fans even defended Bertuzzi's actions at the time; some still do today. But the ideal of the noble enforcer who polices the game to keep it safe had been dealt a crushing blow.*

By the time the sport returned from the lockout in 2005, the ground was already shifting. Fighting in that season fell by nearly half from its 2003–04 rates. The game was faster, and the tough guys were having trouble keeping up. A new wave of analytics arrived, calling into question some of the long-held assumptions about an enforcer's impact on the game. Fans began to hear more about the effects of head injuries; terms like "he just got his bell rung" quickly began to sound like relics of a bygone era. The league eventually moved to outlaw certain types of hits

---

* Bertuzzi himself wasn't an enforcer—he'd been a first-team all-star the year before. But on that night, or at least that shift, that's exactly the role he was playing.

to the head, eliminating many of the open-ice collisions that had filled highlight reels over the years. And one by one, teams began to send their enforcers to the press box or the minors—and eventually to the unemployment line.

Hockey has always been a dangerous game, and with players getting bigger and faster every year, it will stay that way. The league still features hits and blood and the occasional fight; sometimes it even promotes them. But it's not the same as it once was. And for better or for worse, it's all but certain that we can't go back.

FROM THE CANOE TO THE BOXING RING

The long and winding search for an opponent
who could handle Dave Semenko

ON THE EDMONTON OILERS OF THE MID-'80S, EVERYONE had a role to play. Wayne Gretzky's job was to score. Mark Messier's job was to score. Paul Coffey, Glenn Anderson and Jari Kurri's jobs were to score. Grant Fuhr's job was to try to stop the puck often enough that the eight or nine goals everyone else scored would be enough.

And Dave Semenko's job was to destroy anyone who went near any of those other guys.

Semenko wasn't the most-feared fighter of his era; that honour would go to Bob Probert or, before him, someone like Dave Brown or Behn Wilson. But Semenko was the archetypal enforcer, the guy everyone thought of when the role was mentioned. You knew what you were getting with him. If you touched Gretzky, or even came close, you could expect a visit from Semenko. Chances were, he'd skate over, introduce himself with a smile and suggest that you might want to think about knocking it off before he had to end you. Or, as he'd occasionally phrase it: "Why don't you and me go for a little canoe ride?"

Nobody knew quite what that meant, but they knew it wasn't good, and few had any desire to find out much more. So, Semenko kept the peace. His very presence, the thinking went, was enough of a deterrent to give Gretzky and friends room to do their work.

Any time hockey fans talk about famed tough guys, the discussion inevitably turns to a single question: Who was their toughest opponent? That's always good fodder for a debate. Somebody will insist it was Probert, somebody else will back a more obscure pick, and the argument will end over beers and grainy YouTube clips.

In Semenko's case, the answer doesn't lead to much debate. That's because Dave Semenko once stepped into the ring with Muhammad Ali.

Literally.

In 1983, Semenko and Ali squared off in a boxing ring. It was a charity exhibition match,* but it wasn't purely theatre. Semenko trained for weeks to make sure he at least looked like he could hang in with the greatest of all time. The match took place in Edmonton, in front of a reported six thousand fans. Ali, who for some reason was accompanied to the ring by actor Jan-Michael Vincent, soaked up the cheers from the crowd while dodging most of Semenko's punches. The Oilers tough guy did land a few shots, and at one point Ali countered with a flurry that bloodied Semenko's nose. The bout ended after three rounds and was officially ruled a draw. That was being charitable to Semenko, but you have to give him credit for stepping into Ali's office at all.

Sadly, we never did get a rematch in a venue where Semenko would be more comfortable, like a hockey rink . . . or a canoe.

---

* The promoter was Larry Messier, Mark's uncle.

22

THE LEAGUE OF THE LOCKOUT

A decade after failing to implement a cap,
Bettman and the owners get their rematch

EVERYONE SAW IT COMING.

Almost from the moment the 1994–95 lockout ended, the possibility of another work stoppage loomed. Even as the collective-bargaining agreement was extended to help bring the league's players to the 1998 Olympics, it felt as though the two sides were simply kicking the can down the road. Except that this was no ordinary can—it was more like a time bomb, one that would eventually go off and leave behind something that only vaguely resembled the NHL that fans had come to know.

And so, in the years leading up to 2004, the league operated under a shadow. It was there through the bad times, like the bankruptcy of the Ottawa Senators and Buffalo Sabres—hold on just a little longer, guys, because a new financial landscape is on the way. It was there through the good times, like Joe Sakic passing the Stanley Cup to Ray Bourque at the end of the legend's final NHL game—nice moment, sure, but the days of teams like the Avalanche collecting superstars weren't going to last. It hung over every signing, every draft and every game. Something big was coming. We just didn't know quite what.

But Gary Bettman knew. And having learned some hard lessons in 1994, this time he wasn't taking no for an answer.

———

For the first four decades of its existence, the NHL hadn't had to worry much about work stoppages. Sure, there were the occasional wildcat strikes by disgruntled players, like the one that spelled the end of the Hamilton Tigers. But there wasn't the need to keep a players' union happy, because there wasn't an actual players' union. The league president and his owners set the rules, and the guys on the ice either accepted them or they found new jobs.

That changed in 1957, with the first attempt by the players to band together. The effort was driven by Detroit's Ted Lindsay, who argued that the owners weren't being forthcoming with information about player pensions and other key concerns. He met with Bob Feller, then the president of the Major League Baseball players' union, and began to spread the word to his fellow NHLers that it was time to get organized.

The creation of the National Hockey League Players' Association was officially announced in February of 1957, with Lindsay as the president and Doug Harvey as vice-president. At first, the players made it clear that they were generally happy with the state of the league and simply wanted to be treated as more equal partners. But the announcement still landed with a thud inside the executive boardrooms, where some owners felt blindsided that the players had actually gone through with it. The league pushed back, insisting that because the new union's members all had individual contracts, there was nothing to negotiate. Players were threatened with trades or demotions to the minors if they didn't break rank. The players refused to back down, threatening a multimillion-dollar lawsuit if the NHL followed through on its threats.

Eventually, the two sides found enough common ground that a decade of uneasy peace followed. But by 1967, the players were ready to push for more. They formed a second iteration of the NHLPA, this one led by player agent Alan Eagleson. Eagleson had already made a name for himself by negotiating Bobby Orr's first contract with the Bruins, getting the teenaged defenceman a reported seventy-thousand-dollar salary and a signing bonus, resetting the market for top prospects in the process.

Eagleson would go on to head the NHLPA for over two decades. Some players loved him, especially those for whom he negotiated rich new deals. Others grew to worry that he was too cozy with the owners. He became one of the most powerful men in the sport, most familiar to fans for his forays into international hockey. But with other agents pushing back, Eagleson's empire crumbled in 1989 when an audit revealed problems with the NHLPA's books. Players who had trusted Eagleson would come to find out that he'd worked against their interests; Orr would claim he was never told about a contract offer from the Boston Bruins that would have included an ownership stake, leading to his regrettable departure for the Chicago Black Hawks in 1976.

Eagleson was eventually convicted on fraud and embezzlement charges, and he spent time in prison. He was also forced out of his role as executive director of the NHLPA, with the players handing the reins over to his deputy, Bob Goodenow.

Early on, Goodenow drew rave reviews from players. Where Eagleson had been seen as too close to the owners, Goodenow was not, to put it mildly; he was also far more willing to share information and make sure the players understood the issues they faced. As *The Philadelphia Inquirer* wrote on March 8, 1992, "If the players in the NHL were to select a rookie of the year . . . it would probably be a guy who does his job in a jacket and tie. It would probably be Bob Goodenow."

By 1995, Goodenow had beaten Bettman in their first labour showdown. A decade later, it was time for round two.

With the league's CBA set to expire in September 2004, the owners and players held their first negotiations twenty months early. In January of 2003, the two sides met for the first time to see if there was any common ground to be found. The stakes had changed since the mid-'90s, but the faces hadn't—Bettman was still heading up the owners' side, while his nemesis, Goodenow, remained as the head of the NHLPA. To say the two men didn't like each other would be an understatement, and Goodenow had earned a reputation for being every bit as prickly as Bettman.

The goal was to forge a deal, not a lifelong friendship, but it quickly became apparent that having Bettman and Goodenow in the same room wasn't going to work. The two sides agreed to turn much of the early negotiations over to surrogates, with deputy director Ted Saskin representing the NHLPA and NHL vice-president Bill Daly doing much of the talking for the league. That proved effective, and while the process remained a ways away from any breakthroughs, the opposing sides seemed to be at least inching closer together as the winter wore on. But to have any progress, Bettman and Goodenow would have to be brought back into the discussions. The two adversaries would quickly torpedo any existing goodwill.

The key issue, as expected, was a salary cap—although the league tried very hard not to call it that. Various euphemisms were thrown at the wall, with Bettman eventually settling on "cost certainty." Regardless of what the commissioner called it, the league was insisting it needed a limit on how much the players would be paid. The NHLPA refused to consider any such proposal. As Toronto Maple Leafs player rep Bryan McCabe dramatically put it, "If they want a hard cap, we'll sit out the rest of our lives."

Beyond a simple philosophical dispute, the two sides couldn't even agree on the scale of the problem—or whether there was a problem at all. The owners produced scary pronouncements about how much money they were losing, and players would immediately lay out all the reasons the numbers were bunk. If Bettman said the sky was green, Goodenow would be right there to insist that it was red.

To make matters worse, both sides had learned from 1994, when the owners quickly splintered once things got serious. This time, Bettman made sure he had the power to keep everyone in line, including the ability to levy seven-figure fines on any owner who spoke out of turn in public. Goodenow made it equally clear to the players that any wavering from the party line would be kept in-house—or else.* And both sides had prepared well in advance, with Bettman forcing each owner to take out a ten-million-dollar line of credit to weather any stoppage and Goodenow encouraging players to line up alternate employment in Europe or elsewhere.

---

* Canadiens winger Pierre Dagenais found this out the hard way when he was quoted suggesting that some form of a hard cap might be acceptable to some players. He was quickly hauled in front of the media in full backtrack mode.

As 2004 wore on and the deadline neared, the question was no longer whether there would a lockout, but how long it would last. And, more pointedly, whether the NHL would become the first league in North American sports history to lose an entire season to a work stoppage. As the rhetoric ratcheted up on both sides, some observers even started to muse about the possibility of losing multiple seasons. This was shaping up to be the league's Armageddon.

The World Cup went on as scheduled, ending with an abbreviated one-game final on September 14, 2004. The next day, the CBA expired and Bettman made it official: The work stoppage had begun. Now we'd wait to see if the Great Lockout of 2004 would extend into 2005, or 2006 and beyond.

Over its first few months, the 2004 lockout largely followed the script set out in 1994. The players offered some small concessions, just enough to appear to be trying to make a deal. The owners immediately rejected the offers, calling them completely unreasonable. And the two sides would occasionally take a break from sniping at each other to remind fans that they were deeply sorry it had come to this and sincerely wished there was some other way. Oh, and also, they'd just cancelled another few weeks' worth of games.

The first significant break from the posturing came in December, when the players made a surprise offer. Dump the demand for a hard cap, they told the owners, and we'll agree to a luxury tax, limits on rookie salaries, and a 24 percent salary rollback on every existing contract. The tax and rookie cap weren't major departures from the union's previous position, but the rollback was an eye-opener, one that felt like an honest-to-goodness gesture of good faith. Surely the league would have to come back to the table with some major concessions of their own.

Instead, Bettman quickly rejected the offer as not even worth considering. And in an ingenious bit of manoeuvring, he insisted that the player's suggestion of a 24 percent rollback would now be the baseline for any further discussions. As Jonathan Gatehouse put it in his 2012 book *The Instigator*,* "the union had been beaten with its olive branch."

As the calendar flipped to 2005, hopes that the season could be saved were fading quickly. By the same point in the 1994–95 lockout, progress was being made. This time around, the two sides seemed to be moving farther apart. Bettman began to make ominous threats of a deadline after which the season would have to be cancelled, and finally settled on February 16 as his drop-dead date. Meanwhile, Goodenow and the players refused to budge—at least publicly. But behind the scenes, cracks were beginning to form. It was increasingly clear that the owners weren't bluffing about cancelling the season, and if that happened there was a good chance the 2005–06 season would be threatened as well. Players began to wonder whether losing a full year's pay or more was really worth it just to avoid the same sort of cap their colleagues in the NBA and NFL seemed able live with.

On February 13, just three days before Bettman's deadline, there was a genuine breakthrough. For the first time, the players indicated that they'd be willing to consider a hard cap, albeit one that wasn't tied directly to revenue. That set off a flurry of desperate back-and-forth talks, as the two sides tried to come to an agreement on what the number would be. But that burst of hope was short-lived; the gap was too big, and there were simply too many details to sort through. The players had made the big concession that was needed, but it had come far too late.

On February 16, Bettman gathered the media in New York and put on his best sombre face. "As I stand before you today, it is my sad duty to announce that because that solution has not yet been attained, it no longer is practical to conduct even an abbreviated season," he told the hockey world. "Accordingly, I have no choice but to announce the formal cancellation of play for 2004–05."

It was a gut punch for hockey fans. And it came with a final, cruel twist: Just as fans were coming to grips with what they'd witnessed, rumours swirled of a last-ditch effort to save the season. Fresh talks

---

* To this day, the book remains the single best examination of Bettman's tenure ever produced.

spearheaded by Wayne Gretzky and Mario Lemieux started days after Bettman's announcement and spurred hopes that the two stars could pull off yet another dramatic comeback. But their efforts went nowhere, and soon reality set in for good: There'd be no agreement, no Stanley Cup, no season. The NHL really had gone where no big-league sport had ever gone before. We were truly in uncharted territory.

With the season lost, the two sides retreated to their corners for several weeks. When talks resumed in April, it was once again the players who provided the breakthrough by offering to accept a revenue-based cap with a hard ceiling if it came with a floor as well. The offer was crucial in two key respects: It addressed most of what the owners wanted, giving the sides enough common ground to forge a deal. And it was delivered without Bob Goodenow.

The longtime NHLPA head had drawn his line in the sand from the beginning: No hard cap. Period. Now, his players were willing to cross that line in an attempt to get a deal done. With Saskin and NHLPA president Trevor Linden clearly now steering the ship, Goodenow remained as the union's leader in title only and rarely appeared in the bargaining sessions that followed.

The march towards a deal became a sprint by July, and after several days of talks, the announcement finally came on July 13, 2005. The two sides had their CBA, one that would include a thirty-nine-million-dollar hard cap for the coming season. The owners voted unanimously to approve the deal, and rightly so—Bettman had delivered a near-total victory.

For the players, the story wasn't so simple. They'd lost a full season of their careers, and their "never a cap" vows looked hollow in hindsight. But the deal still left room for the cap to grow and big contracts to follow. For one man, though, the agreement represented a clear loss. On July 28, two weeks after the new deal was announced, Bob Goodenow resigned as the NHLPA's executive director. The owners already had their cap; now they had a scalp to go with it.

———

In 1994, Major League Baseball had cancelled its World Series one month into a midseason players' strike. At the time, MLB stood as the only league to lose its postseason to a work stoppage. That strike dragged into the following spring, with the owners threatening to use replacement players, before it finally ended days before the 1995 season was due to start.

The strike had been the league's eighth work stoppage in twenty-two years, a track record that established baseball as a sport plagued by labour disputes. But this time was different. After decades of all-out war between players and owners, both sides seemed to realize that losing the World Series had been a bridge too far. To this day, the 1994 strike remains the last work stoppage to cancel MLB games. Even the hardest of the hardliners seemed in agreement: We simply can't go down this road again. We can't put our fans through this anymore.

The NHL felt no such obligation.

And so, as the years ticked away on the eight-year CBA, the league went into preparation mode for the next lockout—just as it had in 2004. The NHLPA had taken years to recover from Goodenow's departure, churning through leaders and controversies before finally hiring former MLB union head Donald Fehr. Life under a salary cap hadn't been so bad, especially when it became clear that several teams were willing to work around it by signing stars to front-loaded deals stretching over a decade or more. And the league was generating more revenue than ever. It seemed like everyone was winning.

But for the owners, it wasn't enough. And so, as the CBA's 2012 expiry date approached, fans were treated to what was by now a familiar song-and-dance, as Bettman pivoted from bragging about the game's soaring revenues to mumbling about how dire the financial landscape had become.

The 2004 lockout had been painful, but at least fans understood why it was happening. One side said it needed a hard salary cap, while the other refused to play under one. That was a big-picture debate, one without much middle ground, and it would be difficult to solve without sitting out until one side cracked.

By contrast, the 2012 lockout would be about . . . well, something. There was talk of the league wanting to reduce the players' share of revenue from the agreed-upon 57 percent. There was talk of limiting contract lengths to five years, which Daly solemnly pronounced was "the hill we will die on." There was talk of changing the arbitration system, or perhaps tweaking entry-level deals.

Those weren't small issues, but they seemed like the kind of things that could be negotiated in good faith during an off-season. You give me a few percentage points of revenue here, I make a concession on something you want there, and we don't need to miss any games to figure it all out. The league seemed to be in strong financial shape, with average franchise values rising and a new ten-year, $1.9 billion TV deal with NBC.* Daly's rhetoric aside, there were no do-or-die philosophical battles to be fought. Instead, the league's reason for locking out the players this time around seemed simpler: because they could. This was just how the NHL did business.

And so, for the third time in eighteen years, the NHL shut its doors in September 2012. The usual routine of threats, hyperbole and cancelled games followed, with a handful of new twists (including the NHLPA's threat to decertify and pursue an antitrust claim). It was widely assumed that nothing of substance would happen until January arrived and the league could start to threaten credibly to throw another season away. Sure enough, a deal was reached in the first week of the new year, leaving enough time for an abbreviated training camp and the same forty-eight-game schedule that had been played in 1995.

Bettman issued the now-traditional apology to fans when the deal was officially ratified, saying, "I know that an explanation or an apology will not erase the hard feelings that have built up over the past few months, but I owe you an apology nevertheless."

The end result saw the players and owners meet in the middle on a fifty-fifty split of hockey revenues, just as everyone had expected all along. The league settled for an eight-year limit on contracts instead of the five

---

* The TV contract was easily the richest in league history and seemed like a big win for the NHL at the time. However, fees for live sports rights in North America skyrocketed shortly after; within a few years, the NBA had signed a deal of its own worth twenty-four billion dollars.

that it swore had been its hill to die on.* That year's All-Star Game and Winter Classic were cancelled.

But the news wasn't all bad. When the regular season opened on January 19, 2013, the league had made sure to paint THANK YOU, FANS on the ice in every building.

The new deal was for ten years, with both sides holding the right to opt out after eight, meaning the next lockout could immediately be pencilled in for 2020. Today, players signing long-term contracts routinely negotiate "lockout protection" in the form of off-season bonuses for the 2020–21 season. As of this writing, it remains to be seen whether the 2020 lockout will wipe out an entire season or only half of one.

---

* RIP NHL, I guess.

THE NHL'S ONLY STRIKE

Work stoppages aren't always the owners' idea

GARY BETTMAN'S HAT TRICK OF LOCKOUTS REPRESENTS three of the four work stoppages in NHL history. The fourth has been largely forgotten, but it probably shouldn't be, because it laid a lot of the groundwork for the battles to come and may have cost the league president his job. And to this day, it remains the only time in league history that the players have gone on strike, as well as the only time a work stoppage has happened after a regular season had already started.

So, why have so many fans never heard of it? Probably because it only lasted ten days.

The NHL had operated without a collective-bargaining agreement for most of the 1991–92 season.* The players and owners had agreed to continue under the terms of the expired agreement for several reasons, not least of which was that the players were in the process of transitioning out of the Alan Eagleson era. With Bob Goodenow now at the helm, the players finally had someone who was willing to tell them what was going on. And as he settled into the job, he was saying something they'd never heard before: You need to go on strike.

Goodenow's attempts to hammer out a new deal with NHL president John Ziegler had yielded little. While there were no showstoppers like the salary cap, there was disagreement over issues like free agency, pensions, roster sizes, the length of the entry draft and even (believe it or not) revenue from licensing trading cards. The players wanted to make some gains; the owners

---

* Yes, despite what recent history has taught hockey fans, there's nothing that says an expired CBA has to mean an automatic work stoppage.

assumed that the union would quickly fold its hand, since it always had under Eagleson. And so Goodenow pushed for an aggressive strategy: Walk out just days before the playoffs were scheduled to start. Players aren't paid salaries during the postseason, while the owners of playoff teams reap some of their biggest profits. A strike that threatened to wipe out the playoffs after almost the entire regular season had been played would be disastrous for the owners. Goodenow drove that point home to the players, who authorized him to call the strike on April 1 if he didn't have a deal.

A frantic final weekend of bargaining produced little progress, and for the first time in the history of the league, a work stoppage had shut down the season.

Briefly. After several days of each side offering what they swore were really and truly their very final offers, they struck a deal. No games had been lost, the playoffs were saved and the season wrapped up without any further interruption.

The new CBA was only a two-year agreement, retroactive to the start of the 1991–92 season, meaning another battle was just over the horizon.* The owners had learned to take the players seriously, and that the Eagleson days of palling around with the union were over. Ziegler was pushed out shortly after, partly due to dissatisfaction with how he'd handled the negotiations, and the owners went looking for someone who could beat this Goodenow guy at his own game.

As it turns out, ten days can change a lot, even if it doesn't seem like all that big a deal at the time.

---

* That CBA expired after the 1992–93 season, after which the two sides once again agreed to play a year without a deal, setting the stage for the 1994 lockout.

23

GETTING CREATIVE

The NHL changes the rules, welcomes a new star and takes it outside

WHEN THE NHL FINALLY RETURNED TO THE ICE FOR meaningful games on October 5, 2005, a welcome familiarity hung over the proceedings. There were the same thirty teams in the same thirty buildings, featuring most of the same players.* But like an old friend you haven't seen in far too long, the game was different in ways both obvious and less so. In an attempt to free up the play and provide a more entertaining product, the NHL had rewritten much of its rule book in advance of opening night. After years of struggling to win acceptance for even the most minor changes, the league figured—correctly, as it turned out—that fans, media and front offices alike would be so happy to have hockey back that they wouldn't gripe too loudly over some new rules. Several of the revisions had been tested in the American Hockey League during the 2004–05 season, with the NHL carefully monitoring the results.

Some of the new rules had been debated for decades. That was the case for what was commonly referred to as "the elimination of the red line." Confusingly for rookie fans, the centre line itself was still there, but two-line passes that crossed it were now legal. The change was

---

* The year-long lockout had spelled the end for the careers of several veteran stars, including Mark Messier, Scott Stevens, Ron Francis, Al MacInnis and Adam Oates. Brett Hull joined them after just five games.

intended to open up the neutral zone, making it theoretically harder for teams to clog up the ice in the face of the threat of a long-distance pass from a sufficiently skilled defenceman. Many fans had been calling for the change for years, and few bothered to mourn the end of the two-line pass rule.

Other changes were less well received. The addition of a trapezoid behind the net, outside of which goaltenders wouldn't be allowed to handle the puck* seemed to cause more confusion than anything. The idea was to prevent expert puck handlers like Martin Brodeur from acting as a third defenceman, retrieving opposition dump-ins and immediately firing them right back out again; apparently, simply encouraging teams to avoid playing a tedious dump-and-chase style would have been too much to ask.

There was also a small reduction in the size of goaltender equipment, the reintroduction of the tag-up rule for offsides, some tweaks to rink dimensions, and a clever update to the icing rule that prevented the offending team from changing lines on the ensuing break in play.

But the most controversial new feature was one that fans had debated for years. The introduction of the shootout, long a staple of international competition, split the hockey world solidly along old-school and new-school lines. The wrinkle was indisputably entertaining, bringing fans out of their seats with each and every shooter,** but the individual nature of the proceedings seemed to go against the sport's team-first ethos, and the idea that modern hockey fans couldn't handle a good old-fashioned tie rubbed many the wrong way.

The addition of the shootout to decide regular-season games was probably inevitable—for a league starved of entertainment value, sacrificing a little competitive integrity to put an exclamation mark at the end of highlight reels made a certain type of sense. What didn't, and still doesn't, make sense is a decision that failed to get much attention at the time: continuing to award a point to the losing team in a game that goes

---

* For a time, the areas on either side of the trapezoid were creepily referred to as "the forbidden zone." Thankfully, everyone came to their senses and stopped calling it that.

** Ironically, the same argument that old-school fans had long been derided for using in favour of fighting.

past regulation. That rule change had come in 1999, in an effort to discourage teams from putting fans to sleep by playing for the tie in overtime. With no more ties to worry about, the "loser point" had served its purpose and was all set to be taken out behind the barn. But the league kept it, mumbling something about keeping playoff races competitive,* and it has continued to deface the standings ever since.

All in all, the "new NHL" was a mixed bag, although you had to give the league credit for at least trying. Yet despite myriad changes to the rule book, the biggest impact in that first season came from something far simpler: telling the referees to actually use it.

When it came to reducing obstruction, the NHL didn't actually need any new rules at all. It already had plenty, right there in the rule book, and they were clear on what was allowed and what wasn't. You couldn't hook and hold, you couldn't hack and slash, and you certainly couldn't latch onto a star player and water ski behind him down the ice.

Thanks to decades of lax enforcement, though, the NHL product had evolved into a mess of clutching-and-grabbing, interference and occasional outright tackling. Every once in a while, the sight of a player fighting through all that made for a great highlight. But far more often, it smothered play, turning every shift into a slow-moving slog in which fourth-liners could keep up with the game's best players by simply grabbing hold and hanging on for the ride.

In 2005, the league decided enough was enough. Call the rules, officials were told, and if anyone complains, we'll have your back.

So, that's what the officials did. Having awarded teams an average of just over four power plays a game in 2003–04, referees handed out almost six per game in 2005–06. That led to complaints from fans and players alike, as it resulted in choppy games that seemed to be constantly interrupted by whistles. Early on, there was also confusion over what exactly

---

* For the record, the loser point does no such thing. Its main purpose, as far as anyone can tell, is to artificially inflate records around the league, allowing the GMs who insist on keeping the rule in place to lose more games than they win and still boast about finishing "over .500."

constituted a penalty, as players were sent to the box for plays that had been commonplace for a generation. But the NHL stuck with it through those early months, reasoning that the players would figure out the new standards as the season wore on. Between cracking down on obstruction and the other new rules meant to open up the game, surely fans would again see the return of higher scores.

Scoring did go up, and significantly so. The 5.14 goals per game scored in 2003–04 had been the lowest since the 1950s, but the average shot up by a full goal in 2005–06, while goaltenders' average save percentage dropped by ten points. The NHL had finally done it . . . sort of.

A closer look at the numbers painted a less inspiring picture. Yes, scoring had gone up, but almost entirely due to all those extra power plays. When both teams were at full strength, as they were for the vast majority of each game, offence had barely moved. And that led to an obvious question: What happens if the number of power plays comes back to Earth?

It didn't take long to find out. Officials called an average of two fewer penalties per game in 2006–07, and fewer still in the years after. There are two schools of thought on what happened; the league argues that players adapted to the new rules and started committing fewer fouls, while a cynic might suggest that referees simply fell back into their old look-the-other-way habits. Either way, in 2012, power plays were handed out at the lowest rate since the 1970s.

The result was predictable. Even with the presence of two-line passes and trapezoids, scoring dropped back to levels seen during the dead puck era. The relatively heady days of the 2005–06 season were an outlier.

The scoring boost would end up being short-lived, but another key development ahead of the 2005–06 season would have far more staying power. For the first time since Eric Lindros in 1991, the league had a genuine once-in-a-generation superstar on the way in the person of junior hockey sensation Sidney Crosby. A brilliant centre who'd been generating headlines since his early teens, Crosby was a shoo-in to go first overall in the 2005 entry draft.

That presented a problem. Since there hadn't been a 2004–05 season, the league had to figure out a way to determine who deserved that coveted pick. Recycling the 2003–04 standings didn't seem fair, but giving everyone in the league—including 100-point powerhouses like the Detroit Red Wings and Philadelphia Flyers—an equal shot at a projected franchise player didn't either. So the league found the middle ground, settling on a lottery system that awarded each team between one and three Ping-Pong balls based on a variety of factors. Teams lost balls for making the playoffs or picking first overall in recent seasons; only four teams ended up with the maximum three balls. (Purely coincidentally, one of those teams was the league's biggest and most profitable American market, the New York Rangers.)

The draw was held on July 22, 2005, with the results announced in a TV special. The last two teams standing were the Pittsburgh Penguins and Mighty Ducks of Anaheim, and the NHL had Pittsburgh CEO Ken Sawyer stand on stage next to Ducks GM Brian Burke for the big reveal. A grim-faced Gary Bettman opened an envelope and flipped over a card, revealing a Penguins logo and instantly changing the course of the next decade.*

As Sawyer and Burke shook hands, the camera cut to Penguins GM Craig Patrick, who appeared to mouth the words "Wow, that's huge." He'd turn out to be more right than he knew.

Crosby debuted in 2005–06, scoring 102 points as a rookie and finishing second in Calder Trophy balloting to 2004 top pick Alexander Ovechkin. In his second year, Crosby took home both the scoring title and league MVP honours. He led the Penguins to the Stanley Cup final for the first time in 2008, his third season in the NHL.

Early in 2008, Crosby had been front and centre in one of the NHL's occasional bursts of creativity. On January 1, he beat Ryan Miller in a

---

* Years later, Burke (by then the GM of the Toronto Maple Leafs) would go on a memorably profane rant about "the Pittsburgh model, my ass" and how "they won a goddamn lottery." For the record, the Ducks would end up picking Bobby Ryan second and would win the Stanley Cup in 2007, although Ryan didn't debut until the following season.

shootout to earn the Penguins a 2–1 win. That in itself wasn't all that interesting, but both the venue and occasion were: Ralph Wilson Stadium, home of the Buffalo Bills, in the first-ever Winter Classic. The sight of Crosby scoring in front of seventy thousand fans as a light snow fell around him proved irresistible to sports fans around the world, and it was instantly clear that the NHL had a hit on its hands.

The 2008 game wasn't the first regular-season outdoor game in league history. That honour went to the 2003 Heritage Classic, which had pitted the Montreal Canadiens against the Oilers in Edmonton's Commonwealth Stadium. That game had been a success, although the pending lockout and its immediate aftershock delayed any meaningful follow-up. But by the fall of 2006, the league's new chief operating officer, John Collins, was working alongside NBC Sports executive Jon Miller on reviving the concept, this time as an all-American matchup to fill the network's prime sports slot on New Year's Day.

Putting the event together was no small feat, and in previous years the NHL might have wilted from the scope of the project. But Collins drove it forward and the game turned out to be a massive hit with fans and (probably more importantly) corporate sponsors. The league quickly announced a 2009 game, this one featuring the Red Wings and Blackhawks at Chicago's Wrigley Field. While the 6–4 Detroit win wasn't as dramatic as the 2008 edition, the TV ratings were even better and the jaw-dropping shots of an ice rink at Wrigley were instantly iconic.

The hockey world was hooked. The Winter Classic would quickly shove aside the increasingly tedious All-Star Game as the regular season's marquee event. The NHL found itself in the rare position of receiving praise from all corners. Now they had to figure out what came next.

The answer, predictably: Beat the whole concept into the ground.

After a third Winter Classic in 2010, this one between the Bruins and Philadelphia Flyers at Fenway Park, the historic home of the Boston Red Sox, the league announced that *two* outdoor games would be played in 2011. The Winter Classic featured the Penguins and Washington Capitals, both making their second appearance outdoors; it was a fantastic matchup on paper, one that generated a good deal of buzz thanks to the HBO documentary series *24/7*, which followed both teams for weeks in advance of the event. But the game was a letdown, and far worse, it saw Sidney Crosby suffer a season-ending concussion on a blindside hit from Capitals' checking centre David Steckel.*

Meanwhile, 2011 also saw the return of the Heritage Classic, with the Canadiens visiting the Calgary Flames. While the game itself was nothing to write home about, the return of outdoor action to Canada was well received. The league held just one outdoor game in 2012 and none at all in 2013 due to the lockout. But then 2014 arrived and brought with it a turning point, as the league expanded its outdoor slate to a whopping six games. That included a Winter Classic between the Maple Leafs and Red Wings in front of over 100,000 fans at "The Big House" in Ann Arbor, Michigan, as well as a surprisingly successful foray into California at Dodger Stadium and a heavily anticipated debut in Yankee Stadium. But it also featured a second game at Yankee Stadium just days later; a return to Chicago; and a laughable Heritage Classic between the Vancouver Canucks and Ottawa Senators that was actually played *indoors* when the threat of rain resulted in BC Place's retractable roof being closed.**

One outdoor game a year was special. Two was fine. But six was overkill of the highest order, a fact even the NHL seemed to recognize when it dropped back down to a pair of games in 2015. It settled in at four for both 2016 and 2017, and by the end of the 2017–18 season, NHL teams had played either twenty-four or twenty-five regular-season outdoor games, depending on whether or not you count the Vancouver effort.

That seems like a lot for an event that was meant to be unique. But in fairness, the NHL was simply responding to demand from fans, sponsors and teams—all of whom wanted a piece of the outdoor action. The recent glut of outdoor games may be too much of a good thing, but that doesn't change the fact that the concept has been very good indeed, among the

---

* Crosby actually played in the team's next game four days later, but left after a hit from Victor Hedman and didn't return to the lineup until November.

** The only thing anyone remembers from that game was Vancouver coach John Tortorella's decision not to start Roberto Luongo, effectively torpedoing the team's relationship with its star goaltender.

most popular gimmicks that any major pro sports league has ever tried. The NHL doesn't like to get creative, and on the rare occasions when it does, it doesn't always get the result it's looking for. But every now and then, it hits one out of the ballpark. Or the football field.

THE FORGOTTEN OUTDOOR GAMES

A prison yard, an unfinished arena and Vegas, baby

ASK AN NHL FAN WHEN THE LEAGUE PLAYED ITS FIRST outdoor game, and there's a good chance they'll say it was the 2008 Winter Classic. The ones with better memories will point to the 2003 Heritage Classic. That's the right answer if we're talking about games that actually counted in the regular-season standings. But if we're looking for any outdoor games at all, then there are three more to add to the list. And it's safe to say that none of them were "classics" in any sense of the word.

The first came all the way back in 1954, and featured the Detroit Red Wings travelling to Marquette, Michigan. No, Marquette didn't have an NHL team, but it did have a prison, and that's where the Red Wings were headed.

It all began the previous summer, when Ted Lindsay visited Marquette Branch Prison as part of a promotional tour with GM Jack Adams. The star winger got along well with the prison's inmates, and the warden issued an invitation: Come back in the winter for a friendly game. Adams accepted, and on February 2, 1954, the Red Wings arrived to face a pickup team of convicts, surrounded by guard towers and razor wire.

Needless to say, there was significant concern over the safety of those involved, and the potential for acts of serious violence. But once the inmates were assured that Gordie Howe would try to keep his elbows down, the game went ahead as scheduled.

It wasn't much of a contest, with the Red Wings jumping out to an 18–0 lead after one period. That was it for keeping score, and as the game went on, the two sides started swapping players to even things out. Nobody got hurt, the ice held up nicely and the event was deemed a success.

The next outdoor game came two years later, albeit largely accidentally. After missing the playoffs, the Boston Bruins were making a postseason tour through Newfoundland when they arrived in the small town of Bay Roberts. They'd been promised a game against a local team at the new Conception Bay Sports Arena, but arrived to find that the rink wasn't actually finished. With no roof in place, the two teams were left to play in the rain and fog.

Like the Red Wings game, this one wasn't especially competitive, with one scorekeeper's estimate pegging the final at something like 26–1 for Boston. Bruins goalie Terry Sawchuk didn't have much to do, and at one point was reportedly spotted holding an umbrella during the action. But the game would go down in history as the league's second outdoor contest, as well as the first to be witnessed by paying spectators.

Those two games remained the league's only outdoor adventures for thirty-five years. But in 1991, the league revisited the concept during the preseason by having the New York Rangers face the Los Angeles Kings in a Las Vegas parking lot. The September meeting was played in eighty-five-degree heat, which presented its share of challenges. The rink crew laid a tarp over the ice, which overheated in the sun and melted. The blue lines hadn't been created with the customary paint, as players realized when strips of fabric began to peek through the ice. As the game went on, chunks of the playing surface broke off and had to be replaced.

And then there were the locusts.

Yes, in what may stand as the closest the NHL has come to an all-out biblical plague (that didn't involve a Vancouver Canucks jersey redesign), the ice was periodically invaded by swarms of insects. That wouldn't have been a major problem under normal circumstances, since the bugs were just passing through. But when they hit the ice, they froze to it, giving large swaths of the rink a crunchy, insect-based coating.

The Kings won the game 5–2, and we all figured that would be the last we'd see of outdoor games . . . and NHL hockey in Las Vegas.

24

THE PARITY ERA

With a cap in place, the age of "competitive balance"
arrives . . . at least until it's time to hand out the Cup

THE 2005–06 SEASON WAS A HELL OF A LOT OF FUN.

Sure, we were all thrilled to have hockey back and probably would have cheered just about anything, but that return season served up so many twists and turns that it was impossible not to get sucked back in. The double cohort of freshmen meant that two of the best rookies in history debuted at the same time, with Sidney Crosby and Alexander Ovechkin both topping 100 points. Five players hit the fifty-goal mark, including San Jose's Jonathan Cheechoo, who managed an unlikely fifty-six-goal season. The eventual Art Ross and Hart Trophy winner, Joe Thornton, was traded after twenty-three games.* And as we'd been promised, small-market teams were able to compete against the big boys, with the Ottawa Senators, Carolina Hurricanes and Buffalo Sabres all topping 110 points.

But not everything had changed, and briefly disoriented fans searching for a bit of familiarity didn't have to look any further than the top of the standings. The Detroit Red Wings had been the league's model franchise before the lockout, and they somehow came out of it looking even better. They won fifty-eight games and put up 124 points under new head coach

---

* He remains the only player to win either trophy while splitting the season between two teams.

Mike Babcock. With Steve Yzerman slowed by age and injury, late-round picks Pavel Datsyuk and Henrik Zetterberg emerged as stars, and the Wings finished second in both goals for and against to head into the play-offs as the prohibitive Cup favourites.

And then it all fell apart. In a stunning upset, the Wings were knocked out in six games by the eighth-seeded Edmonton Oilers. It felt like just about the perfect signpost for the new NHL: a small-market underdog taking out the star-studded favourite. This is what parity looked like.

The Oilers' miracle run took them all the way to the Stanley Cup final, where they ran into another small-market club, the Hurricanes. The matchup might have looked like a nightmare to TV executives, but it was a compelling series, especially after an injury to Edmonton starter Dwayne Roloson in the opening game restored the Oilers' underdog status. Carolina eventually emerged with a hard-fought win, taking the Cup on home ice in a dramatic seventh game.

It was a fitting end to one of the most unpredictable seasons that fans had ever seen. "This is a new era," the hockey gods seemed to be telling us. "Pay attention, because anything can happen."

Far from settling into predictability with one season of the salary cap era behind it, the league continued to churn through storylines. Both the Oilers and Hurricanes missed the playoffs in 2006–07, marking the first time ever that both of the previous year's finalists did so. It was an especially painful year in Edmonton, where Chris Pronger forced a trade out of town; the team wouldn't make the playoffs again for a decade.

Crosby won his first MVP award and scoring title in just his second season, and the addition of Evgeni Malkin spurred the Penguins to their first playoff appearance in six years. The Sabres captured the Presidents' Trophy but failed to make it out of the third round, then saw the core of their team flee in free agency. And in Anaheim, the Ducks dropped the "Mighty" from their name but lifted the franchise's first Stanley Cup, beating Ottawa in five games. (The Senators could at least claim to have scored that season's Cup-winning goal, with defenceman Chris Phillips accidentally beating his own goalie, Ray Emery, on a wraparound while the Ducks were changing lines.)

The following two seasons delivered back-to-back Red Wings-Penguins finals, the first Stanley Cup rematch since the Oilers and Islanders traded titles in the '80s. Detroit took the 2008 matchup in six games, while Crosby and the Penguins won the 2009 meeting in seven.* That series ended with Marc-André Fleury stoning Nicklas Lidstrom from in close in the final seconds of the deciding game, preserving a 2–1 Penguins win.

When the final horn sounded on the 2009 final, the NHL had its fourth champion in the first four seasons of the cap era, with all four having been built in decidedly different fashions. For the first time, the league really was starting to look like one where any team could win and the days of the dominant dynasty were dead. But in the Western Conference, a pair of up-and-coming clubs had other ideas.

From the start of the 1997–98 season through the end of the 2007–08 campaign, the Chicago Blackhawks won just one playoff game. They finished under .500 in eight of those seasons and in the bottom three overall in both 2003–04 and 2005–06. Even more stunning, from today's perspective, the United Center sat half-empty for home games; the Blackhawks finished twenty-ninth in league attendance in 2007, well behind teams like the Phoenix Coyotes, Florida Panthers and even the soon-to-move Atlanta Thrashers.

Through it all, Chicago fans mostly shrugged. Longtime owner Bill Wirtz had made it clear that he had little interest in spending the sort of money it would take to push the team into contention, and fans reacted accordingly. It would be nice to be able to describe a feel-good turning point, but the reality is somewhat more macabre. Wirtz died shortly before the start of the 2007–08 season, and his sons took over the team. When a ceremony honouring the deceased owner was held at the home opener, Chicago fans booed.

---

* Marian Hossa played for the losing team in both series. His luck would get better in 2010.

Fortunately, the rebuilding Hawks already had some key young pieces in place, largely thanks to a pair of lucky breaks at the draft. In 2006, Chicago held the third-overall pick, behind the Blues and Penguins. After St. Louis took American defenceman Erik Johnson, the Penguins decided their roster needed a two-way Canadian centre. They picked Jordan Staal, leaving Jonathan Toews for the Blackhawks.* Chicago followed that by winning the 2007 lottery, jumping four slots in the draft order and landing winger Patrick Kane with the first-overall pick.

With new ownership, a pair of blue-chip forwards and a solid core that included defenceman Duncan Keith, the 2007–08 Blackhawks put together their best season in years, finishing with eighty-eight points and narrowly missing the playoffs. They followed that with a breakthrough 104-point season that saw them go all the way to the 2009 Western Conference final before falling to the Red Wings.

Meanwhile, in Los Angeles, the Kings were in the process of building a contender of their own. The team had won just a single playoff round in the fifteen seasons since its Cup final run in 1993 and had missed the post-season in every year from 2003 through 2009. But the Kings had nabbed centre Anze Kopitar and goaltender Jonathan Quick in the 2005 draft and had the good fortune of holding the second-overall pick in a 2008 draft with two slam-dunk franchise players up for grabs. The Tampa Bay Lightning used the top pick on Steven Stamkos, leaving the Kings to happily snap up defenceman Drew Doughty.

Heading into the 2009–10 season, the Blackhawks signed coveted free agent Marian Hossa to the sort of massive contract that "Dollar Bill" Wirtz would have never allowed. Hossa turned out to be the final piece of a championship puzzle, and the Hawks rolled to their first Stanley Cup since 1961.

The season was a success for the Kings as well, as they finally made the playoffs, where they put up a decent fight against a strong Vancouver team. Those Canucks would hit their peak in 2010–11, running away with

---

* Staal ended up being a decent enough player, but the thought of the Penguins adding Toews to a roster that already featured Crosby and Malkin is slightly terrifying.

the Presidents' Trophy before falling to Tim Thomas and the Bruins in a heartbreaking Cup final that saw them blow a 3–2 series lead.[*] Vancouver would lead the league again in 2011–12, but find itself knocked out in the first round by the eighth-seeded Kings. In the moment, it felt like a major upset. In hindsight, it was the start of one of the most dominating playoff runs ever seen, as the Kings rolled through the postseason, winning fifteen of their first seventeen games. The sixteenth win proved slightly trickier, as the Devils pushed back to extend the final, but LA closed the series on home ice in game six.

The Cup was the first in Kings franchise history, and it marked the seventh different Cup winner since the lockout. The salary cap era finally got a repeat champion in 2013, when Chicago won its second title with the Toews-Kane combination up front. Chicago and Los Angeles traded Cups for two more seasons, with the Kings taking it home in 2014 and the Hawks battling back in 2015. That was followed by Crosby and the Penguins winning back-to-back Cups in 2016 and 2017.

The regular season had never seen more parity—or, to use the league's preferred phrasing, "competitive balance." That was a good thing, as far as the NHL was concerned, and the league took every opportunity to boast about tight games, close playoff races and frequent upsets. Not everyone agreed, and there were times when the whole thing started to feel dangerously close to flipping coins, although it was hard to deny that the league had never been more unpredictable.

But the league found itself in an awkward position when the playoffs arrived and the same three teams kept winning. Between them, the Hawks, Kings and Penguins took home eight of the nine Stanley Cups awarded from 2009 through 2017, which seemed at odds with the anything-can-happen vibe the league was pushing.

Any concerns that the postseason was becoming too predictable were at least temporarily laid to rest during the 2018 playoffs, which ended with the Washington Capitals finally winning the Stanley Cup

---

[*]   The series is probably best remembered for Vancouver fans rioting in the streets after the loss in game seven.

after years of falling short when it mattered. It was an unexpected run, one that followed an underwhelming regular season and started with the team facing a 2-0 series deficit against the Columbus Blue Jackets. The Capitals recovered, although it took a lucky bounce in overtime of game three to set the comeback in motion, and eventually vanquished the Penguins, too, on their way to the first title in franchise history.

But if the Capitals' win was a surprise, their opponent in the final was an outright shock. Despite being written off by virtually everyone before the season began, the expansion Vegas Golden Knights capped off one of the most stunning seasons in pro-sports history with a run that fell just three wins short of a championship. Hockey in Las Vegas hadn't just worked, it had been a hit beyond anyone's imagination. For one season at least, anything really could happen in the NHL.

A league marked by parity, where anyone can win on any given night, is great news for the teams involved . . . assuming, of course, that they actually do want to win.

"Tanking" has always been a touchy subject in the NHL. In theory, losing on purpose goes against everything in the hockey ethos, and accusing anyone of giving anything less than their absolute best at all times can amount to a mortal insult. On the other hand, well, hockey fans have eyes. And they have common sense. So, when they see a team suddenly flatline just as a generational talent appears on the horizon, they can put two and two together.

That's what happened in 1984, when the Penguins and Devils staged a turtle derby for the right to draft Mario Lemieux. And it sure seemed to happen again in 1993, when Senators owner Bruce Firestone allegedly told reporters his team had thrown its final games to ensure it would get Alexandre Daigle.* That ultimately led the league to introduce a draft

---

* Firestone later denied that there'd been any such plot, and as *Sports Illustrated* reported, he also noted that his comments had come during an off-the-record session with reporters in which he'd had "eight, maybe nine beers."

lottery; Daigle, of course, ended up being one of the biggest busts in league history.

To be clear, nobody really thinks that the players themselves are trying to lose. Why give half an effort just so some hotshot draft pick can show up at next year's training camp and take your job? But a GM with an eye to the future, perhaps helped along by a coach with some job security, might decide that icing a less-than-ideal lineup is the smartest long-term move.

All of which brings us to the 2014–15 season, in which a bunch of teams suddenly got very bad just in time to have a shot at drafting Connor McDavid.

In the age of parity, truly bad teams are rare. In both 2009–10 and 2010–11, only one team, the Oilers, finished with fewer than seventy points. In 2011–12, only the Columbus Blue Jackets did. But in 2014–15, four teams finished below that mark. The Oilers and Toronto Maple Leafs were bad, but the real race was between the Coyotes and Sabres, who went down to the wire while putting up two of the worst seasons of the modern era.

It wasn't hard to figure out what was going on, and the whole thing turned farcical as the season drew to a close. At one point, the Sabres hosted the Coyotes in a game that went into overtime. When the Coyotes scored the sudden-death winner, Buffalo fans cheered.

In the end, it didn't matter—the Oilers won the draft lottery, "earning" the first-overall pick for the fourth time in six years. McDavid ended up being even better than expected, duplicating Crosby's feat of winning the Hart Trophy in his second pro season. Meanwhile, the NHL changed its lottery rules starting in 2016, theoretically removing the incentive for teams to blatantly tank, and thereby solving a problem the league insists it never had in the first place.*

---

* And no, as a Toronto fan I can assure you that the 2015–16 Maple Leafs didn't tank to land Auston Matthews. It's perfectly reasonable for a team to place every half-decent player in the organization on long-term injured reserve at the all-star break.

THE CASE OF THE MISSING CUP

When the guest of honour is running a bit late

"TONIGHT, FANS, THE STANLEY CUP IS IN THE BUILDING."
Those are words that every hockey fan looks forward to hearing. They mean that a team is one win away from a championship, with a chance to capture the legendary trophy that very night. And they conjure up the dramatic image of the trophy waiting in the wings while gladiators battle it out on the ice to determine whether its services are required.

But as confused fans learned in 2015, the announcement isn't always accurate.

One of the neat things about covering the Stanley Cup final as a member of the media is that, when the deciding game is over, you get to head out onto the ice to conduct your interviews with the winning team. Assuming you can get past the crippling fear of slipping and face-planting on live television, it's a lot of fun. But as the Blackhawks were wrapping up their win over the visiting Lightning to close out the 2015 final in six games, it quickly became apparent to those of us who'd watched the series from the press box that something was wrong.

Members of the media line up near the ice as the game is still being played so that we'll be ready to go as soon as the Cup presentation ends. But on that night, as the Chicago crowd counted down the final seconds before erupting at the team's third championship in six years, the mood among the league's behind-the-scenes staff seemed tense. Then downright unhappy. And then, just maybe, a little frantic. At one point, Gary Bettman stormed by, which didn't seem all that unusual until you remembered that he was supposed to be on the ice already.

Soon, a sheepish explanation was released: The Stanley Cup wasn't in the building.

As it turns out, the league likes to wait as long as possible to bring the Cup to the arena. Usually, that still means it arrives in plenty of time for the final buzzer. But on this night, the Chicago area had been hit with torrential rains.* The deluge had let up during the game, but had caused flooding. Some of the roads to the arena were impassable, and those that were still open were clogged with traffic.

The league was eventually able to arrange for a police escort, with ESPN reporting that the race to the rink reached speeds of 100 miles per hour. The Cup finally arrived after a noticeable delay. In what was no doubt an admirable feat of understatement, one league executive told the *Toronto Sun* that "the commissioner was not pleased."

All's well that ends well, and for a trophy that's been kicked into the Rideau Canal,** left on the side of the road*** and stolen multiple times,**** being fashionably late for a party is hardly the worst thing in the world. Still, the league has reportedly tweaked its policy to make sure the Cup arrives early for future celebrations. So, the next time you're told that the Stanley Cup is in the building, who knows? It might even be true.

---

* Tornado sirens were heard in the hours before the game, and at one point during the pregame warm-up, the roof of the United Center started leaking.

** By the 1905 Ottawa Senators.

*** By the 1924 Montreal Canadiens.

**** Including once by Guy Lafleur, who tossed it into the trunk of his car and made off with it in 1979.

25

THE FUTURE

A look at the next 100 years

SO, NOW WHAT?

After 100 seasons, today's NHL doesn't look much like the 1917 version. It's gone from four teams to thirty-one, revised its rules, grown into a multibillion-dollar industry and seen players take to the ice under an open sky for reasons other than their arena being on fire.

So, where do we go from here? When the sequel to this book comes out in 100 years, what sort of league will it be describing?

Making predictions is a fool's game, of course. But that's never stopped a sportswriter before, so let's wrap up our look back at the NHL's first century by peering into its murky future.

Some of the calls are easy enough. For example, the league welcomed its newest franchise in 2017, when the Vegas Golden Knights took to the ice, then stunned everyone by steamrolling the Pacific Division. But we won't stay at thirty-one for long. If expansion plans for a thirty-second team haven't been announced by the time you're reading this, they will be soon. That team will almost certainly be in Seattle, balancing out the conferences and seeing the league finally arrive in the city that won the last pre-NHL Stanley Cup. And given what the Golden Knights did in their first season, that Seattle team will face a landscape where expansion teams are expected to compete right away.

The bigger question will be how much more the league can grow. There are still a handful of American markets that could host a team.

Houston seems the next in line. Maybe we give it another try in Cleveland or Kansas City, or see one-time candidates like Milwaukee re-emerge. (I'm still holding out hope for those Hampton Roads Rhinos.) But once a thirty-second team is in place, the focus could also shift north of the border to Quebec City or Hamilton, or to figuring out a way to get second franchises in hotbeds like Toronto or Montreal. It wouldn't be surprising to see teams eventually arrive in all of those markets—if not by expansion, then perhaps via the relocation of struggling franchises like the Florida Panthers or Arizona Coyotes—at which point those abandoned markets would immediately become candidates for future expansion or relocation.

Or maybe the league thinks even bigger, making its way to Europe or someday even Asia. Back in 2008, Bill Daly predicted that European expansion could be possible "within ten years' time," and while having teams outside North America would present some logistical challenges, an all-overseas division doesn't feel quite as far-fetched as it would have a generation ago.

On the ice, we can expect the game to continue to evolve. Again, some of this isn't all that hard to forecast based on the trends of the last decade or two. It sure seems as if fighting will be an increasingly rare sight, even if the league never does get around to actually outlawing it. Big hits are probably headed that way too, as the league looks to minimize the impact of concussions on its players.[*]

That's the right thing to do, but there's also an element of self-preservation here; the NHL is currently facing lawsuits from former players over its handling of concussions, and some of the dollar values being thrown around are enough to shake the league to its foundation. And if you really want to see an impact on the way the game is played, wait until there's a reliable test for CTE[**] that can be administered to living

---

[*]   Ken Dryden's 2017 book, *Game Change*, made a convincing case for banning all hits to the head.

[**]   Chronic traumatic encephalopathy is a degenerative brain disease that can lead to early dementia and other symptoms and has been posthumously diagnosed in many former pro athletes. As of this writing, it can only be diagnosed after death.

athletes; the first still-in-his-prime superstar found exhibiting early signs of the disease will raise a host of new ethical questions.

The emphasis on safety will extend to equipment, with the next generation of fans looking at throat protection and cut-resistant gear the same way we look at helmets and goalie masks now. The idea of playing without a visor will seem ludicrous, and the days of full facial protection probably aren't that far off. We'll hear complaints about "soft" players and the loss of the league's tough-guy identity, but they'll fade quickly. Here's hoping that those changes happen because of common sense, and not because a preventable tragedy forces the league's hand.

The ice surface will grow, although we may need to wait for the next wave of new arenas for that to happen. It will look different too, since the NHL loves nothing more than adding a line here and moving a circle there. It's been shown that teams that have to change lines on the bench farther from their own net give up more goals, so someday the rink may be flipped, so that teams have that long change twice instead of once. There will be ads on the jerseys that we'll hate at first but get used to, just as we did when they started showing up on the boards and ice. At some point, they'll finally get around to fixing the delay-of-game penalty, figuring out a way to treat a puck shot over the glass in the same way as a puck shot over the bench or down the length of the rink for icing. We'll still have shootouts, but not as many as we do now, because overtime will be longer.

Technology will solve some of the league's problems for us. Some sort of microchip in the puck will eliminate debates over whether it crossed the goal line, while also doing away with lengthy offside reviews. A new era of player tracking will lead to a revolution in stats and analytics, and concepts like Corsi will seem almost adorably quaint in retrospect. We'll figure out a way to make sticks that don't shatter whenever someone breathes on them. And hand-wringing over TV deals will eventually fade, as an increasingly fractured audience forces the league to focus on maximizing revenue-per-fan instead of overall audience.

The loser point will be gone—the standings will be based on a three-point system—and young fans will ask the rest of us why we were okay with everything being so messed up for years. We won't have a good answer for them.*

It will be fascinating to see whether the league embraces bigger, more fundamental changes. That could include eliminating offsides altogether, allowing teams to use the full two hundred feet available to them. If widening the rinks doesn't free up enough open ice, the league could move to four on four as the even-strength standard (reducing rosters and payrolls in the process). Maybe we'll do away with the draft lottery—or even the draft itself. Granted, all of those ideas seem radical now, but so did shootouts not all that long ago. A lot can change in a decade or two.

Oh, and the nets will be bigger. They'll have to be, because eventually the league will run out of meaningless tweaks to minor rules and decide it's finally time to see some goals. Everyone will scream when it happens; then, after a few months, nobody will remember why we ever had a problem with the idea in the first place.

This being the NHL, the bigger headlines will often come off the ice. History tells us that we'll almost certainly have a lockout of some kind when the current collective-bargaining agreement expires, although how long it lasts and how acrimonious it gets remains to be seen. That could depend on which hill the owners decide to pretend to be willing to die on this time; if it's just about squeezing a few more percentage points out of hockey-related revenue, a deal could get done reasonably quickly, but if they go after a bigger prize, like guaranteed contracts, we may lose another season. Either way, a new CBA will get signed eventually, at which point we'll start the clock again counting down to the next lockout.

Of course, those future work stoppages will hinge on what looms as perhaps the biggest story on the league's short-term horizon: the end of the Gary Bettman era. Bettman turned sixty-six in 2018; Clarence Campbell was considered old when he retired in 1977 at the age of seventy-one. That's not a perfect comparison—it was a different era

---

* Seriously, you know the confusion you feel when you see photos of players in Cooperalls? That's how the loser point is going to look to the next generation.

and Campbell was already in poor health—but it brings home the point that Bettman can't keep this up forever. He may not even want to. At some point, the NHL is going to find itself under new leadership, and it's hard to imagine a decision that will hold bigger ramifications for the future of the league.

It's possible that the owners decide to stay the course, looking internally at someone like Daly to simply extend the Bettman era. It would be hard to blame them—as we're reminded incessantly whenever Bettman's legacy is discussed, revenues are at an all-time high. But then again, revenues are at an all-time high in every sport these days, and given where the league was when Bettman arrived, it would have been virtually impossible for him to do *anything but* improve the bottom line. Still, hockey people tend to be conservative, and it's not hard to imagine them deciding that good enough is good enough before seeking out a Bettman sequel that's as faithful as possible to the original.

But maybe not. Maybe they recognize the need for fresh thinking and look outside the league, just like in 1992. Or maybe they even hand the reins over to a former player who also has ties to management and ownership. Maybe a Steve Yzerman or Brendan Shanahan or even a Wayne Gretzky could navigate both sides of the aisle in the way Bettman never could, combining a player's respect for the game and its traditions with a manager's view of the bottom line.

One way or another, the decision will say a lot about where the league is headed. And after more than twenty-five years, hockey fans won't have Gary Bettman to kick around anymore. (Except for when the Bettman hologram shows up to present the Stanley Cup. This is the NHL, after all—some things will never change.)

Despite all the uncertainty, we can close by making one prediction about the next century with some degree of confidence: We'll enjoy the hell out of it.

How could we not? We're hockey fans. And at its best, this sport is still all sorts of fun, in spite of the league that brings it to us. And yes, if we're being honest, sometimes it's even fun precisely *because* of the league, warts and all.

As perplexing, frustrating and embarrassing as the NHL's first century has often been, at least we can give the league this much: It certainly keeps us on our toes. We may never know what to expect, but by now we realize that's half the fun.

So, someday down the line, when the next generation's version of the yellow raincoats come out, the locusts hit the ice and nobody can manage to read the novelty crown-and-anchor wheel, hockey fans will be there, ready to do what we always do: make eye contact with the nearest fellow fan, shake our heads, and chuckle, "Can you believe this freaking league?"

Of course we can. It's the NHL.

ACKNOWLEDGEMENTS

THIS BOOK WOULDN'T HAVE BEEN POSSIBLE WITHOUT THE work of countless hockey historians and writers over the years who've shared the stories of the sport and the NHL. Many of their books were indispensable throughout this project, including *The Instigator: How Gary Bettman Remade the League and Changed the Game Forever* by Jonathon Gatehouse; *Hockey: A People's History* by Michael McKinley; *Behind the Net: 106 Incredible Hockey Stories* by Stan Fischler; *Changing the Game: A History of NHL Expansion* by Stephen Laroche; *Breakaway: From Behind the Iron Curtain to the NHL* by Tal Pinchevsky; and *The NHL: 100 Years of On-Ice Action and Boardroom Battles* by D'Arcy Jenish.

I'd also like to thank everyone involved in building and maintaining the many excellent resource sites that I relied on while researching this book. Those include the indispensable hockey-reference.com, as well as newspapers.com, nhltradetracker.com, prosportstransactions.com, greatest-hockeylegends.com, hockeydb.com and historicalhockey.blogspot.com.

I also owe my thanks to those whose ongoing work in spreading NHL history continues to inform and entertain. If you're a hockey fan on Twitter, make sure your follows include names like Dave Stubbs (@Dave_Stubbs), Mike Commito (@MikeCommito), Liam Maguire (@liams_hockey) and @NHLhistorygirl.

On a personal level, I owe a debt of gratitude to the many kind people within the sports media world who've helped make it possible for a lifelong fan to build a career in sports writing. The full list would be longer than this book itself, but includes Bruce Arthur, Bob McKenzie, Sarah Larimer,

Bill Simmons, James Duthie, Greg Wyshynski and Ian Mendes, as well the talented teams at ESPN, VICE Sports and Sportsnet. And a special thanks to the readers who've been along for the ride, and who've helped me build an audience by sharing feedback and spreading the word. I quite literally couldn't have done it without you.

Thanks to Craig Pyette, Pamela Murray, Evan Rosser, Lloyd Davis and Linda Pruessen for their tireless work on this book, as well as to my agent Brian Wood for making it all happen. All of you, please stop sending me files to edit.

Thank you to my wife, Marcie, who has spent the last twenty-five years pretending to be interested as I rambled on with what turned out to be the rough draft of this book over beer and chicken wings.

And finally, thanks to my children, Erica and Douglas, for inspiring me every day. I can only hope that someday I'll be able to write a hockey list as insightful as "Ven Renstrik" or come up with a joke as funny as "hamper time."

INDEX